SOCIAL STUDIES

MACMILLAN

Macmillan Social Studies

COMMUNITIES
PEOPLE AND PLACES

SENIOR AUTHOR
John Jarolimek

Ruth Pelz

Macmillan Publishing Company
New York
Collier Macmillan Publishers
London

Macmillan Publishing Company
866 Third Avenue, New York, New York 10022
Collier Macmillan Canada, Inc.

Printed in the United States of America
ISBN 0-02-147340-4
9 8 7 6 5 4

CONTENTS

Maps

Charts, Diagrams, and Graphs

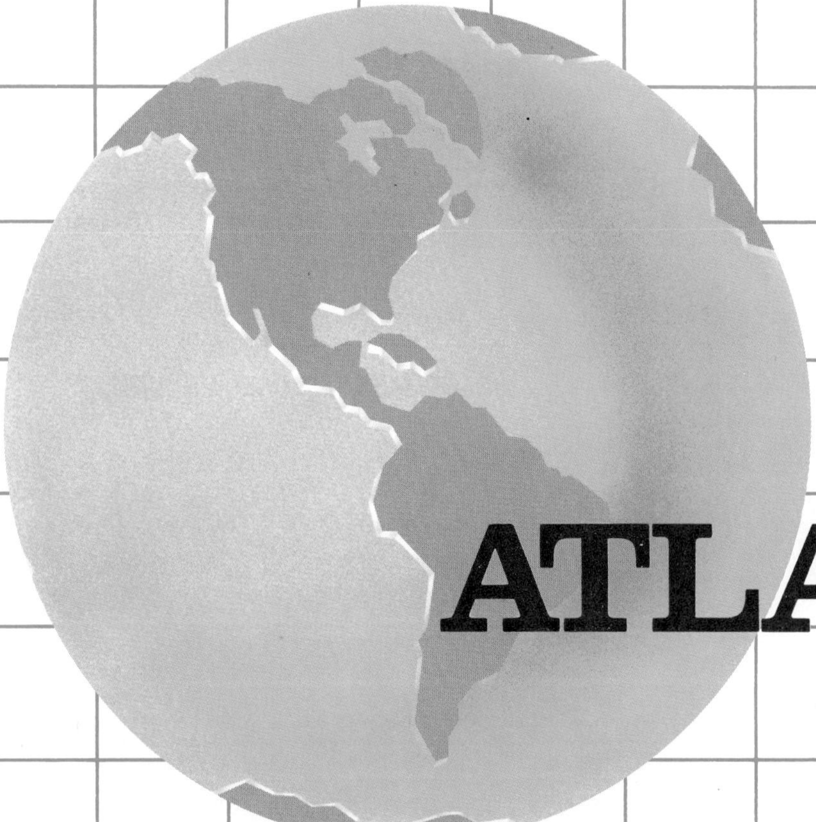

ATLAS

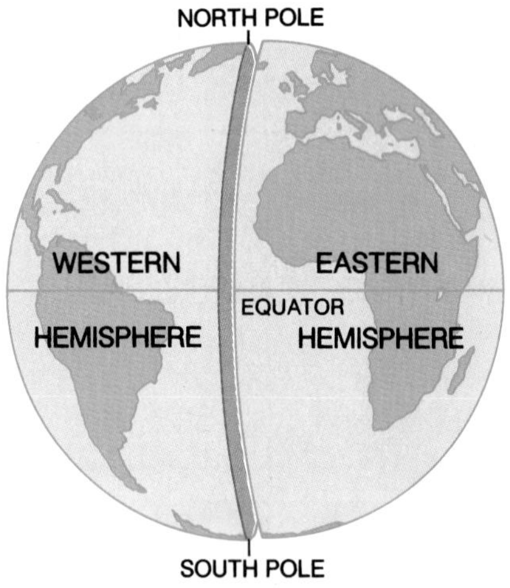

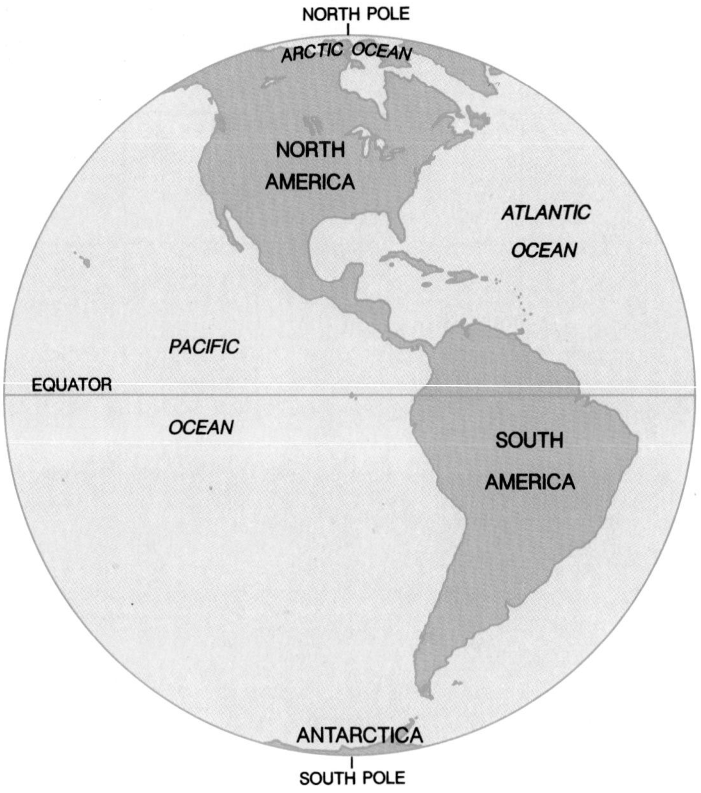

WESTERN HEMISPHERE

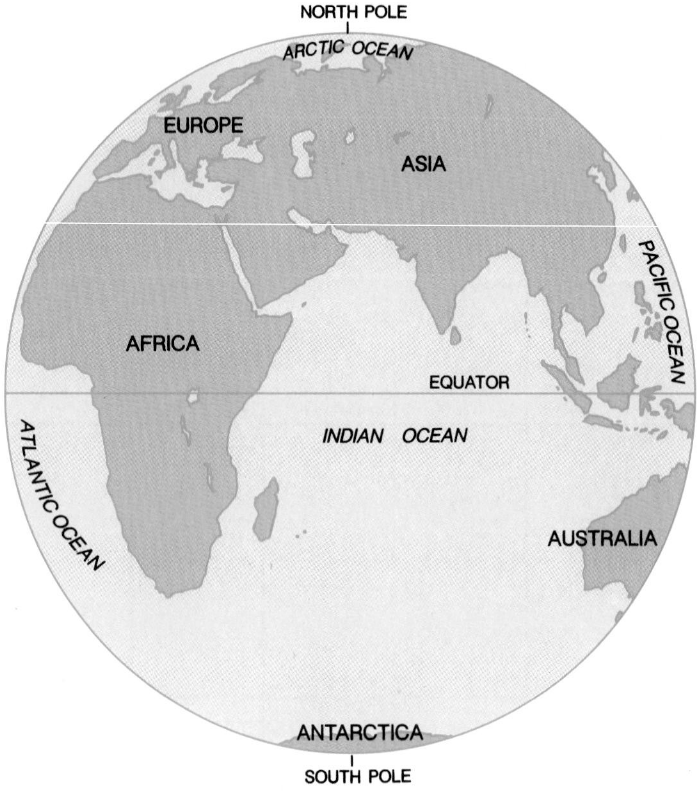

EASTERN HEMISPHERE

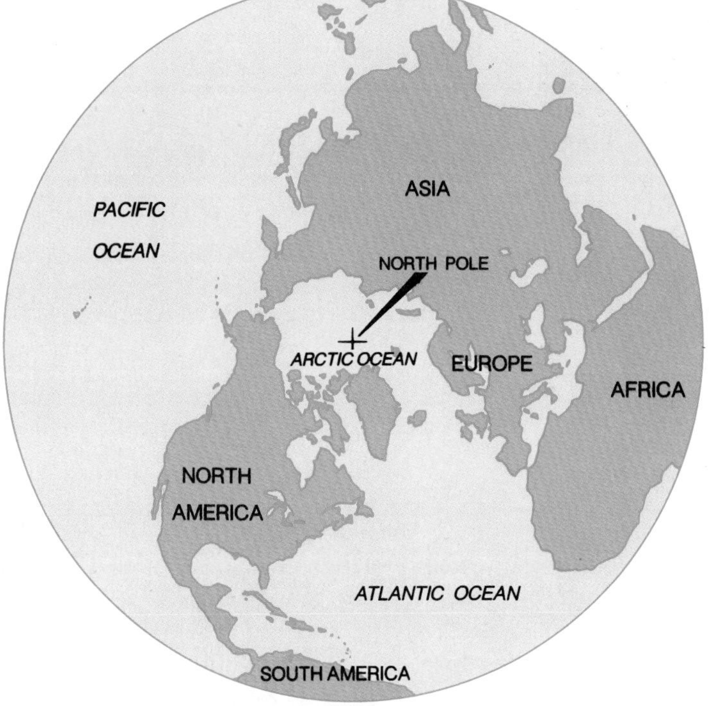

NORTHERN HEMISPHERE

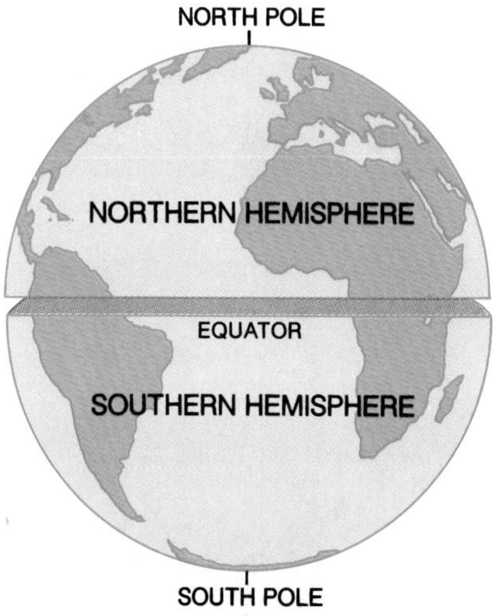

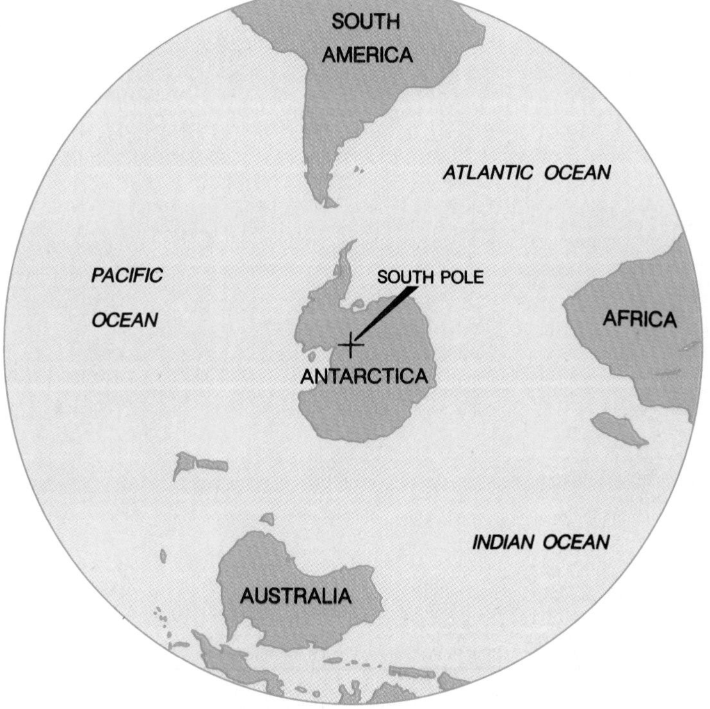

SOUTHERN HEMISPHERE

THE WORLD: POLITICAL

GREENLAND
(Denmark)
ALASKA
(U.S.)
ICELAND
CANADA
NORTH
AMERICA
IRELAND
PORTUGAL
UNITED STATES
MIDWAY
ISLAND
(U.S.)
BERMUDA
(G.B.)
HAWAII
(U.S.)
BAHAMAS
MEXICO
CUBA
HAITI
DOMINICAN
REPUBLIC
PUERTO RICO (U.S.)
JAMAICA
DOMINICA
BELIZE
HONDURAS
GUATEMALA
EL SALVADOR
NICARAGUA
BARBADOS
GRENADA
TRINIDAD AND TOBAGO
COSTA RICA
PANAMA
VENEZUELA
GUYANA
SURINAME
FRENCH GUIANA
(Fr.)
COLOMBIA
CAPE
VERDE
ISLANDS
MAURITANIA
SENEGAL
GAMBIA
GUINEA-
BISSAU
SIERRA
LEONE
LIBERIA
EQUATOR
GALAPAGOS
(Ecuador)
ECUADOR
PACIFIC
OCEAN
PERU
SOUTH
AMERICA
BRAZIL
ATLANTIC
OCEAN
AMERICAN
SAMOA
(U.S.)
WESTERN SAMOA
TONGA
BOLIVIA
PARAGUAY
FRENCH POLYNESIA
(Fr.)
CHILE
EASTER
ISLAND
(Chile)
URUGUAY
ARGENTINA
N
W
E
S
FALKLAND
ISLANDS
(G.B.)
SOUTH
GEORGIA
(G.B.)

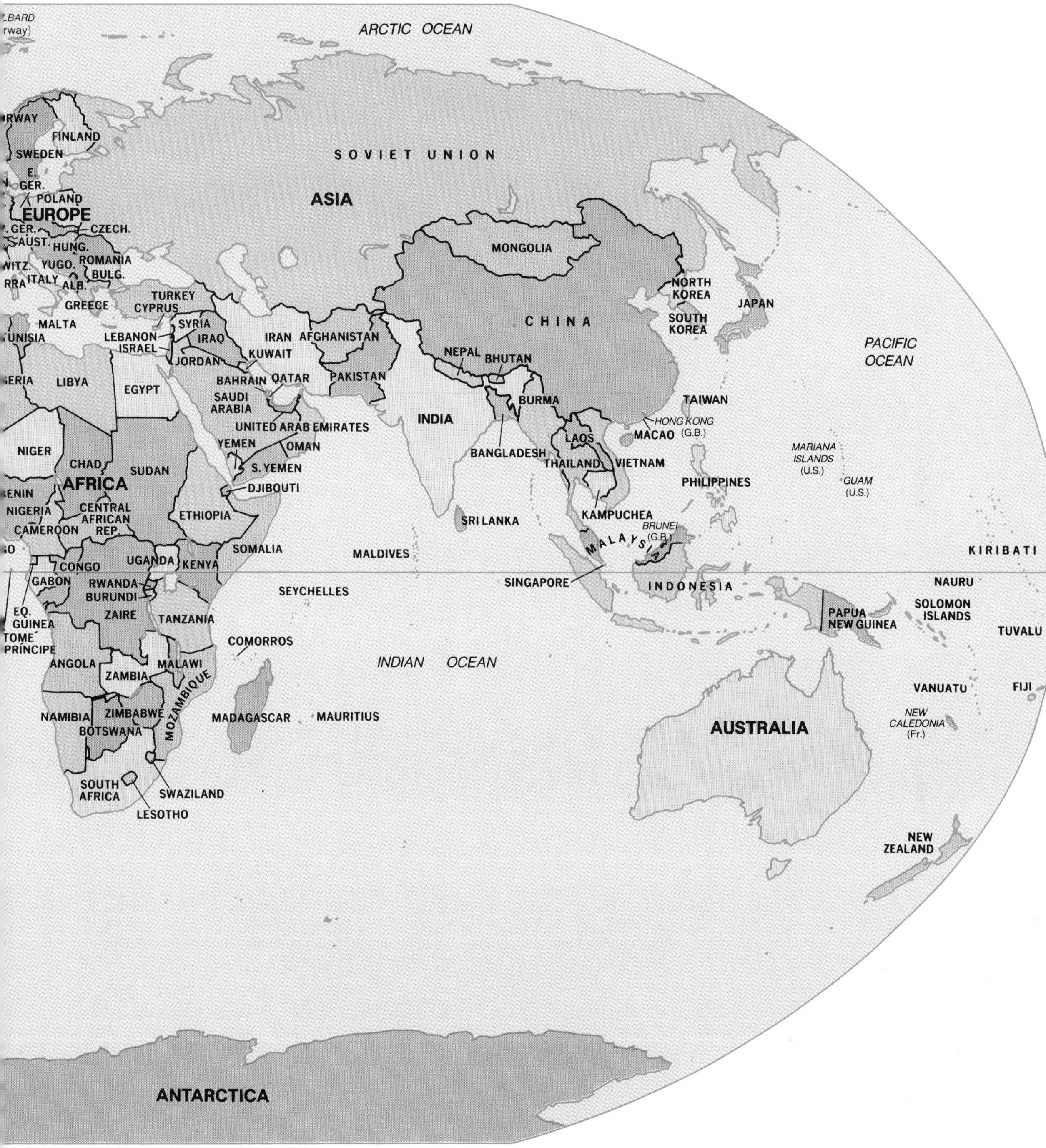

ARCTIC OCEAN
SOVIET UNION
ASIA
EUROPE
FINLAND
SWEDEN
E. GER.
POLAND
CZECH.
AUST.
HUNG.
ROMANIA
YUGO.
BULG.
ITALY
ALB.
GREECE
TURKEY
CYPRUS
MALTA
SYRIA
LEBANON
ISRAEL
IRAQ
IRAN
AFGHANISTAN
KUWAIT
JORDAN
BAHRAIN
QATAR
PAKISTAN
LIBYA
EGYPT
SAUDI ARABIA
UNITED ARAB EMIRATES
YEMEN
OMAN
S. YEMEN
DJIBOUTI
NIGER
CHAD
SUDAN
AFRICA
NIGERIA
CENTRAL AFRICAN REP.
CAMEROON
ETHIOPIA
SOMALIA
CONGO
UGANDA
KENYA
GABON
RWANDA
BURUNDI
ZAIRE
TANZANIA
EQ. GUINEA
COMORROS
ANGOLA
ZAMBIA
MALAWI
NAMIBIA
ZIMBABWE
MOZAMBIQUE
BOTSWANA
MADAGASCAR
MAURITIUS
SOUTH AFRICA
SWAZILAND
LESOTHO
SEYCHELLES
MALDIVES
INDIAN OCEAN
MONGOLIA
CHINA
NORTH KOREA
SOUTH KOREA
JAPAN
NEPAL
BHUTAN
INDIA
BANGLADESH
BURMA
TAIWAN
HONG KONG (G.B.)
MACAO
LAOS
THAILAND
VIETNAM
PHILIPPINES
KAMPUCHEA
SRI LANKA
BRUNEI (G.B.)
MALAYSIA
SINGAPORE
INDONESIA
PACIFIC OCEAN
MARIANA ISLANDS (U.S.)
GUAM (U.S.)
KIRIBATI
NAURU
PAPUA NEW GUINEA
SOLOMON ISLANDS
TUVALU
VANUATU
FIJI
NEW CALEDONIA (Fr.)
AUSTRALIA
NEW ZEALAND
ANTARCTICA

WASHINGTON
Seattle
Olympia
Spokane
Columbia River
OREGON
Portland
Salem
Eugene
PACIFIC OCEAN
IDAHO
Boise
Pocatello
Snake River
MONTANA
Great Falls
Helena
Billings
NORTH DAKOTA
Bismarck
SOUTH DAKOTA
Pierre
Missouri River
WYOMING
Casper
Cheyenne
Platte River
NEBRASKA
CALIFORNIA
Sacramento
San Francisco
Oakland
San Jose
Los Angeles
Long Beach
San Diego
NEVADA
Reno
Carson City
Las Vegas
UTAH
Great Salt Lake
Ogden
Salt Lake City
Provo
Colorado River
COLORADO
Denver
Colorado Springs
Pueblo
Arkansas River
KANSAS
Sali
Wic
ARIZONA
Phoenix
Tucson
NEW MEXICO
Santa Fe
Albuquerque
El Paso
Rio Grande
OKLAHO
Oklahom City
TEXAS
Fort Wo
Austin
San Antonio
MEXICO
PACIFIC OCEAN
HAWAII
Honolulu
Hilo
0 300 Miles
0 400 Kilometers
ALASKA
Nome
Fairbanks
Anchorage
Juneau
Yukon River
0 400 Miles
0 600 Kilometers
PACIFIC OCEAN
GULF OF ALASKA
N
W
E
S

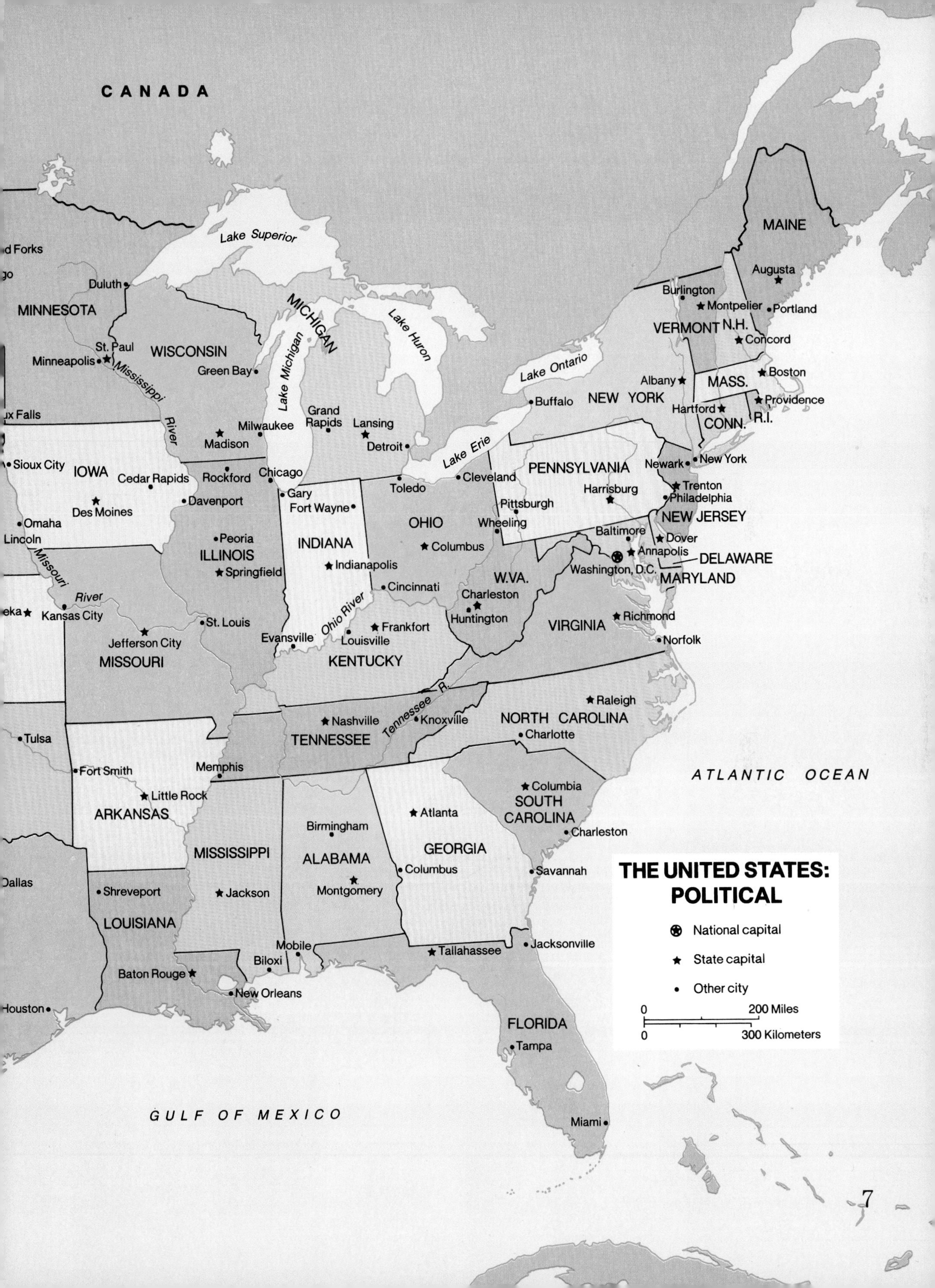
CANADA
Lake Superior
Lake Michigan
Lake Huron
Lake Ontario
Lake Erie
d Forks
go
Duluth
MINNESOTA
St. Paul
Minneapolis
Mississippi River
WISCONSIN
Green Bay
MICHIGAN
Milwaukee
Madison
Grand Rapids
Lansing
Detroit
ux Falls
Sioux City
IOWA
Cedar Rapids
Rockford
Chicago
Gary
Davenport
Des Moines
Omaha
Lincoln
Missouri River
Peoria
ILLINOIS
Springfield
eka
Kansas City
St. Louis
Jefferson City
MISSOURI
INDIANA
Fort Wayne
Indianapolis
Evansville
Ohio River
Toledo
Cleveland
OHIO
Columbus
Cincinnati
Louisville
Frankfort
KENTUCKY
Wheeling
W.VA.
Charleston
Huntington
PENNSYLVANIA
Pittsburgh
Harrisburg
Philadelphia
NEW YORK
Buffalo
Albany
New York
Newark
Trenton
NEW JERSEY
Baltimore
Washington, D.C.
Annapolis
Dover
DELAWARE
MARYLAND
VIRGINIA
Richmond
Norfolk
MAINE
Augusta
Portland
Burlington
Montpelier
VERMONT
N.H.
Concord
MASS.
Boston
Providence
Hartford
CONN.
R.I.
Tennessee R.
TENNESSEE
Nashville
Knoxville
Memphis
NORTH CAROLINA
Raleigh
Charlotte
Tulsa
Fort Smith
Little Rock
ARKANSAS
SOUTH CAROLINA
Columbia
Charleston
Atlanta
GEORGIA
Columbus
Savannah
Birmingham
ALABAMA
Montgomery
MISSISSIPPI
Jackson
Dallas
Shreveport
LOUISIANA
Mobile
Biloxi
Baton Rouge
New Orleans
Houston
Tallahassee
Jacksonville
FLORIDA
Tampa
Miami
ATLANTIC OCEAN
GULF OF MEXICO
THE UNITED STATES: POLITICAL
National capital
State capital
Other city
0
200 Miles
0
300 Kilometers

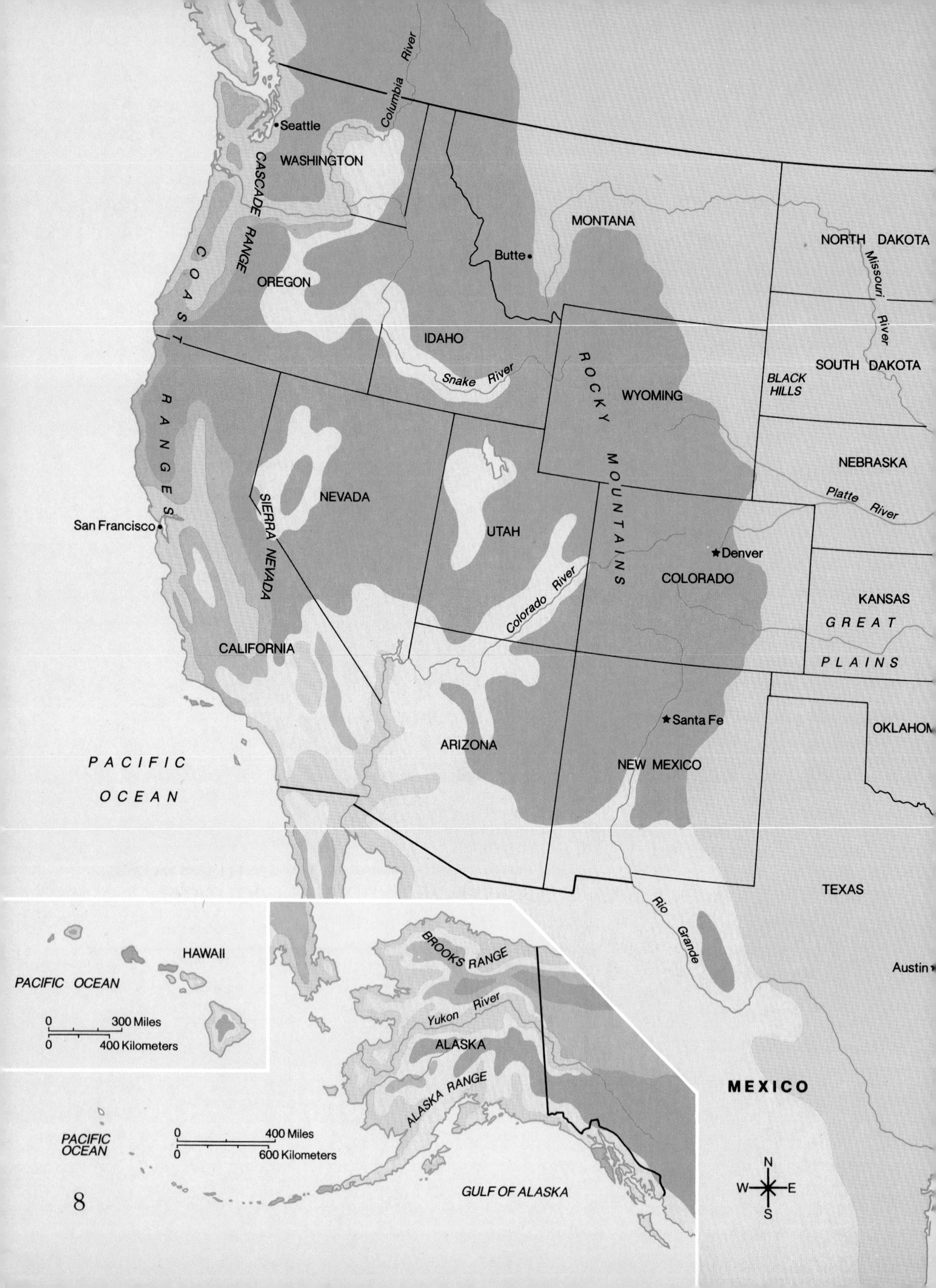

Columbia River
Seattle
WASHINGTON
CASCADE RANGE
COAST RANGES
OREGON
MONTANA
Butte
NORTH DAKOTA
Missouri River
IDAHO
Snake River
ROCKY MOUNTAINS
WYOMING
SOUTH DAKOTA
BLACK HILLS
NEBRASKA
Platte River
NEVADA
SIERRA NEVADA
UTAH
San Francisco
Denver
COLORADO
Colorado River
KANSAS
GREAT PLAINS
CALIFORNIA
Santa Fe
OKLAHOM
ARIZONA
PACIFIC OCEAN
NEW MEXICO
TEXAS
Rio Grande
Austin
HAWAII
PACIFIC OCEAN
0 300 Miles
0 400 Kilometers
BROOKS RANGE
Yukon River
ALASKA
ALASKA RANGE
MEXICO
PACIFIC OCEAN
0 400 Miles
0 600 Kilometers
GULF OF ALASKA
N
W
E
S

THE UNITED STATES: PHYSICAL
National capital
State capital
Other city
Mountains
Hills
Plateaus
Plains
CANADA
Lake Superior
Lake Michigan
Lake Huron
Lake Ontario
Lake Erie
MINNESOTA
WISCONSIN
MICHIGAN
IOWA
ILLINOIS
INDIANA
OHIO
PENNSYLVANIA
NEW YORK
VERMONT
NEW HAMPSHIRE
MAINE
MASS.
CONN.
RHODE ISLAND
NEW JERSEY
DELAWARE
MD.
WEST VIRGINIA
VIRGINIA
KENTUCKY
MISSOURI
TENNESSEE
NORTH CAROLINA
SOUTH CAROLINA
GEORGIA
ALABAMA
MISSISSIPPI
ARKANSAS
LOUISIANA
FLORIDA
Chicago
Kansas City
St. Louis
Boston
New York
Washington, D.C.
Atlanta
New Orleans
Miami
Mississippi River
Missouri River
Ohio River
Tennessee River
Arkansas River
Savannah River
Hudson River
Connecticut River
OZARK PLATEAU
APPLACHIAN MOUNTAINS
ATLANTIC COASTAL PLAIN
GULF COASTAL PLAIN
ATLANTIC OCEAN
GULF OF MEXICO
0
200 Miles
0
300 Kilometers

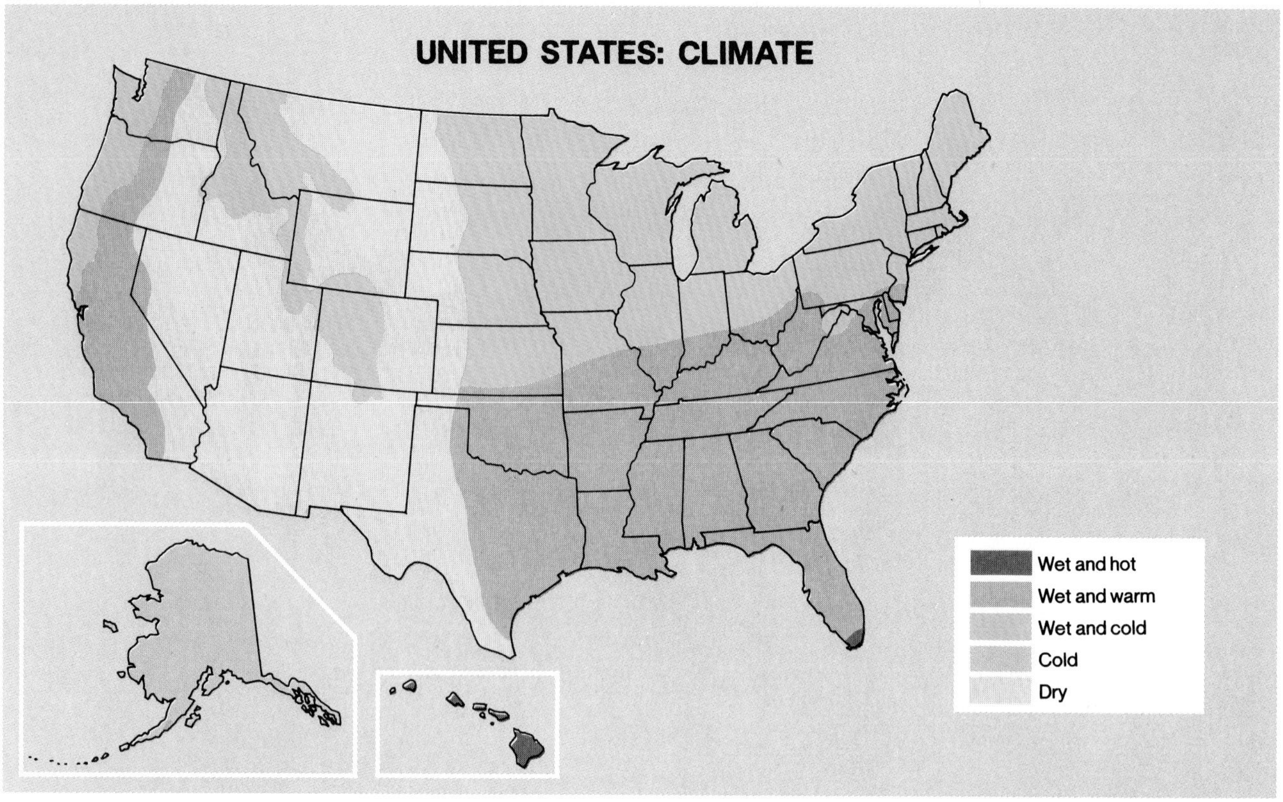
UNITED STATES: CLIMATE
Wet and hot
Wet and warm
Wet and cold
Cold
Dry

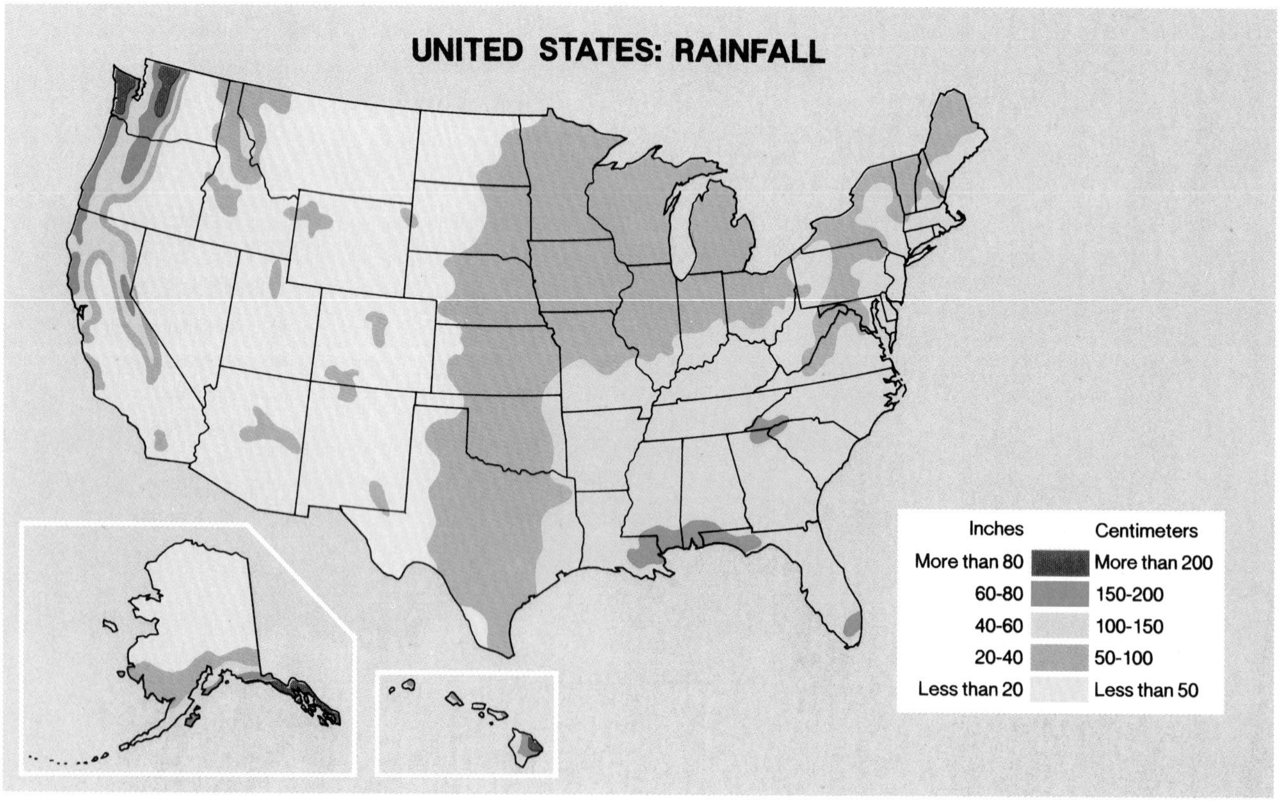
UNITED STATES: RAINFALL
Inches
Centimeters
More than 80
More than 200
60-80
150-200
40-60
100-150
20-40
50-100
Less than 20
Less than 50

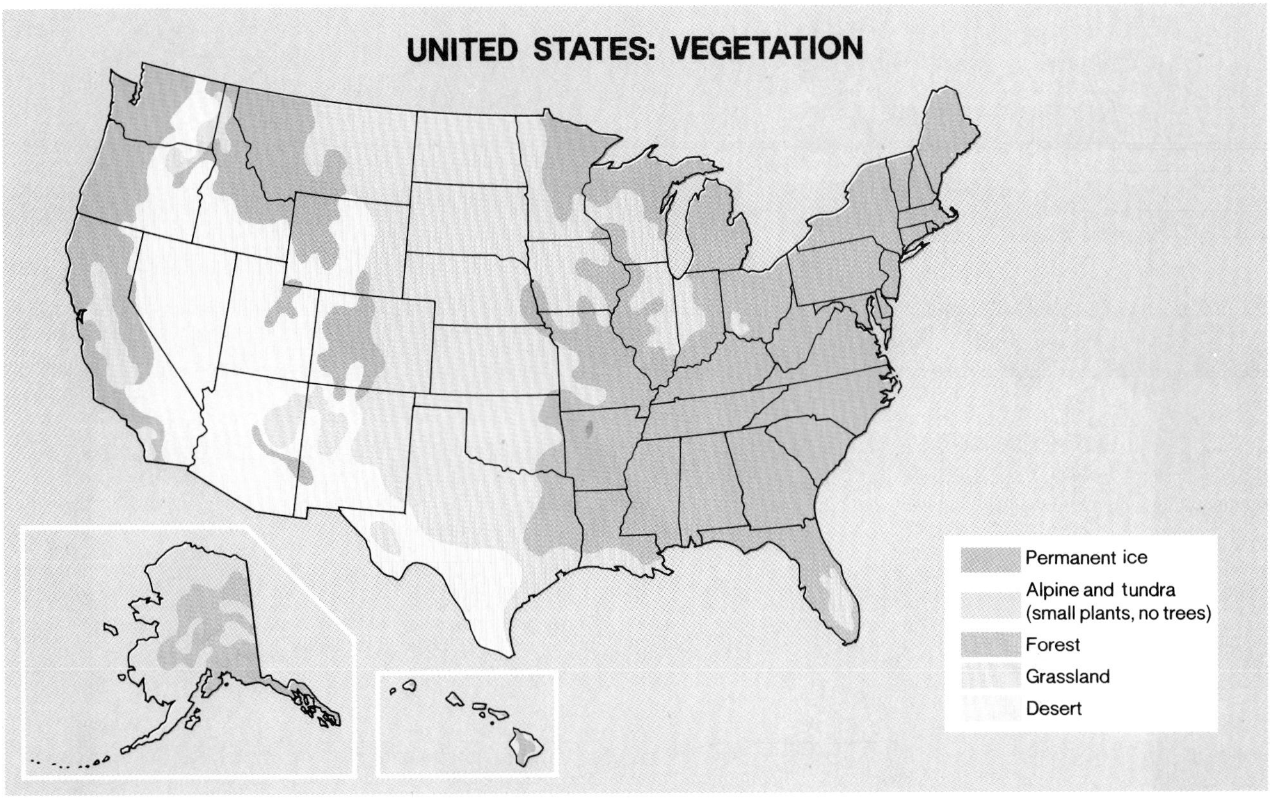
UNITED STATES: VEGETATION
Permanent ice
Alpine and tundra (small plants, no trees)
Forest
Grassland
Desert

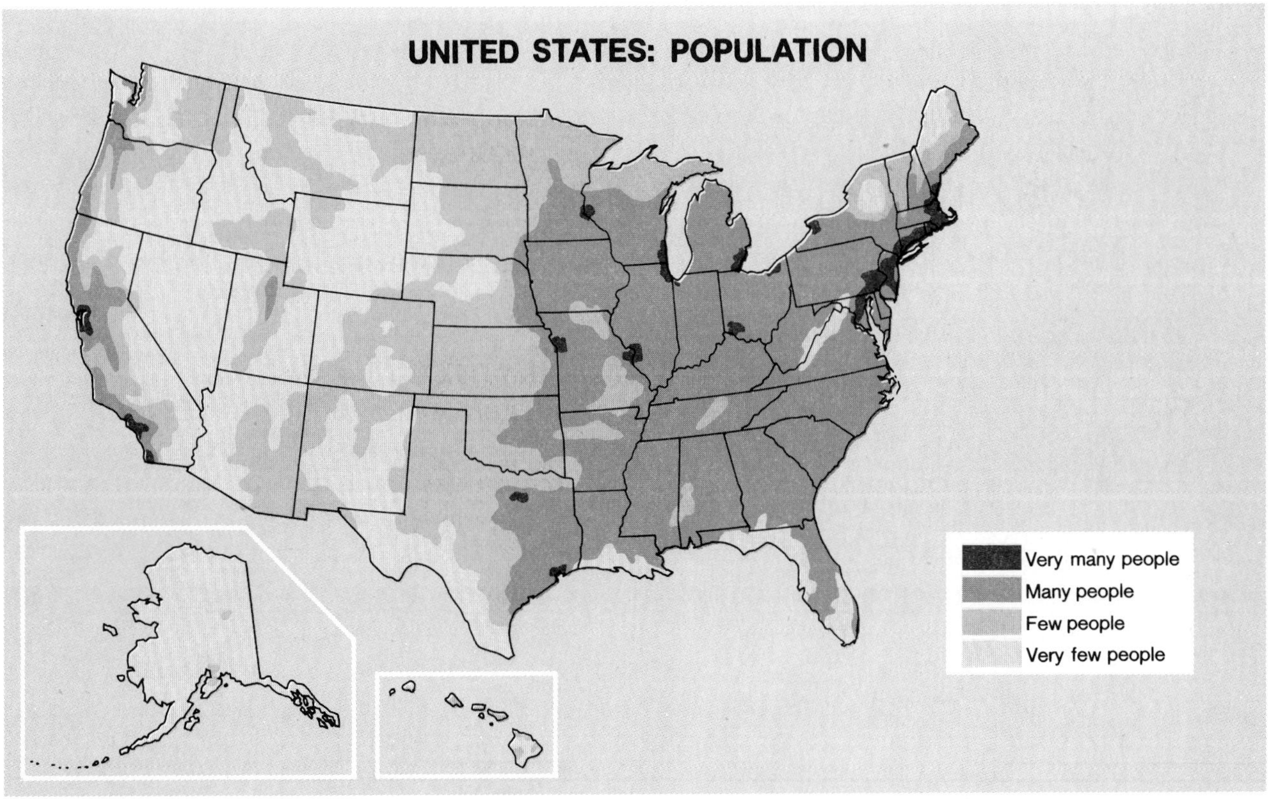
UNITED STATES: POPULATION
Very many people
Many people
Few people
Very few people

Dictionary of Geographical Words

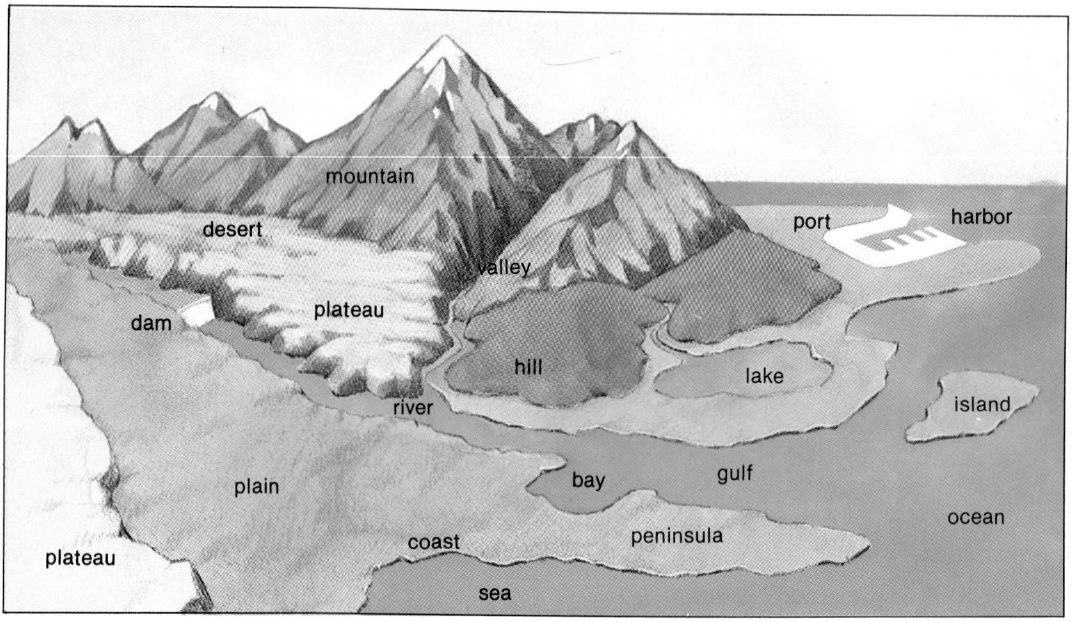

bay (bā): part of a body of water that extends into the land, usually smaller than a gulf

coast (kōst): land along a sea or ocean

dam (dam): a wall built across a river to hold back the water

desert (dez′ ərt): a very dry area where few plants grow

gulf (gulf): part of a body of water that extends into the land, usually larger than a bay

harbor (här′ bər): a protected place on an ocean, sea, or river where ships can anchor safely

hill (hil): a rounded and raised landform, not as high as a mountain

island (ī′ lənd): a body of land entirely surrounded by water, smaller than a continent

lake (lāk): a body of water entirely surrounded by land

mountain (mount′ ən): a high rounded or pointed landform with steep sides, higher than a hill

ocean (ō′ shən): the whole body of salt water that covers nearly three fourths of the earth's surface; the sea

peninsula (pə nin′ sə lə): land extending from a larger body of land, nearly surrounded by water

plain (plān): an area of flat or almost flat land

plateau (pla tō′): flat land with steep sides, raised above the surrounding land

port (pôrt): a place where ships load and unload goods

river (riv′ ər): a large stream of water that flows across the land and usually empties into a lake, ocean, or another river

sea (sē): a large body of water partly or entirely enclosed by land; another term for ocean

valley (val′ ē): an area of low land between hills or mountains

Map Symbols

Map symbols vary from map to map. Some maps use the same or similar symbols. Other maps use quite different symbols. You will see some of the commonly used symbols shown below on the maps in this book.

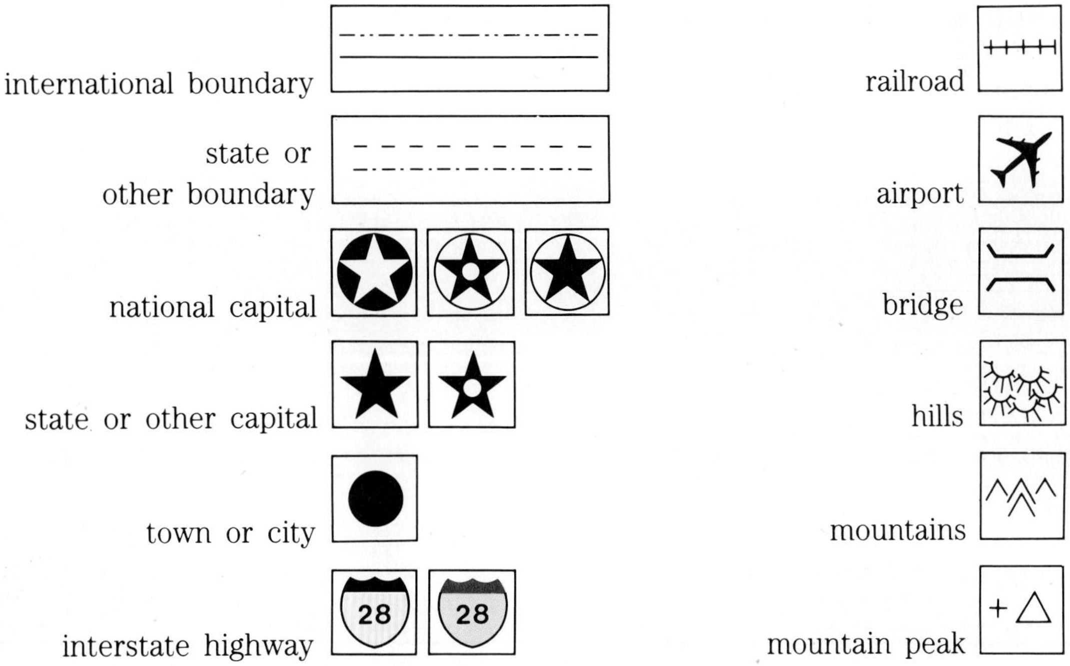

1

WE ALL LIVE IN COMMUNITIES

This year you will be studying all about communities. What are communities and why are they so important? Communities are places where people live, work, and play. The people in communities help us meet our needs.

Looking Ahead

1. This picture shows children in a community. What are they doing?
2. Where do you play in your community?

Words to Learn

community	location
town	transportation
village	port
city	capital
suburbs	museum

1 What Are Communities?

Each day you go to many different places. You leave your home and go to school. You go to stores to shop and to parks to play. Each day you see many different people. You see your family and friends. You see the people who live and work nearby.

All these places and people are part of your community (kə myo͞o′nə tē). A community is a place and the people who live and work there. What makes a community? Why do people live in communities?

A community is a place and the people who live and work there. People enjoy spending time with others in their community.

To answer these questions, think what your life would be like if you lived all alone. What would you miss? What do you need that the people in your community help you get?

Meeting Basic Needs

There are some things that all people need in order to live. These things are called basic needs. No one can live without food, clothing, and shelter.

The people in our community help us meet our basic needs. Look at the pictures on this page. How are the people in the pictures meeting their basic needs? How does your family meet these basic needs?

People in communities meet their basic needs in many ways. Shopping for food may be a family activity. Some people sew their own clothes.

Working in a Community

Most people cannot meet their basic needs alone. They depend on the work that other people do. Some workers produce goods, such as bread, bicycles, coats, or books. Other workers provide services that help people. Doctors, teachers, firefighters, and police officers are some of the people who provide services in our communities.

Workers in a community provide goods and services. The picture on the right shows people buying goods in a store. What service is being provided below?

Many communities have a parade to celebrate the Fourth of July.

Customs in a Community

People in a community also have good times together. There are some special times that everyone in a community shares. All communities have holidays. Every year on the Fourth of July Americans celebrate our country's birthday. Some communities have fireworks. Other communities have picnics and parades.

The things we do on holidays are examples of customs. Each community has its own customs, or special ways of doing things. Customs are something that the people in a community share.

Do You Know?

1. What is a community?
2. Name the three things that all people need in order to live.
3. What are three services provided by people in communities?

2 How Are Communities Different?

Almost everyone lives in a community. There are many different kinds of communities. One important difference is size. Communities can be large or small.

Rural Areas

A small community is called a town (toun). A very small community is sometimes called a village (vil′ij). Towns and villages provide goods and services for the people who live in the surrounding area.

Towns and villages usually are found in rural areas. Rural areas have few people. Houses may be far apart.

A town is a rural community.

Urban Areas

A city (sit′ē) is a very large community. Many people live in a city. Most buildings in a city are close together. Large numbers of people live in apartment houses. People work at many kinds of jobs.

A large city usually is surrounded by smaller communities called suburbs (sub′urbz). Houses in a suburb are farther apart than in a city. There is more open space in a suburb. Many people live in a suburb but work in a city.

A city and its suburbs make up an urban area. Urban areas have many, many people. They have many stores, houses, and large buildings.

A city is part of an urban area.

A community's location makes a difference in the kind of work people do.

Location of Communities

Communities can be found almost anywhere in the world. Some communities are in the mountains. Others are near the ocean. There are communities near good farm land or near forests. The location (lō kā′shən), or place, of a community makes a difference in the kind of work people do.

A community located near a forest may be a logging community. People in the community may have jobs cutting trees and hauling logs. Others may work in mills that make lumber from the logs. The logs and lumber may be sent to other places.

Location is important for other reasons. A community needs many goods it cannot make itself. Goods must be brought from other places. All communities must have good transportation (trans′pər tā′shən). The moving of people and goods from place to place is called transportation.

New Orleans is a busy port city on the Mississippi River.

New Orleans, Louisiana, is a port (pôrt) city on the Mississippi River. A port is a place where ships load and unload goods. Port cities grew up along harbors, or protected places, on many rivers and other bodies of water.

Albuquerque (al′bə kur′kē), New Mexico, is a railroad center. Trains come in and out of this community every day. Many communities grew up because of their location near a railroad.

Good transportation can help a community grow. Most large urban areas are located near ports or railroads. They also are near airports and big highways.

Do You Know?

1. What kinds of communities are in rural areas?
2. What kinds of communities make up an urban area?
3. Why do communities need transportation?

Before You Go On

Learning About a Grid Map

The map on the next page shows part of a community. The map key shows what the symbols on the map stand for. Symbols stand for real things. What symbol stands for a house? What symbol stands for a railroad? Some symbols are not shown on the key. The river and the lake are named on the map. They are blue to help you tell that they are bodies of water.

This map also has a grid. The grid helps you locate places on the map. A grid is a set of squares. Each square has a letter and a number. The letters are shown on the left of the map. The numbers are shown on the top of the map.

Here is how to use the grid. Point to the hospital on the map with your finger. Now slide your finger to the left. What letter do you come to? Now move your finger up from the hospital. What number do you come to? The hospital is in square C-3.

Practicing Your Skills

Use the map and the map key to answer these questions.

1. In what squares are there schools?
2. How many stores are in square B-2?
3. In what squares are there parks?
4. How many bridges are shown on the map?
5. In what square is the firehouse?
6. Through what squares does the railroad pass?

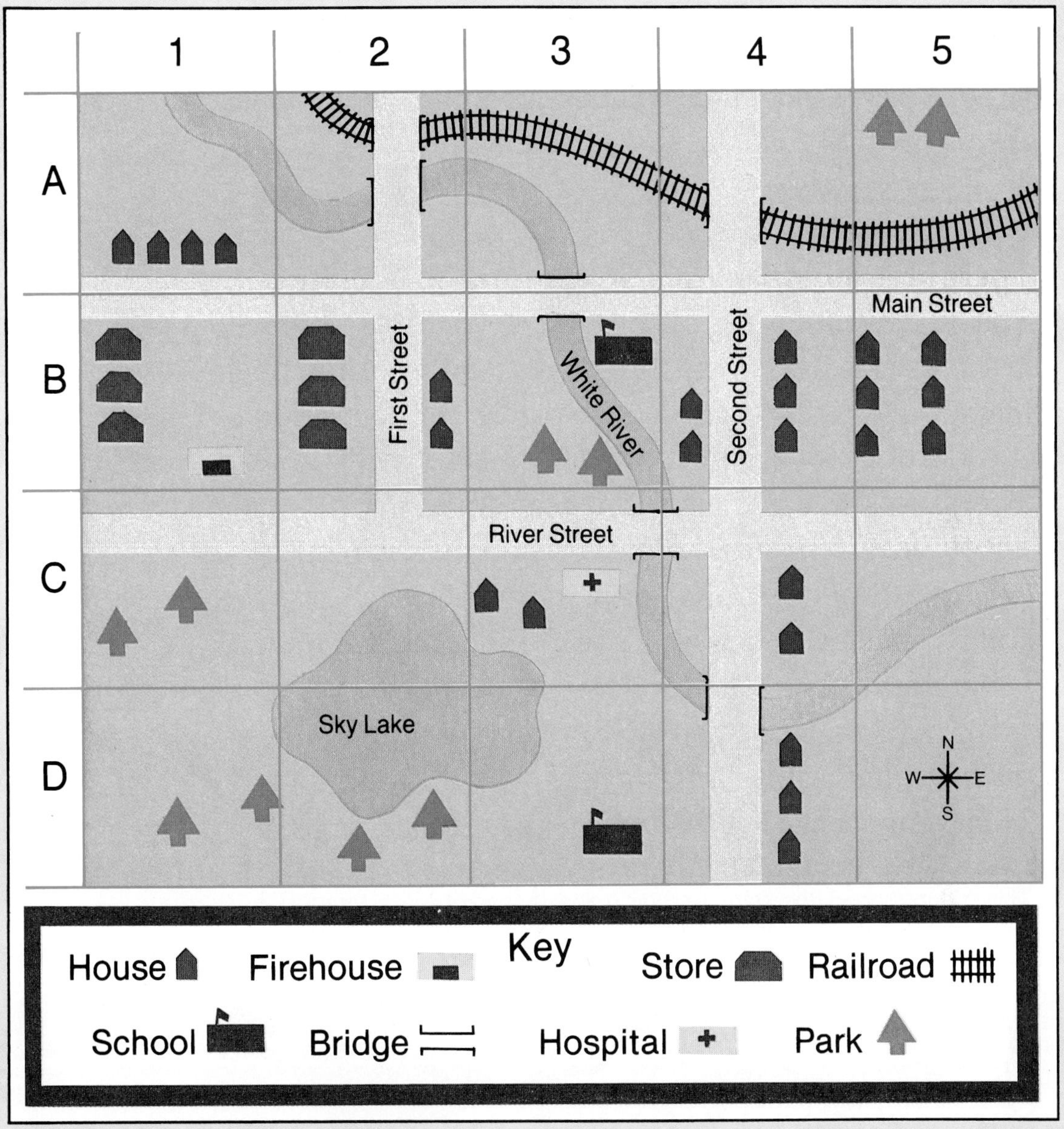
1
2
3
4
5
A
B
C
D
Main Street
First Street
Second Street
White River
River Street
Sky Lake
N
W
E
S
Key
House
Firehouse
Store
Railroad
School
Bridge
Hospital
Park

3 We Live in the United States

Do you know the name of the state in which your community is located? Find your state on the map of the United States on pages 28-29.

Our 50 States

There are 50 states in our country. The United States map shows the borders of each state. Borders are places where one state ends and another begins. Maps have lines that show borders. In some places the border is formed by a body of water. The map also shows several cities in each state.

One city in each state is the state capital (kap′it əl). The capital city is the place where the state's leaders meet and work. Find the capital of your state on the map.

Each state is special. But all the states share many things. They are all part of the same country. They work together in many ways.

This picture shows the state flag, bird, and flower of West Virginia. What is the flag, bird, and flower of your state?

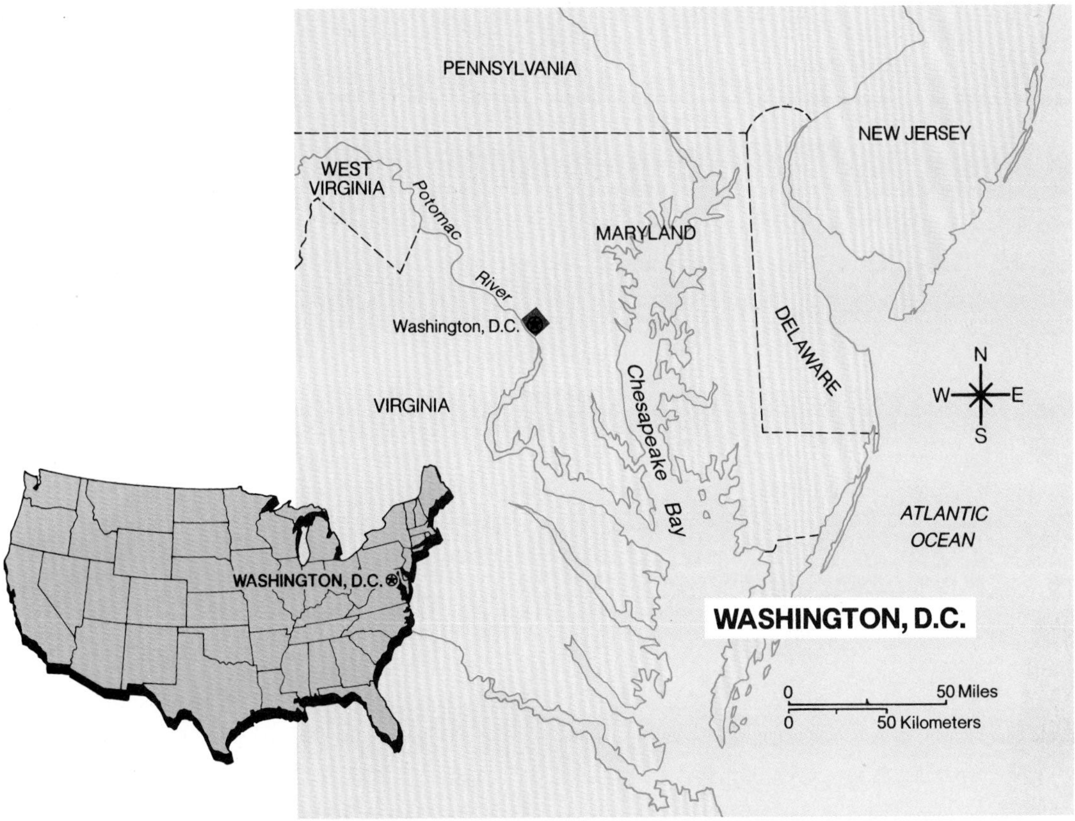

Washington, D.C., is the capital of the United States. Find the city on the map. On what river is it located?

Another word for together is united. The name of our country is the United States of America. That is a long name. Our country also has several shorter names. These names are the United States, the U.S., the U.S.A., and America.

Our country has a capital city too. It is the city of Washington, D.C. The country's leaders meet and work in Washington, D.C.

Washington, D.C., is the only community in our country that is not located in a state. It is between the states of Maryland and Virginia, but is not part of either state. This is a way of showing that the capital of the United States belongs to the whole country. It belongs to the people of every state.

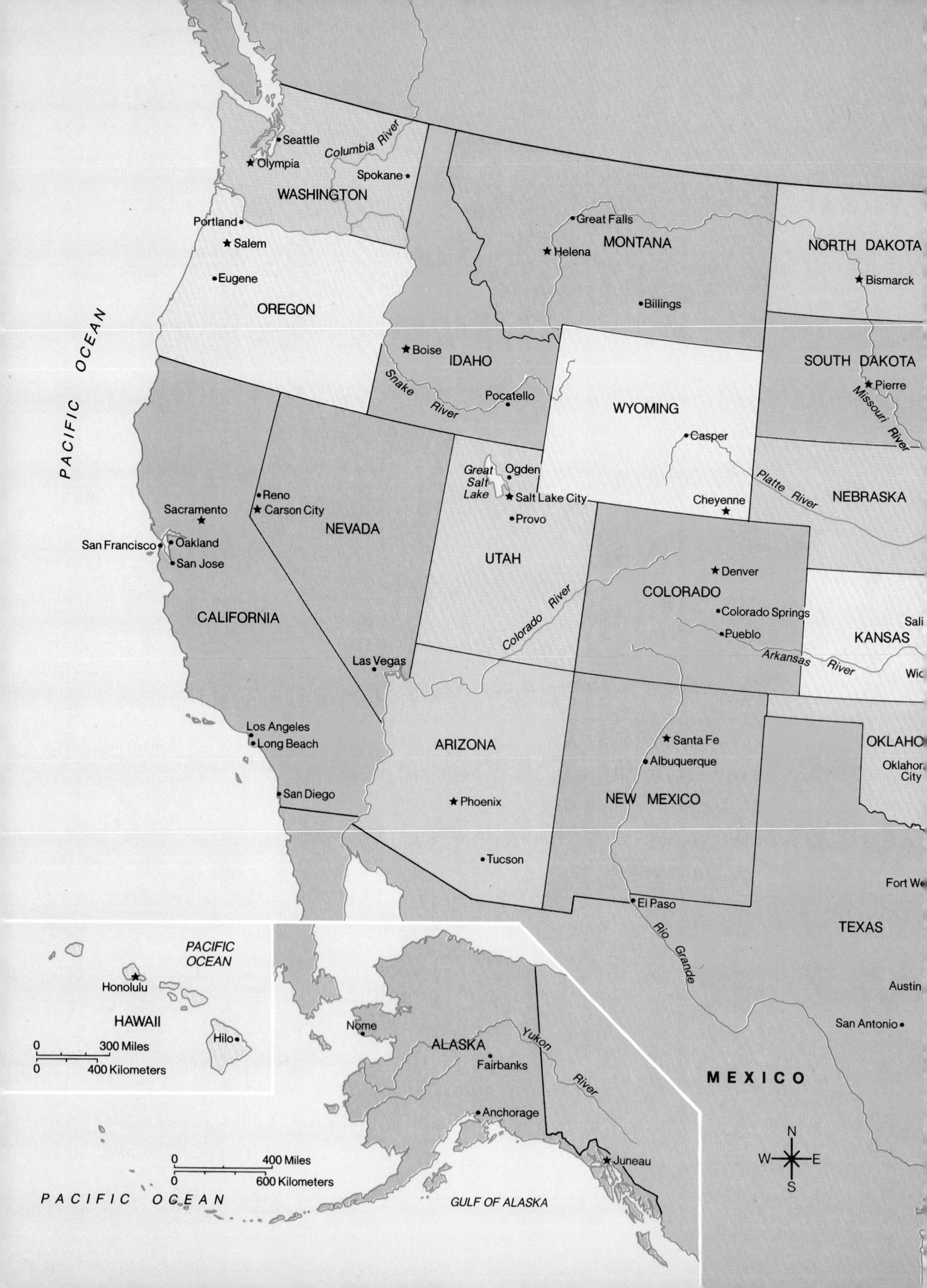
WASHINGTON
Seattle
Olympia
Columbia River
Spokane
Portland
Salem
Eugene
OREGON
PACIFIC OCEAN
MONTANA
Great Falls
Helena
Billings
NORTH DAKOTA
Bismarck
IDAHO
Boise
Snake River
Pocatello
WYOMING
Casper
Cheyenne
SOUTH DAKOTA
Pierre
Missouri River
Platte River
NEBRASKA
Great Salt Lake
Ogden
Salt Lake City
Provo
UTAH
NEVADA
Reno
Carson City
Sacramento
San Francisco
Oakland
San Jose
CALIFORNIA
Las Vegas
Colorado River
COLORADO
Denver
Colorado Springs
Pueblo
Arkansas River
KANSAS
Sali
Wic
Los Angeles
Long Beach
San Diego
ARIZONA
Phoenix
Tucson
NEW MEXICO
Santa Fe
Albuquerque
El Paso
Rio Grande
OKLAHO
Oklahor. City
Fort W
TEXAS
Austin
San Antonio
MEXICO
PACIFIC OCEAN
Honolulu
HAWAII
Hilo
0 300 Miles
0 400 Kilometers
ALASKA
Nome
Fairbanks
Yukon River
Anchorage
Juneau
0 400 Miles
0 600 Kilometers
PACIFIC OCEAN
GULF OF ALASKA
N
W
E
S

THE UNITED STATES: POLITICAL

Mexico City is the capital of Mexico. Mexico City is a big city with busy streets and many tall buildings.

North America

Each state has borders. So does our country. Find the borders of the United States on the map on page 31. These lines show where the United States ends and another country begins.

We share our borders with two other countries. They are Mexico and Canada. Find these countries on the map. Which country is south of the United States? Which country is north of most of the states and east of Alaska?

The United States, Canada, and Mexico are all located on the continent of North America. A continent is a very large area of land. What other countries are located on the continent of North America?

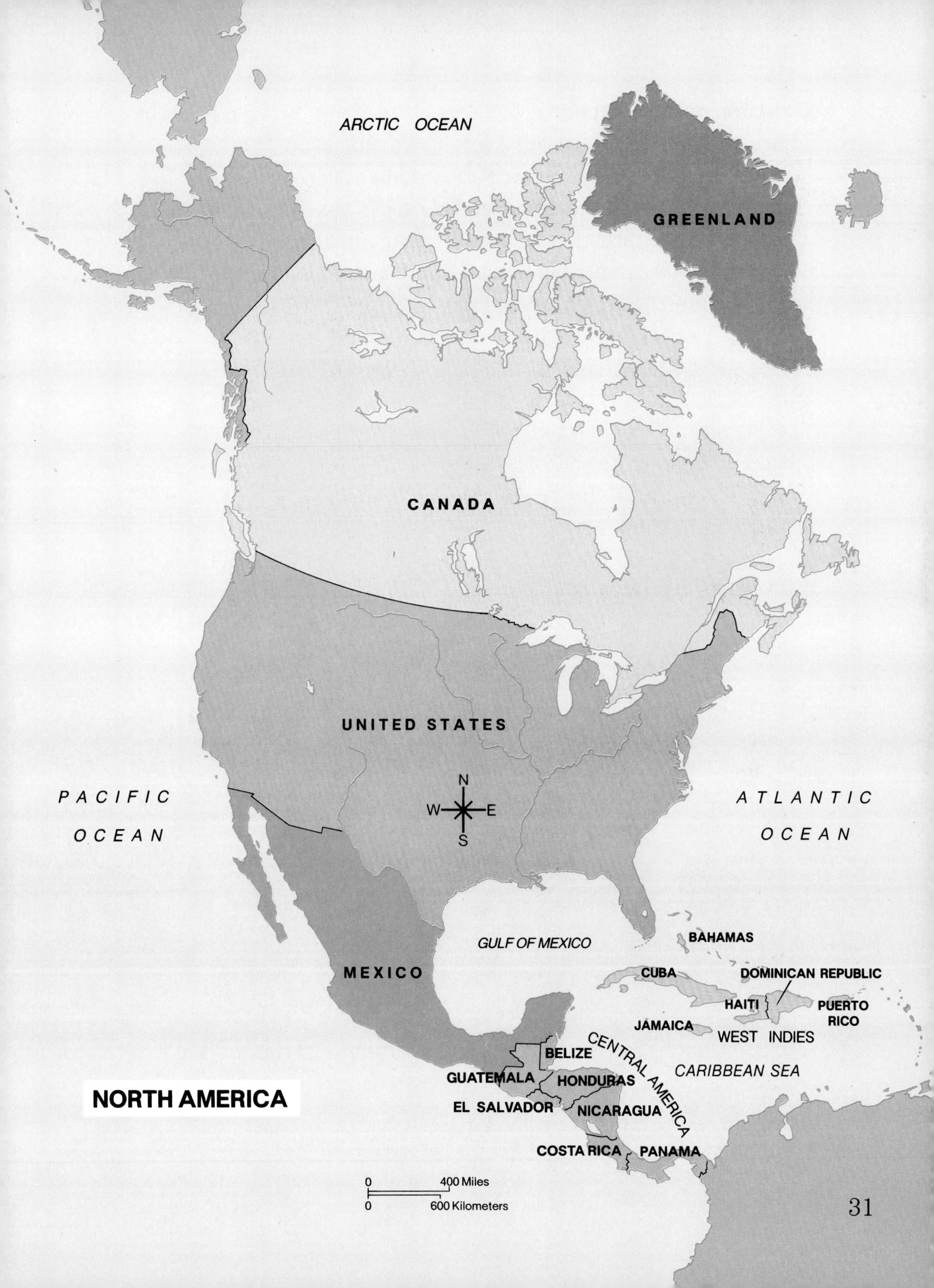
ARCTIC OCEAN
GREENLAND
CANADA
UNITED STATES
PACIFIC OCEAN
ATLANTIC OCEAN
N
W
E
S
GULF OF MEXICO
BAHAMAS
CUBA
DOMINICAN REPUBLIC
HAITI
PUERTO RICO
JAMAICA
WEST INDIES
MEXICO
CENTRAL AMERICA
BELIZE
CARIBBEAN SEA
GUATEMALA
HONDURAS
EL SALVADOR
NICARAGUA
COSTA RICA
PANAMA
0
400 Miles
0
600 Kilometers

NORTH AMERICA

Continents and Oceans

There are seven continents in the world. Find them on the map below. What are they called? To which continent is North America connected?

Continents are the largest bodies of land. Most continents have many countries and a very, very large number of cities and towns.

The largest bodies of water are called oceans. There are four oceans in the world. North America and South America are located between two oceans. The Atlantic Ocean is east of these continents. Which ocean is west of them? The other two oceans are the Indian Ocean and the Arctic Ocean. Find these oceans on the map.

CONTINENTS AND OCEANS

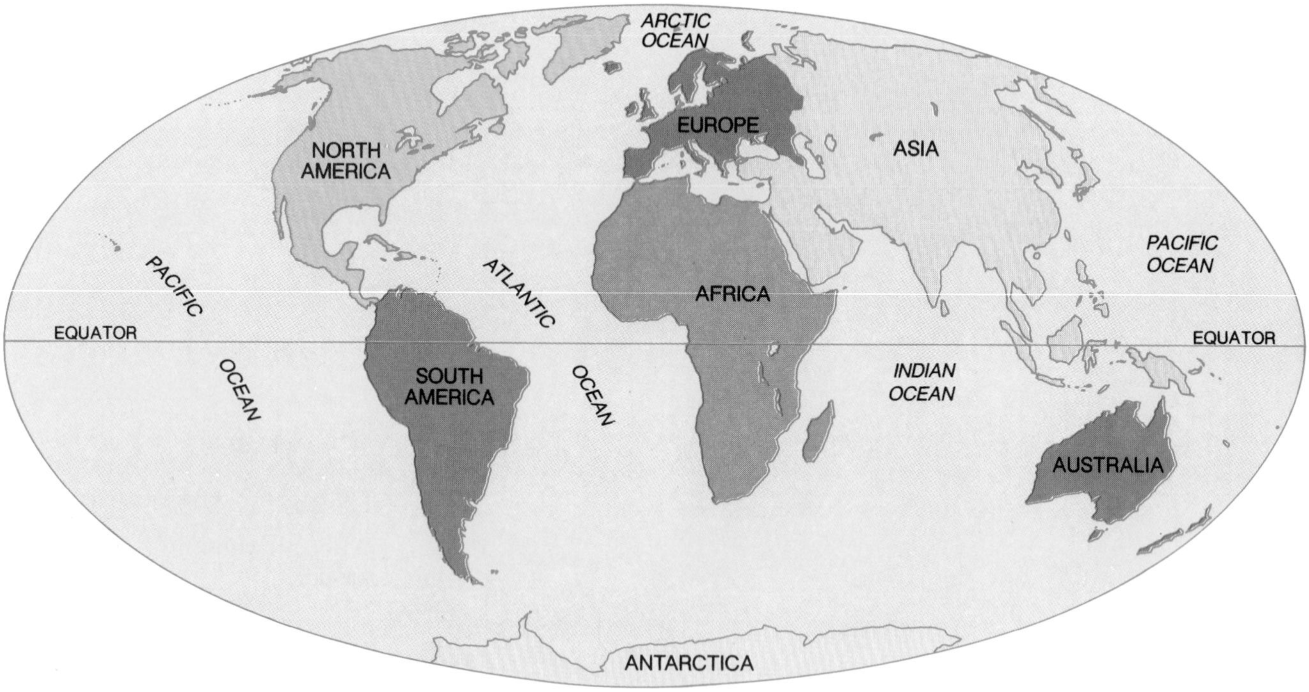

This map shows the earth's continents and oceans. The United States is on the continent of North America. What continent is south of North America?

The picture on the left shows shoppers in Japan.
The picture below shows shoppers in Peru.

Other Countries

Most of the communities you will read about in this book are in the United States. You also will study communities in other countries. You will read about communities that are alike in many ways and about communities that are different.

The pictures on this page show communities in other countries. How are they alike? How are they different?

Do You Know?

1. What is the capital of the United States?
2. Name the continent on which the United States is located. Which state is not on a continent?
3. What two countries share borders with the United States?
4. What are the largest bodies of land called?

4 Learning About Your Community

Sara was studying about communities in school. She decided she wanted to learn about her own community. She lives in the city of Hampton, Virginia. The first thing Sara did was write a list of things she wanted to know.

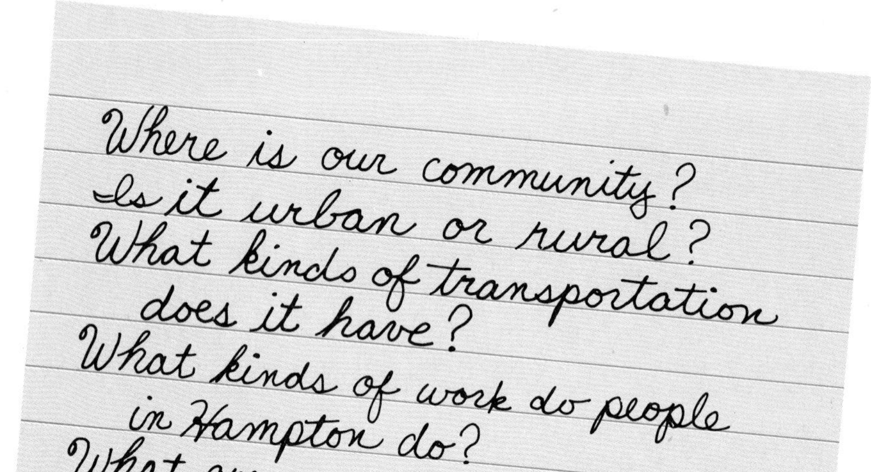

Where is our community?
Is it urban or rural?
What kinds of transportation does it have?
What kinds of work do people in Hampton do?
What are some fun things to see and do?
What was our community like in the past?

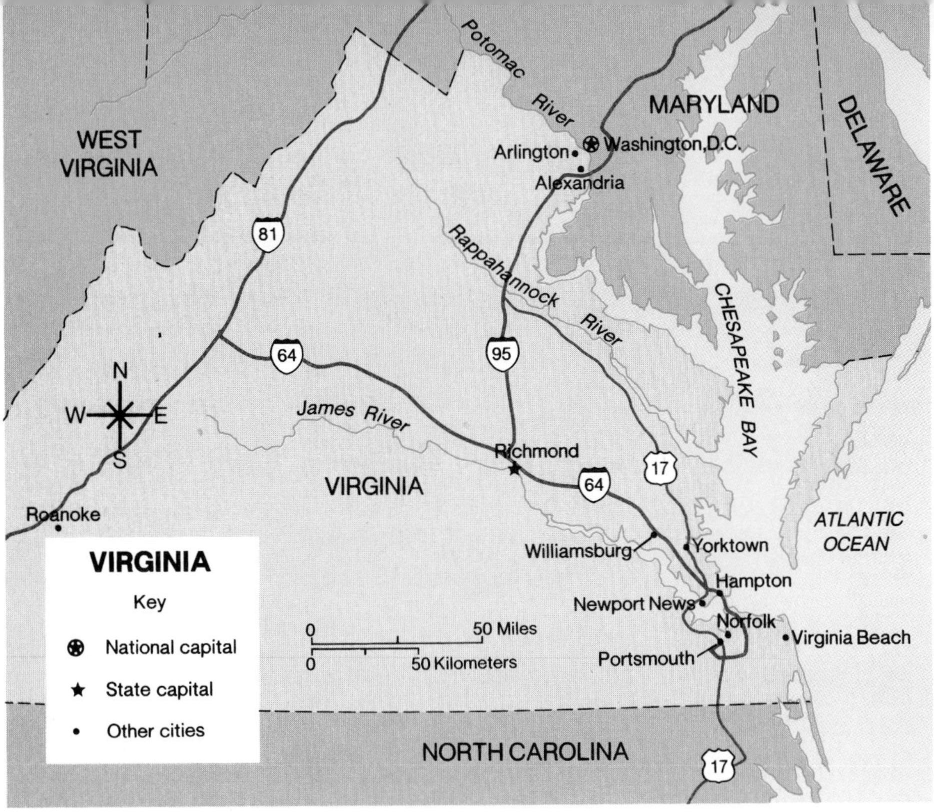

What is the capital of Virginia? How can you tell?

Using Maps

Sara found the location of Hampton on a map of Virginia. She learned that Hampton is located on a peninsula in the southeastern part of the state. A peninsula is a body of land that extends from a larger body of land and is nearly surrounded by water.

The map also showed Sara that the city of Newport News is located nearby, on the same peninsula as Hampton. Across the water to the south is the city of Norfolk. Sara's mother explained that Hampton, Norfolk, Newport News, and several other cities and suburbs are all part of a large urban area.

"These cities," said Sara's mother, "are connected by many kinds of transportation. There are roads, bridges, and tunnels for cars, trucks, and buses. Railroads, airplanes, and ships also come into our urban area."

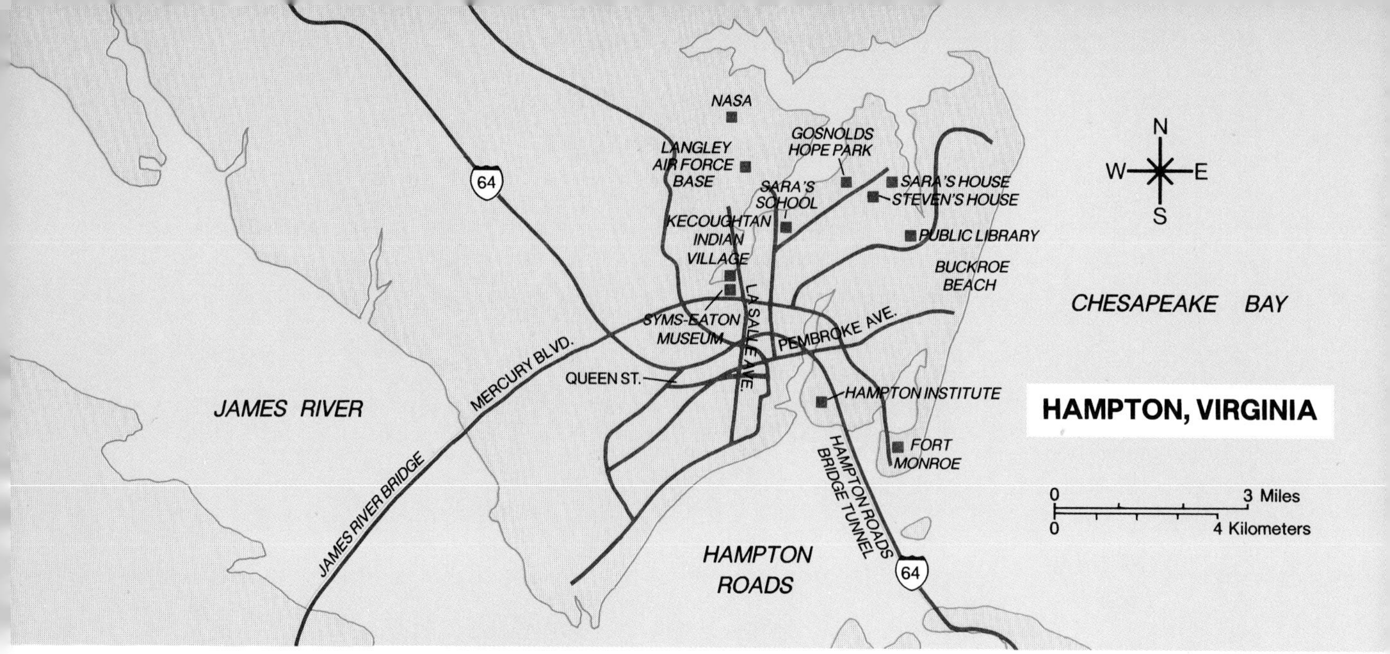

This is a map of Hampton, Virginia. Find Sara's house. In what direction is her house from Fort Monroe?

Sara's father suggested that she locate their home on a map of Hampton. "A map of our community," he said, "shows the location of many places. It can help you learn many things about our city." Sara also found her friend Steven's house on the Hampton map. She found her school and the public library. The map also showed Sara the location of many other places in Hampton.

Jobs in Hampton

Next Sara wanted to learn about jobs in Hampton. Her father told her to write a letter to the Chamber of Commerce. He said that this group of business people would send her information about the places where people work. Sara found the address of the Chamber of Commerce in the telephone book.

The Chamber of Commerce sent Sara information about many companies in and near Hampton. She learned that Hampton is a center for fishing. It has many companies that package seafoods such as fish, clams, oysters, and crabs.

Sara discovered that many people in Hampton work for the government. Some work at the army post called Fort Monroe, for example. Some work at the NASA Langley Research Center. These workers helped our astronauts land on the moon.

Hampton also is a center for education. Sara learned that Hampton Institute was one of the first colleges for black people in the United States. It was opened as a college for freed slaves.

Sara went to visit Fort Monroe. To get inside she had to cross the moat (mōt), or deep ditch, that surrounds the fort.

Hampton's History

Sara's mother told her that she could learn about Hampton's history at the Syms-Eaton Museum (myo͞o zē′ əm). A museum is a building where interesting things are shown. They decided to spend Saturday morning at the museum.

Their first stop was the Kecoughtan (kē kō tan′) Indian Village right next to the museum. The Kecoughtan Indians were the first people to live in the Hampton area. In the village Sara met Kingston Winget. He is in charge of the museum. Mr. Winget offered to show Sara around.

He told Sara that the houses she saw were built the same way the Kecoughtans had built them. They are made of young trees and reeds woven together. Reeds are a kind of tall grass that grows in wet lands. "The Kecoughtan women did most of the work in building their homes," Mr. Winget told Sara.

He also showed her a garden. "We are growing the same kinds of foods the Indians grew," said Mr. Winget.

Inside the museum Sara learned that Hampton is one of the oldest cities in the United States. English settlers began the city in 1610. "The English forced the Indians to leave," said Mr. Winget. "Then they built their town in the place the Indians had lived."

Mr. Winget showed Sara around the Kecoughtan Indian Village. She saw houses built just the way the Kecoughtans had built them. She learned how the Kecoughtans lived long ago.

Mr. Winget also took Sara through the museum. He showed her many interesting things that had been used by early settlers in Hampton.

Sara saw many old drawings and maps that showed what Hampton looked like long ago. She also saw things that were made long ago. The museum has dishes, teapots, glasses, and other things used by the early people in Hampton.

Your Own Community

Sara learned many interesting things about her community. You can learn about your community too. Look again at the list of things Sara wanted to know. What questions about your community would you add to her list?

Do You Know?

1. Where is Hampton located?
2. Tell three ways Sara learned about her community.
3. Name two kinds of work people in Hampton do.
4. Tell two things Sara learned at the museum.

1 TO HELP YOU LEARN

Using New Words

Read the words in the box. Choose the best word to complete each sentence. Write the completed sentences on a sheet of paper.

community	location	village	museum
transportation	capital	suburbs	town
city	port		

1. New York City became a ________ city because it has a good harbor on the Atlantic Ocean.
2. Smaller communities near cities are called ________.
3. Trains and airplanes are kinds of ________.
4. A town is an example of a ________.
5. A very small community in a rural area is sometimes called a ________.
6. The ________ of the United States is Washington, D.C.
7. People enjoy looking at interesting things in a ________.
8. In a ________ you usually can see large buildings and many people.
9. A ________ is a small community in a rural area.
10. Many communities grew up because of their ________ near good transportation.

Finding the Facts

1. Give examples of two services provided by workers. Give two examples of goods produced by workers.
2. What two kinds of communities make up an urban area?
3. How many states are in the United States?
4. Name the only community in our country that is not located in a state.
5. Between which two oceans is the continent of North America located?
6. In what state is Hampton located?

Using Study Skills

1. Use the index on pages 288–294 to answer these questions.

    a. On what page will you find information about Albuquerque, New Mexico?
    b. List all the pages where you can read about transportation.
    c. On what pages will you find information about Hampton, Virginia?
    d. What is the first page where you can read about suburbs?
    e. List all the pages where you can read about Washington, D.C.

2. Tommy's mother buys some apples every week. The picture graph below shows how many apples she has bought in the last four weeks.

Use the graph below to answer these questions.

a. How many apples did Tommy's mother buy in Week 1?

b. In which week did Tommy's mother buy the fewest apples?

c. In which week did she buy the most apples?

d. In which weeks did Tommy's mother buy more than five apples?

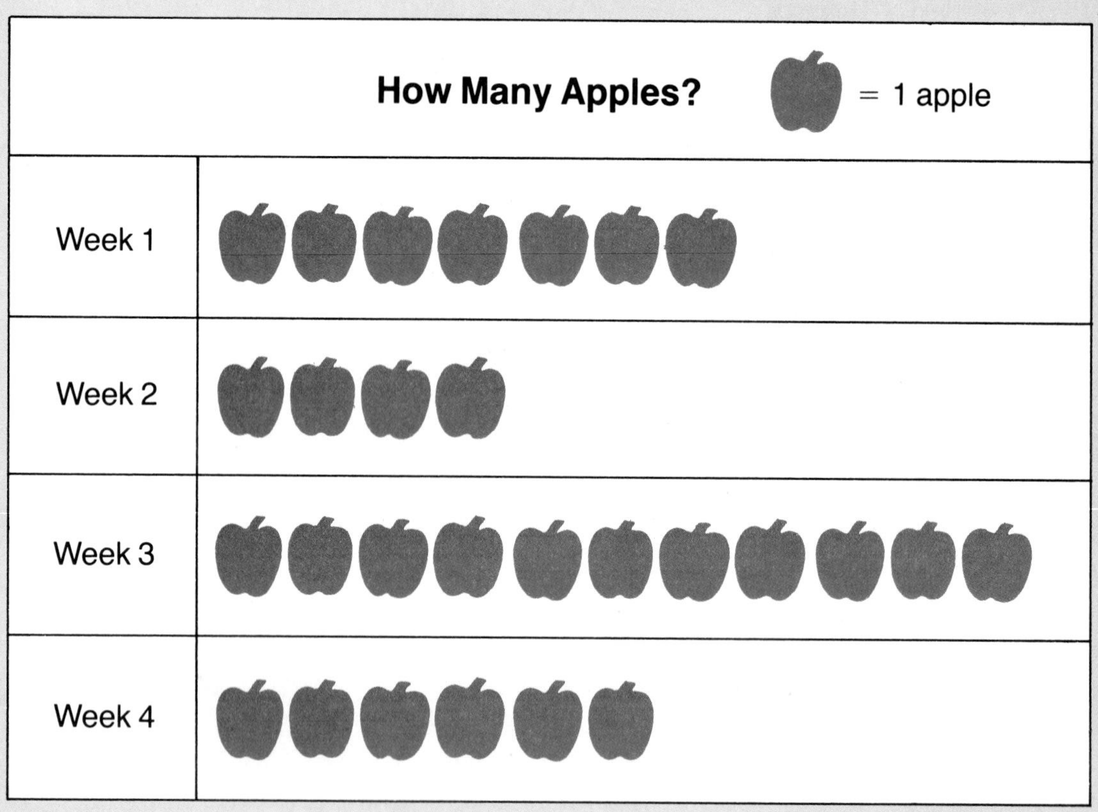

Things to Think About

1. Name two ways towns and cities are different.
2. What kinds of transportation are important in your community?

Things to Do

1. Find a map of your community. Locate these places on the map: your home, your school, the public library, a store in which you have shopped, a park.
2. Cut out pictures of cities, suburbs, towns, and villages from newspapers and magazines. Place them on the bulletin board in your classroom. Decide if they show urban or rural communities.

Learning About Your Own Community

Some communities are small. Other communities are large. Is your community a town, village, city, or suburb? What kinds of communities are located near where you live?

Learning from Maps

1. Turn to the map of the United States on pages 28–29. How can you tell the borders of each state? Name one state where a border is formed by a body of water. What states border your state?
2. Turn to the map of North America on page 31. What country is north of the United States? What country is south of the United States?

B. FRANKLIN
PRINTER

2

PEOPLE BUILD COMMUNITIES

The history of communities is the history of our country. Communities in America have been built by many groups of people. The first people here were the American Indians. They were followed by colonists from many countries. Later the colonists created a new country. The United States was born on July 4, 1776.

Looking Ahead

1. This painting shows Philadelphia during colonial times. How can you tell this is a community of long ago?
2. In what way is this community the same as a community today?

Words to Learn

cultures	population
independence	trade

1 Indians Were the First Americans

The first people in North America were the people we now usually call American Indians. Sometimes they are called Native Americans. A native is a person who was born in a place. The words Native American remind us that these were the first people on our continent.

The First Americans

There are many different groups of Indian people. Indian groups are often called tribes. Each tribe once spoke a different language. The Indian groups were different in other ways too. They had different beliefs and customs. They had different ways of meeting their basic needs.

Indian groups had different <u>cultures</u> (kul′chərz). A culture is the way of life of a group of people. All people have a culture. The food we eat and the clothing we wear are part of our culture. Our language and the things we believe are part of our culture.

This painting shows parts of the <u>culture</u> of the Sioux (sōō) Indians. How can you tell that horses were important to the Sioux way of life?

The games people play are part of their culture. What games shown in this painting do you play?

Many Different Cultures

The Indian groups met all their basic needs from the land around them. The ways they met their needs depended on their location and their culture. The tribes built houses from the materials they found in their area. They ate the plants and animals that lived in the area. The customs of Indian tribes were not the same from one part of America to another.

The map on page 48 shows the location of just some of the many Indian tribes of North America. The cultures of all the tribes in the same area were very much alike. The map shows the main culture areas on our continent when only Indian people lived here. Each culture area is shown in a different color.

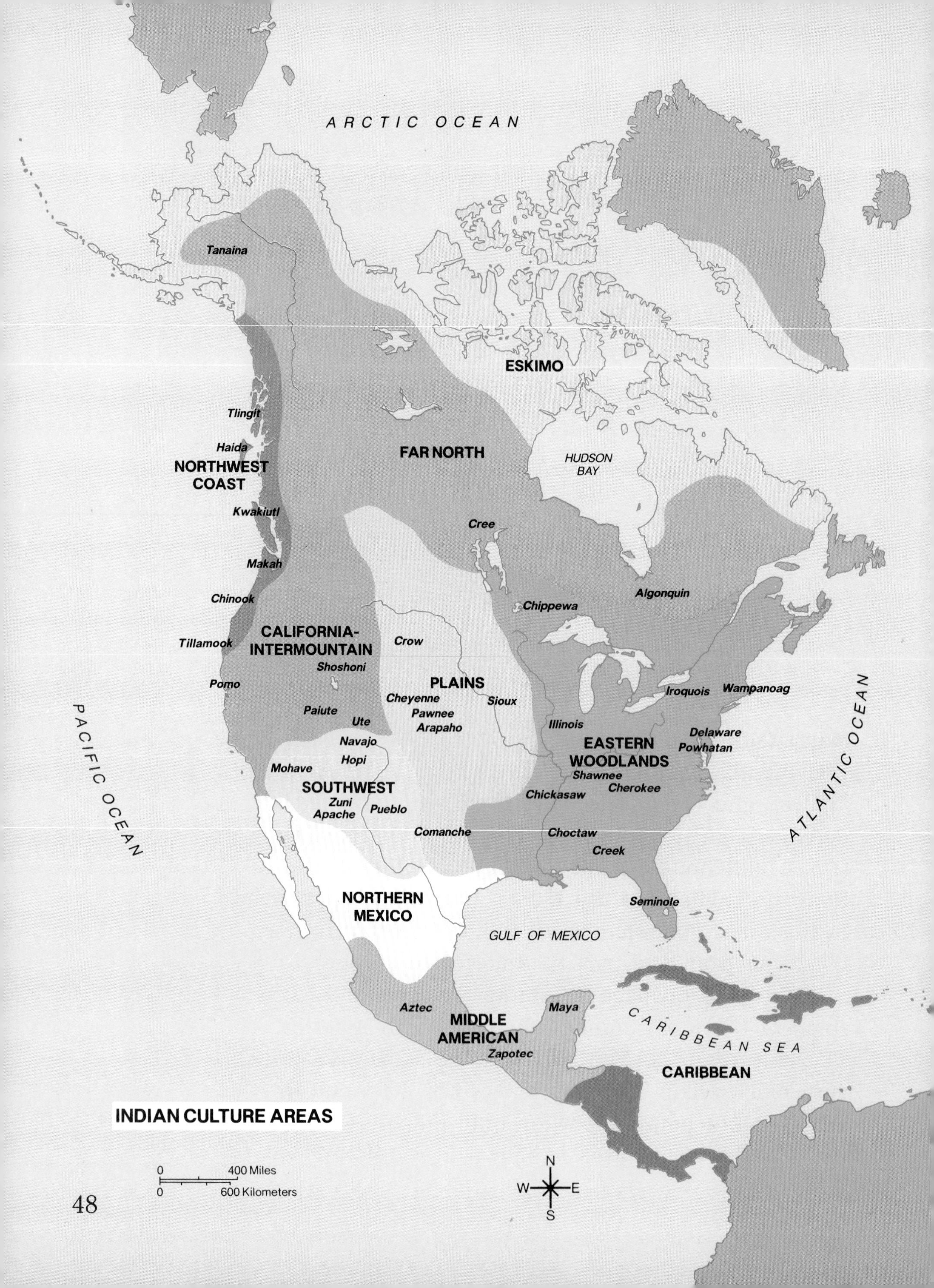

ARCTIC OCEAN
Tanaina
ESKIMO
Tlingit
Haida
NORTHWEST COAST
FAR NORTH
HUDSON BAY
Kwakiutl
Cree
Makah
Algonquin
Chinook
Chippewa
CALIFORNIA-INTERMOUNTAIN
Tillamook
Crow
Shoshoni
PLAINS
Pomo
Cheyenne
Sioux
Iroquois
Wampanoag
PACIFIC OCEAN
Paiute
Pawnee
Ute
Arapaho
Illinois
Navajo
Delaware
EASTERN WOODLANDS
Powhatan
Hopi
Mohave
Shawnee
SOUTHWEST
Cherokee
Chickasaw
Zuni
Apache
Pueblo
ATLANTIC OCEAN
Comanche
Choctaw
Creek
NORTHERN MEXICO
Seminole
GULF OF MEXICO
Aztec
MIDDLE AMERICAN
Maya
CARIBBEAN SEA
Zapotec
CARIBBEAN
INDIAN CULTURE AREAS
0 400 Miles
0 600 Kilometers
N
W
E
S

An Indian Community

The way of life of many Indian groups has changed. Many communities are gone today. But there are still many Indian communities in our country. The town of Neah (nē′ə) Bay, Washington, is one example.

Neah Bay is a community of the Makah (mə kä′) Indians. The Makah are part of the Northwest Coast culture area. The town of Neah Bay is near the tip of a peninsula.

The Makah Way of Life

Long ago, the Makah people lived in small villages along the water. Behind the villages were great forests. The Makah got nearly everything they needed to meet their basic needs from the forests and the water.

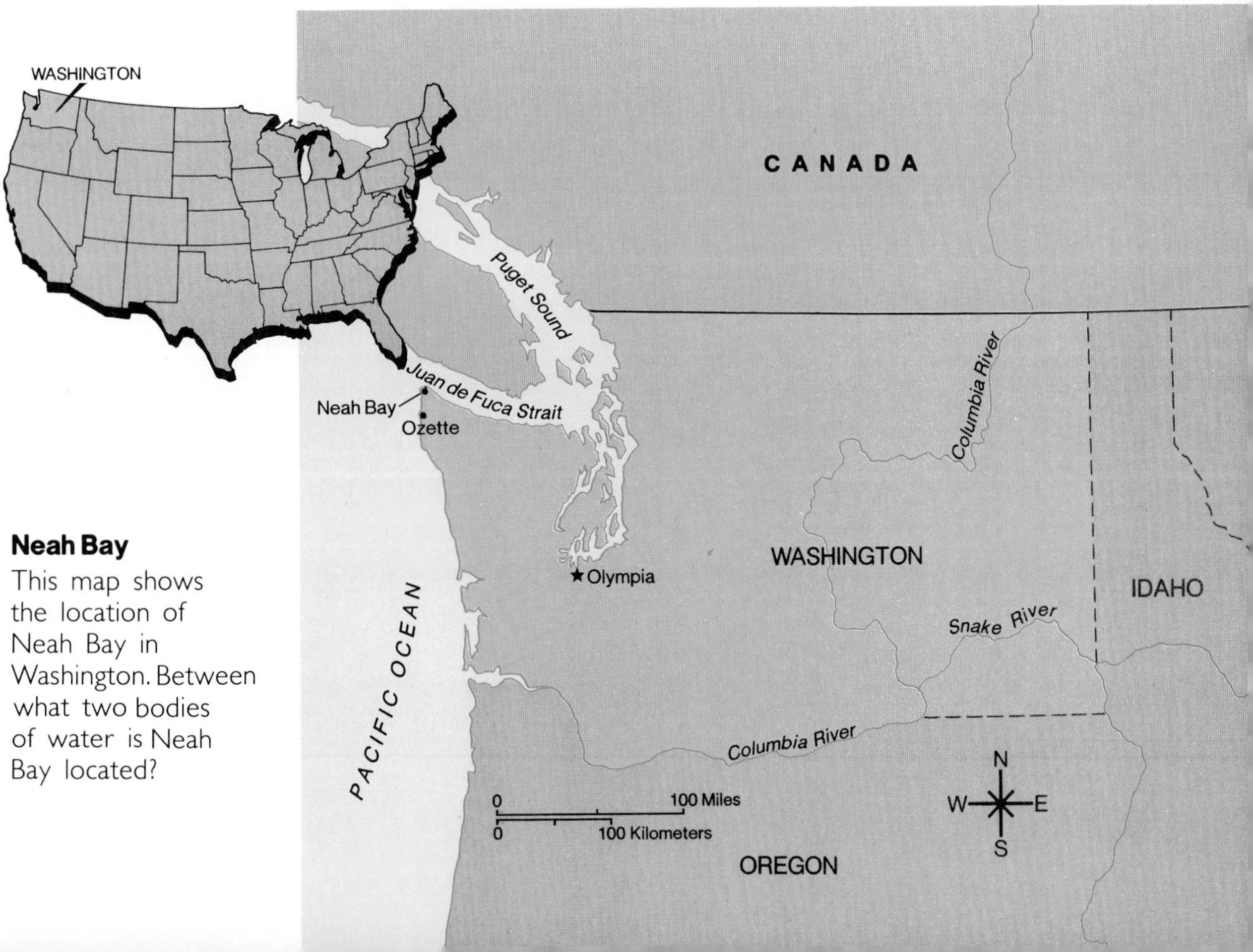

Neah Bay
This map shows the location of Neah Bay in Washington. Between what two bodies of water is Neah Bay located?

The Makah were part of the Northwest Coast culture area. Northwest Coast Indians met their basic needs from the forest and water nearby.

From the trees in the forest, the Makah got wood to build their homes. These were large buildings where several families lived. The Makahs made wooden bowls and spoons for eating, wooden boxes for storing things, and large wooden canoes for transportation. They even made clothing from the bark of the trees! The Makah lands are very rainy. People used rain hats and capes made of bark to stay dry.

The Makahs also found food in the forests. They found many kinds of berries. They trapped some forest animals to eat too.

Most of the Makah's food came from the water. They gathered clams on the beaches and they caught fish. The most important fish were halibut. At halibut fishing time, everyone in the village was busy.

The Makahs also hunted whales. This was dangerous work, but the whale hunters had great skill. They were important people in the Makah village.

Of course, there was also time for play. A popular game was the fish trap game. Three children were the fish. They ran ahead. About ten other children were the fish trap. They held hands and tried to catch each "fish" by joining hands and making a circle around that child.

The Potlatch

The Makah and their neighbor tribes had an interesting custom, called the potlatch (pät′lach′). This was a celebration families gave for special days such as weddings. At potlatch time, people came from other villages. First, family members sang special songs and did special dances. They gave everyone food. Then they gave each guest a gift. In the Makah culture, the way to show you were rich was to give many things away.

The potlatch was a custom of the Makah and other Northwest Coast tribes. People came to this celebration from villages near and far.

Old Ways and New

Today the life of the Makahs at Neah Bay is a mix of old ways and new. Fishing is still important in the community, but the ways of fishing have changed. The Makahs now have motor boats and other new tools to help them catch fish.

In school, Makah children study the same subjects as other children in the United States. They also learn about the culture of the Makah tribe. For example, they learn about Makah woodcarving. Like other Indian groups in the area, the Makah are famous for their woodcarving art.

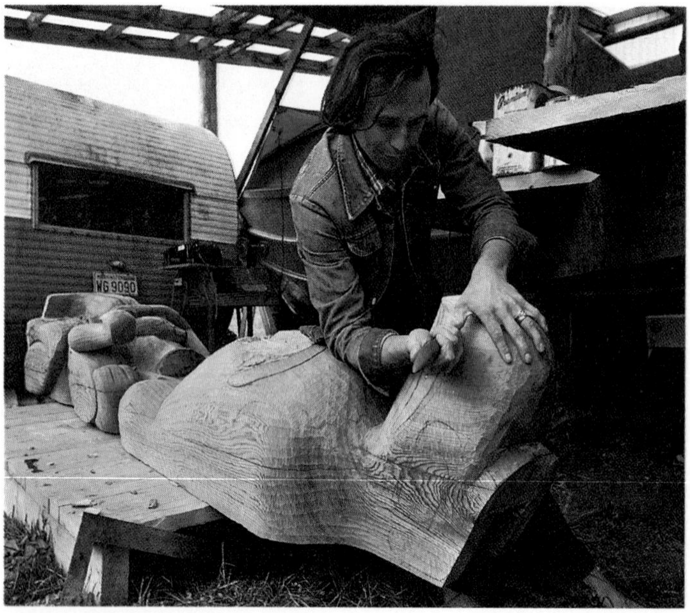

Woodcarving has always been part of the Makah culture. Today Greg Colfax is a Makah woodcarver. His art is sold all over the country.

Greg Colfax

Makah woodcarving is still being done today. Greg Colfax is one of the new Makah artists. He was born in Neah Bay in 1947. After finishing college, he began working as a woodcarver. He goes to museums to learn about old ways of woodcarving. Today Greg Colfax's art is sold in many parts of the country.

Neah Bay is still a community of the Makah Indians. How is this community the same as the one on page 50? How is it different?

Learning About the Past

The Makah people want to remember their past. They also want other people to learn about the Makah way of life. On special summer days, there are old-time canoe races and halibut feasts in Neah Bay.

Near Neah Bay is an interesting place called Ozette (ō zet′). An old Makah village once stood here. But many years ago all the people left. They moved to Neah Bay so the children could go to school there. Recently people dug carefully through the ruins and found many things from the old village.

Many of these old Makah things are now at the Makah Museum. People can visit the Makah Museum to learn about the past.

Do You Know?

1. How did the Makahs meet their basic needs?
2. Tell what the Makahs did at a potlatch.
3. How do the Makahs remember their past?

2 Colonists Settle America

Indians were the only people in North America for thousands of years. Then people began coming here from other countries. Some of them started colonies. A colony is a community settled by people from another country. The people who live in colonies are called colonists.

Colonists from Many Countries

The first colonies in North America were started by people from Spain. St. Augustine, Florida, built as a Spanish colony in 1565, is now the oldest city in the United States. Today St. Augustine still has parts of the old Spanish buildings.

St. Augustine is the oldest city in the United States. This fort was built when the city was a Spanish colony. There also are other old Spanish buildings in St. Augustine.

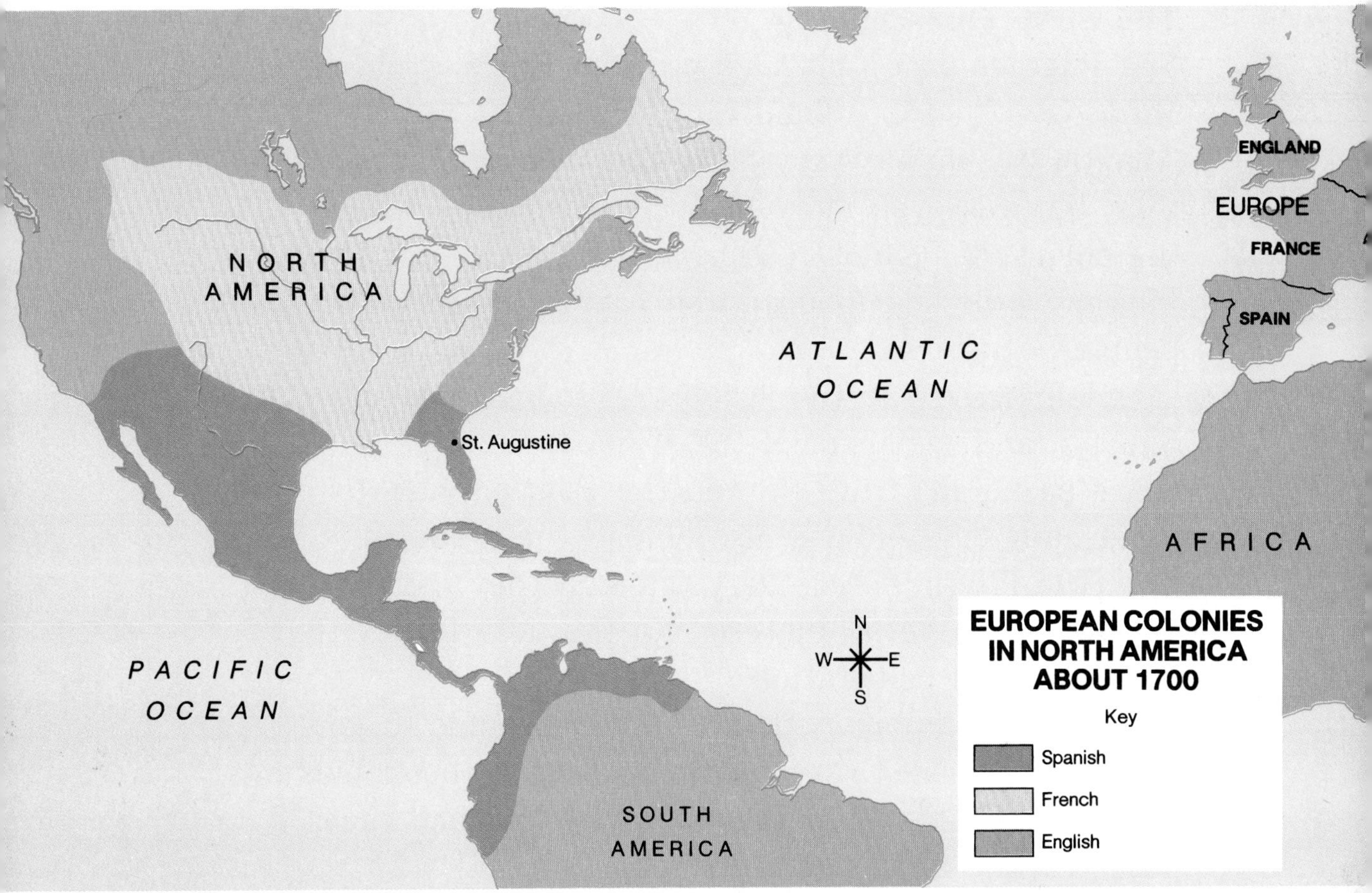

This is a historical map. It shows the Spanish, French, and English colonies in North America. What color on the map shows Spanish colonies? Where on the map did you look for the answer?

People from other countries in Europe also started colonies here. The most important were colonists from England and France. You can see the English, French, and Spanish colonies on the map on this page. What ocean did the European colonists have to cross to come to North America?

Each group of colonists brought their language and culture to the new lands. Each group also learned from the Indians who were already living on those lands. The story of the Pilgrims shows how the colonists learned from the Indians.

The First Thanksgiving

The Pilgrims sailed to America from England on the *Mayflower* in 1620. Their long trip across the Atlantic Ocean was very hard. But in many ways their life was even more difficult when they settled the colony of Plymouth. During the first winter the Pilgrims had little food and only a few houses. Many people became sick.

Help arrived in the spring. An Indian named Squanto and members of the Wampanoag (wäm′pə nō′ag) tribe showed the Pilgrims how to plant corn. The Indians also helped them hunt and fish. The Pilgrims were very thankful they could harvest, or gather, a big crop. In the fall of 1621 they held a special celebration.

The Pilgrims invited their Indian friends to join them for a feast. Everyone ate and ate at big tables full of food. Then they played games and had races. This was the first Thanksgiving.

This painting shows the artist's idea of how the Pilgrims and Indians celebrated the first Thanksgiving.

Thirteen English colonies grew up along the Atlantic Coast. The colonies declared their independence from England on July 4, 1776.

The Colonies Become a Country

More and more people came to North America. They settled 13 colonies along the Atlantic Coast. These colonies were ruled by England. But the colonists wanted to rule themselves. They wanted to be free.

On July 4, 1776, the colonists declared their independence (in′di pen′dəns) from England. Independence is freedom from the control of others. The colonists had to fight a war against England to win their independence.

When the war was over, the colonies were free. A new country was born. Now each colony became a state. There were 13 states in the new United States of America. Americans celebrate the birth of our country every year on the Fourth of July.

Do You Know?

1. Who started the first colonies in North America?
2. Why did the Pilgrims celebrate the first Thanksgiving?
3. Why did the colonists fight a war against England?

Before You Go On

Learning About Bar Graphs

What was the population (pop′ yə lā′ shən) of the United States when it won its independence? Population is the number of people who live in a place. Soon after the United States was born, Americans decided to find out the population of their country. In 1790 they made a count, or census, of the population.

Americans learned many things from the first census. They learned that Virginia had the largest population. They learned that Delaware had the smallest population. They also found out which cities had the most people.

The graph on the next page is called a bar graph. Bar graphs use bars of different lengths to show amounts. This bar graph shows the population of the five largest cities in the United States in 1790.

Look at the bottom of the graph. It shows the names of the cities. Now look at the numbers on the left side of the graph. The numbers stand for numbers of people living in the cities.

Find the bar for Charleston. Move your finger to the top of the bar. Now slide your finger to the left until you come to the numbers. Your finger should be just above the number 15,000. The population of Charleston was a little more than 15,000 in 1790.

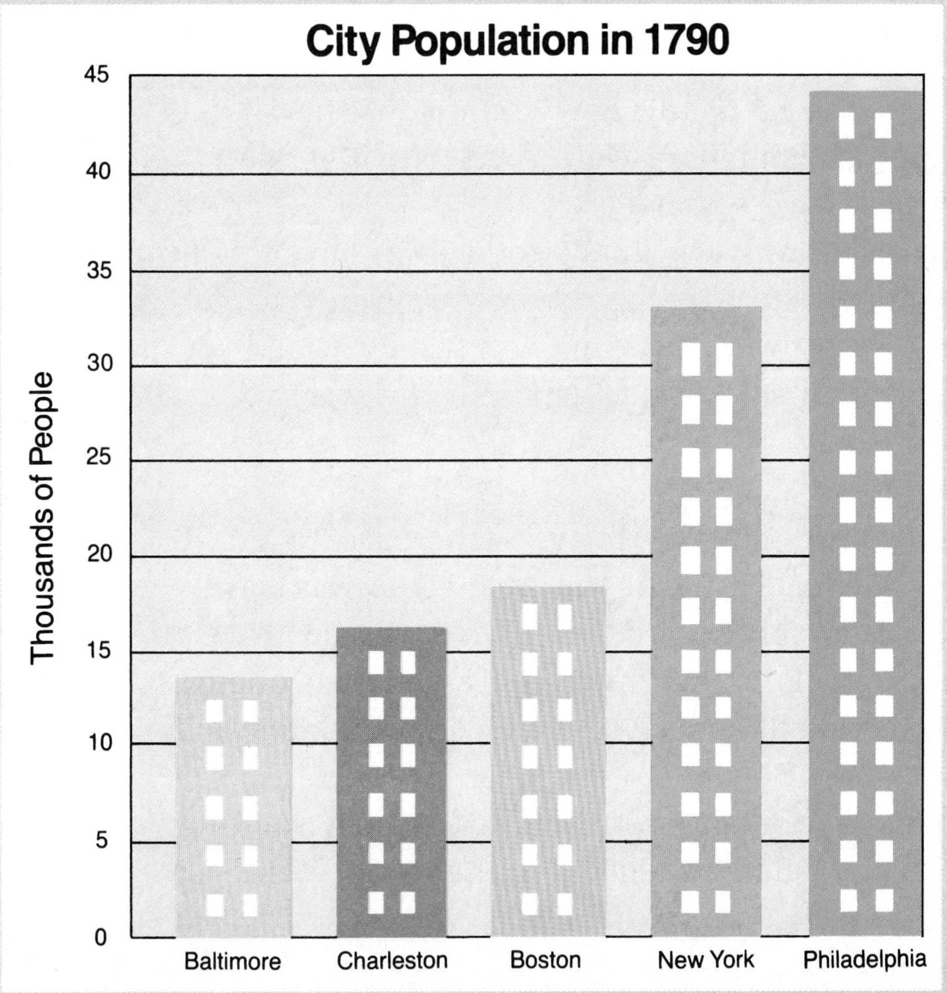

Practicing Your Skills

Use the bar graph to answer these questions.

1. Which city had the largest population in 1790?
2. Which city had the fewest people?
3. Which cities had fewer than 20,000 people?
4. Which cities had more than 30,000 people?

3 The Country Grows

Many people came to the new country of the United States. New communities were formed. Cities grew up. New farms were started.

Soon there was not much good farm land left in the 13 states. But there was more farm land in the west, and it cost very little money to buy. Many families decided to move to lands in the west.

Pioneers

People who lead the way to new lands are called pioneers. Starting a life in the new lands was hard. There were no shops or cities. There was no place to buy food or tools or clothing. There were no doctors or hospitals. Families had to make or bring along everything they needed to live.

A pioneer woman wrote this list of just some of the things her family needed for their trip west. What else would you take along?

flour	salt	pots and dishes
sugar	medicines	rope
cornmeal	seeds	chickens
dried fruit	blankets	plow
bacons and hams	clothing	horses
soap	ax and saw	
	rifle	

The pioneers traveled west in wagon trains.
Their trip was long and hard.

Traveling West

Pioneers traveled west in covered wagons. These were pulled by horses or strong cattle called oxen. Families often traveled together in a wagon train, with one covered wagon behind another in a long line.

The trip west was not easy. There were no roads across the mountains or through the forests. There were no bridges across the rivers. Sometimes pioneers built large wooden rafts to travel on a river or a lake. Rafts are flat boats. People loaded their wagons onto the rafts and floated along.

Travel was very slow. The wagon trains traveled 12 hours a day. Sometimes the pioneers had to stop to make a path for the wagons to cross. Wagons often broke or got stuck in the mud. Then other families would stop to help. The trip west might take as long as six months.

A Busy Life

There was no time to rest when the pioneers reached the new lands. They had to cut down trees and build homes. They had to plow fields and plant their crops.

Pioneer houses were small and plain. Usually they had just one or two rooms. Each house had a fireplace for cooking and heat. Pioneers did not have glass for their windows. Instead, they used pieces of cloth or deerskin.

Their main crops included wheat, corn, potatoes, fruits, and vegetables. Most families raised chickens for eggs. They got milk from their cows.

The pioneers made all their own clothing. The skins from animals they hunted were turned into leather for shoes and jackets. They made their own

Pioneer families lived far from their neighbors. They led a very busy life.

candles from animal fat. Soap was made from fat and ashes. Everyone in the family had jobs to do.

Pioneer life was hard, but there was still time for fun. In the evening the family sang songs or played guessing games. They also played cards and checkers. Often one family member read aloud to the others.

Homes usually were far apart, and people did not see their neighbors very often. But several times a year all the families in an area got together to have a good time.

Sometimes pioneer families got together with friends. Then they wore their best clothes and had a party.

Pioneer Schools

The earliest pioneer communities did not have schools. Sometimes one of the mothers taught several children in her home. The other parents paid her with food they had grown or hunted.

Pioneer children did not have much time for school. In what ways is this classroom the same as yours? In what ways is it different?

Later, schools were built. Usually there was only one teacher in a school. Children of all ages studied in the same room. Many of them had to walk a long way to school each day. They carried their lunch in buckets. When they arrived at school they were warmed by the fire in a large stove in the classroom.

Pioneer children were too busy to go to school every day. They had to stay home to help when there was extra work to be done on the family farm. The school year usually was short.

Do You Know?

1. How did the pioneers travel west?
2. Name two ways that pioneer families got food.
3. How were pioneer children taught before a school was built?

4 A Cattle Town

As more and more pioneers moved west, many new towns grew up across the United States. By the 1870s, railroads linked the new western towns with the cities of the east. The railroads made it possible to bring many different kinds of goods to the west. They also could carry the crops grown by the pioneers to the east.

Trading Centers

The towns along the western railroads became important trading centers for the lands around them. In these towns, pioneers sold some of their crops and animals. They bought things that they could not make or grow. This is an example of trade (trād). Trade is the buying and selling of goods.

Cheyenne (shī en′), Wyoming, grew up as a trading center for cattle. The cattle were raised far away in Texas. But railroads had not yet been built

By the 1870s railroads linked the eastern and western parts of the country. Towns along the railroad became centers of trade.

in Texas. The Texas ranchers had to find a way to get their cattle north to the railroad towns. Then the cattle could be sold and shipped to eastern cities where people wanted to buy the meat.

How could the Texas ranchers get their cattle to the railroad towns? They decided to walk their cattle there. In those days very few people lived in the southwestern United States. There were no fences. The cattle could travel for days along trails through open spaces. It was the job of the cowhands to move the cattle along the trails. The trip was called a cattle drive.

Cheyenne was the trading center at the end of one of the most important cattle trails. Find the trail that ended in Cheyenne on the map on this page. What was life like on a cattle drive?

This map shows the routes of the cattle drives. What symbol shows the cattle trails? On what railroad is Cheyenne located?

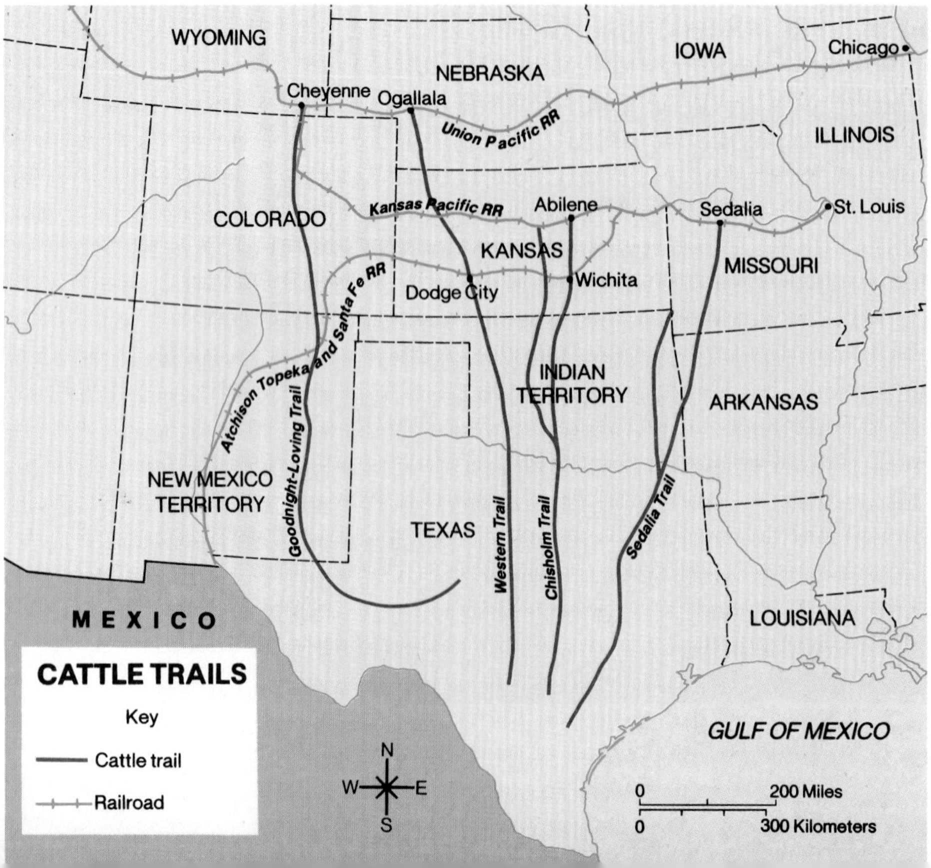

The Thomas Gilcrease Institute of American History and Art, Tulsa, Okla.

Life was hard for cowhands on a cattle drive. They had to work 24 hours a day. They even had to work in rainstorms!

The Cattle Drive

Cattle drives began in the spring so that there would be plenty of grass for the animals to eat on the trail. There were hundreds of cattle in each herd. The cowhands rode beside the herd on horses. They made sure that all the animals stayed together.

Sometimes the cattle were frightened by a loud or strange noise. Then the whole herd stampeded, or ran wildly. The cowhands had to chase the cattle and get them together again. The cattle's long, sharp horns made this dangerous work. Cowhands had to be skilled at riding horses to be able to get out of the way in a hurry!

Most of the day was not as exciting. The cowhands just rode and rode in the dust and hot sun. Remember, there were no towns or stores along the way. All the cowhands had to eat was the food they brought with them. They did not see any other people for weeks at a time. A cowhand's life could be hard and lonely. To pass the time, they often sang songs about their life.

After the long cattle drive, the cowhands finally arrived at the trading center. Here they sold the cattle and were paid for their work.

Cheyenne

Today the people of Cheyenne remember its history as a cattle town. Every year there is a six-day celebration called Frontier Days. A popular event of Frontier Days is the rodeo. This is a show with contests to see which cowhands have the best skills. Some contests in a rodeo include seeing who can tie up a steer fastest and who can ride a bull the longest.

A rodeo is held every year in Cheyenne. This rider is trying to stay on the bull while holding on with only one hand!

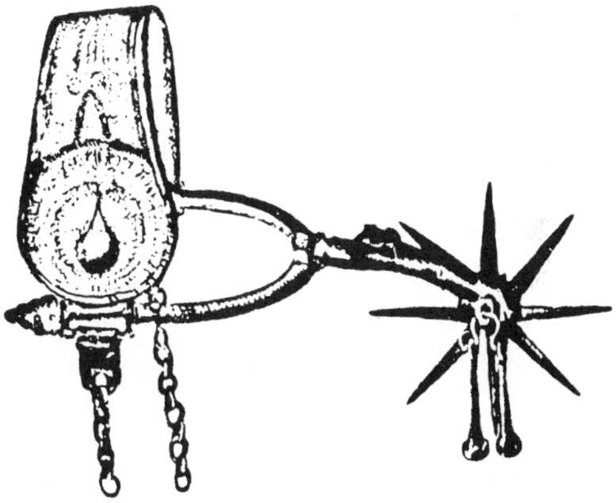

Bill Pickett appeared in rodeos in the United States and in other countries. He and other cowhands always wore spurs on their boots.

Bill Pickett

Bill Pickett was a cowhand who became a famous rodeo star. His special skill was bulldogging. In this contest the cowhand jumps onto a running steer from a horse. Then the cowhand grabs a horn of the steer and tries to pull the animal to the ground. The winner is the person who gets the steer to the ground and ties its legs in the least time.

Do You Know?

1. What did the pioneers do in trading centers?
2. What was the purpose of the cattle drive?
3. Tell what happens at a rodeo.

2 TO HELP YOU LEARN

Using New Words

Match each word with its meaning. Write each word and its meaning on a sheet of paper.

1. culture
2. independence
3. population
4. trade

a. buying and selling goods
b. the number of people in a place
c. the way of life of a group of people
d. freedom

Finding the Facts

1. Give two examples of how the life of the Makahs is a mix of old ways and new ways.
2. Which European country started the first colonies in North America? What other countries also started colonies in America?
3. What did the Indians teach the Pilgrims living at Plymouth?
4. Why is the Fourth of July an important holiday for Americans today?
5. Describe the houses of the pioneers.
6. Why did Cheyenne, Wyoming, become an important trading center for cattle?

Using Study Skills

1. The events listed below are mentioned in Unit 2. On a sheet of paper write the events in the order in which they happened.

   - Colonists declare their independence from England.
   - Indians live in America.
   - Pioneers move west.
   - Cattle drives take place.
   - The Pilgrims celebrate the first Thanksgiving.

2. Look closely at the painting on page 67. It shows a cowhand on the long drive. Use the picture to answer these questions.
   a. What is happening in this painting?
   b. How does the artist show that life was hard on the long drive?

Things to Think About

1. Give three examples that show how the location of Neah Bay was important to the culture of the Makah Indians.
2. Both the Pilgrims and the pioneers went to live in a new place. How did each group travel to its new home? How were the lives of the Pilgrims and the pioneers the same?
3. How were pioneer schools the same as schools today? How were they different?

Things to Do

1. Find out about the Indians who first lived near your community. Make a poster showing some of their customs.
2. Imagine that you are a cowhand on the long drive. Write a letter to your family telling them about life on the trail.

Learning About Your Own Community

The people of Cheyenne remember the history of their community during Frontier Days. How do the people of your community remember its history? Are there special celebrations or parades? Are there statues or buildings named for famous people in your community's history?

Learning from Maps

1. Turn to the map of Indian culture areas on page 48. Name the culture areas shown on the map.
2. Turn to the cattle trails map on page 66. What cattle trails are shown on the map? Through what towns did each trail pass?

3. The grid map below shows part of Cheyenne, Wyoming. Use the map to answer these questions.
   a. In which square is there a hospital?
   b. In which squares is the park?
   c. Through which squares does Central Avenue go?
   d. In which square is City Hall?
   e. Through which squares does 23rd Street go?

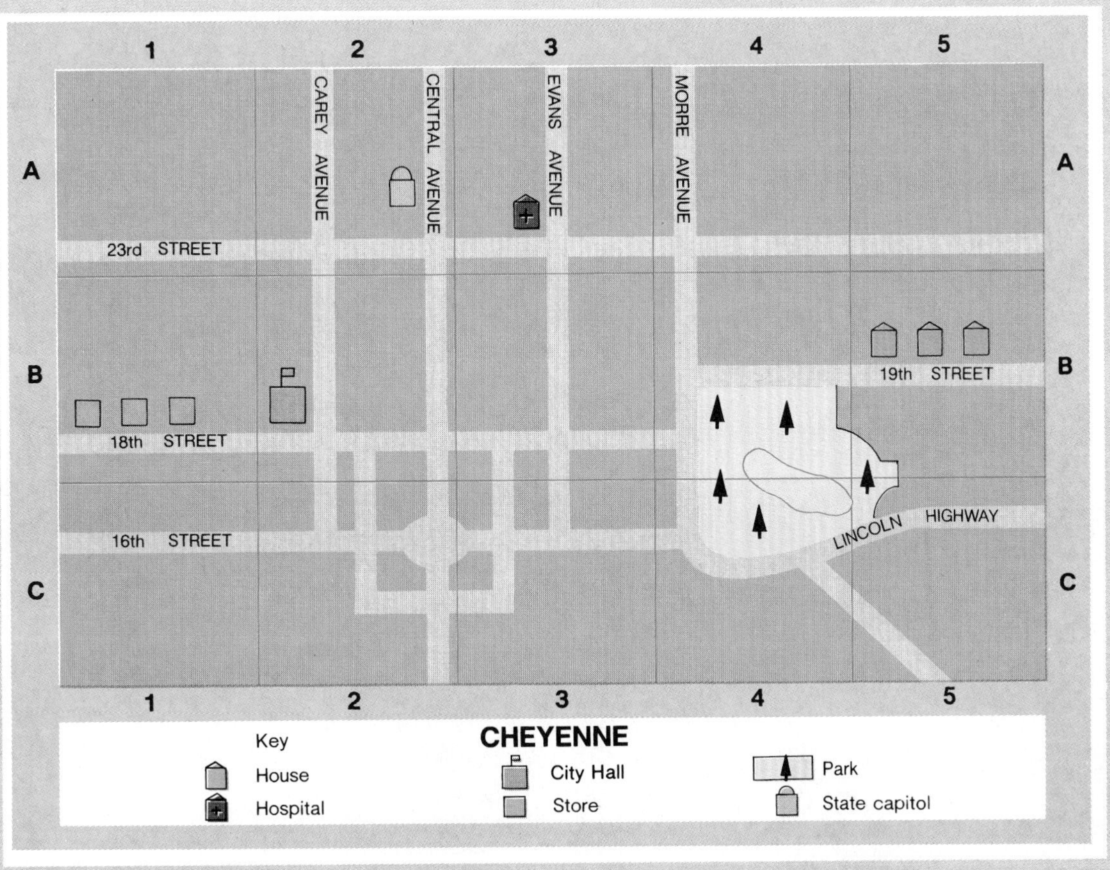

3 RURAL COMMUNITIES

Towns and villages are rural communities. They are trading centers for the people who live and work in the surrounding area. Town schools, banks, churches, hospitals, and libraries provide services for the rural population.

Looking Ahead

1. This picture shows a rural community. How can you tell that this is a rural area?
2. Many rural communities grew up near natural resources. What natural resource is this community near?
3. What kind of work do you think is done by many people in this community?

Words to Learn

mining	pipeline
income	conservation
weather	national parks
climate	tourists
fuel	pollution

1 Living and Working in a Town

Like the cattle towns in the west, most towns first grew up as trading centers. Many trading centers grew up in areas rich in natural resources. Natural resources are things in nature that people can use.

Towns and Natural Resources

There are many important natural resources in the United States. Forests, farm land, rivers, fish, and wild animals are natural resources.

Other natural resources, called minerals, are found in the earth. Important minerals include gold, silver, iron, coal, and oil. The work of digging minerals from the earth is called mining (mī′ning).

This picture shows coal mining. Today workers use large machines to dig the coal out of the earth.

Many people who live in towns have jobs that depend on the natural resources in the surrounding area. They may work as loggers in nearby forests or as miners in nearby coal mines. Other people have jobs turning natural resources into goods that can be sold. They may pack fish or fruit into cans or cut logs into boards.

People in towns also work at other kinds of jobs. Some may work in factories that make many different kinds of products. Others may provide goods and services for those who live in the surrounding area.

Towns are trading centers for the people in the surrounding area. This town is in the state of Montana.

Towns and the Surrounding Area

People who live on farms or ranches or in small villages use the town as a trading center. They bring their goods to town to sell and they shop in the town's stores.

Towns are the center of many activities in rural areas. Towns have hospitals, restaurants, movies, libraries, parks, museums, and other things that smaller rural communities may not have. Children who live in rural areas often go to school in town.

The town of Tillamook provides goods and services for the people who live nearby.

Tillamook

Tillamook (til′ə mək′) is a town in northwestern Oregon. Not far from the town there are good fishing areas in the Pacific Ocean. There are good oyster growing areas in Tillamook Bay. Some people in town have jobs in the fish and oyster business.

The fields around Tillamook have thick, green grasses. There are many dairy farms in this area. Cows raised on these farms eat the grasses and produce lots of good, sweet milk.

The dairy farmers milk their cows twice a day. Then trucks carry the milk to the Tillamook creamery. A creamery is a place where cheese and

Tillamook Bay has good oyster growing areas. Some people who live in Tillamook have jobs in the oyster business.

other dairy products are made. Tillamook is famous for its cheeses. Many people in town have jobs making cheese at the creamery.

Tillamook also has schools, stores, and restaurants where people work. Fishers and dairy farmers and their families come into town to go shopping. They come to visit the parks, the library, and the history museum. Tillamook is an important service center for the people who live in northwestern Oregon.

Do You Know?

1. Why did towns grow up in areas rich in natural resources?
2. What is mining?
3. Tell how towns are important to people in rural areas.

Oranges can be grown only in a place that has a warm climate. Many people earn an income from growing oranges.

2 Working on a Farm

Farming today is very different than it was in pioneer times. Pioneer families raised all the food they needed to meet their basic needs. Today farmers usually raise just one or two crops. They sell their crops and use the money they earn to buy the goods and services they need. Money earned from providing goods or services is called income (in′kum′).

Different crops grow well in different places. Oranges are an important crop in Florida and in California, but they are not grown in most other states. Do you know why?

Weather and Climate

You notice the weather (weth′ər) where you live all the time. Weather is what it is like outdoors each day. It may be hot or cold. It may be rainy or sunny. You may not notice the climate (klī′mit) of your area though. Climate is the kind of weather a place has over many years.

The kinds of crops that can grow in an area depend on the climate. Oranges are grown in southern Florida and southern California because these places have warm climates. Wheat is a crop that can grow in several different climates.

There are two kinds of wheat, winter wheat and spring wheat. The kind of wheat grown in a place depends mostly on its climate.

Winter wheat is grown in mild climates. It is planted in the fall and gets a start before the cold weather begins. It stops growing in the winter and begins growing again in the spring. Winter wheat is harvested in early summer. Spring wheat is grown in places with very cold winters. It is planted in the spring and harvested in the summer, just a few months later.

Both winter wheat and spring wheat are grown in the United States. Find the major wheat growing states on the map on this page.

Find the states where wheat is grown. In what states is winter wheat grown? In what states is spring wheat grown? Does the United States grow more winter wheat or more spring wheat?

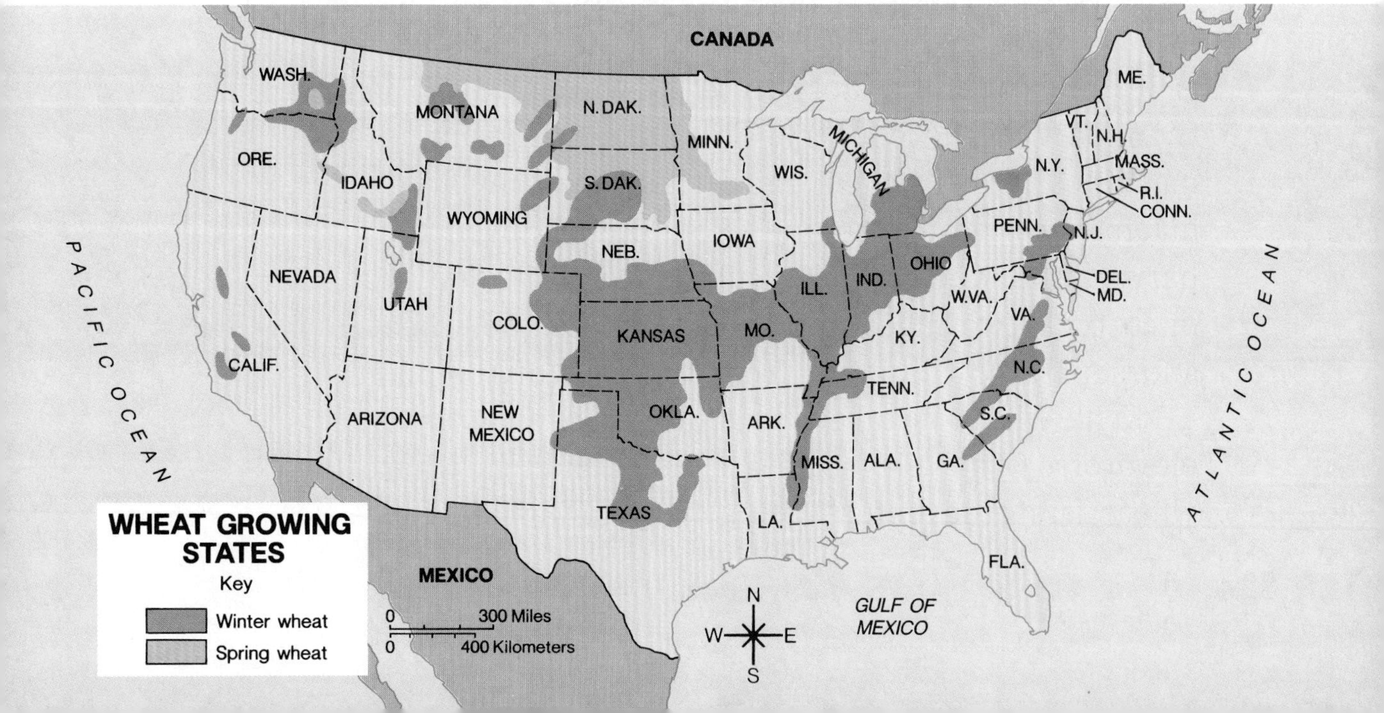

The Block family uses a combine to harvest wheat on their farm. The use of a combine means that the Blocks can harvest more wheat in less time than ever before.

A Wheat Farm

The Block family's wheat farm is located in northwestern Kansas. It is one of the best wheat farming areas of the country. The farm was started by Mr. Block's grandfather almost 100 years ago.

The Blocks are able to grow winter wheat in their part of the country. They use many big machines to help them raise their crop. A large machine called a combine (kom′bīn) is used to harvest the wheat. The combine does the job that once took two machines to do. It cuts the wheat and separates the grain from the rest of the plant.

The wheat is taken by truck to nearby grain elevators. Grain elevators are tall buildings where the wheat is stored before going to flour mills.

PIONEER
PIONEER

From Wheat to Bread

Wheat is taken by trains and trucks from the grain elevators to flour mills. At the mills, wheat is ground into flour. Then the wheat flour is used to make bread, crackers, cakes, and many of the other foods we eat. Wheat and foods made from United States wheat are sold in many countries of the world.

Most bread in the United States is made in large bakeries. How many different kinds of bread can you name in the large picture?

Cyrus McCormick's reaper made wheat harvesting faster and easier. Farmers using this machine could plant and harvest more wheat.

Cyrus McCormick

Growing wheat today is very different than it was long ago. In pioneer days, farmers had only horses and simple tools to help them. They had to work very hard to harvest a field of wheat.

Then in 1831 Cyrus McCormick made a machine called a reaper that changed the way wheat was harvested. McCormick's reaper was pulled by a horse. It could cut more wheat in an hour than a person with the old tools could cut in a whole day! Since then, there have been many changes in the way wheat is harvested. What differences do you see in the way wheat is being harvested in the pictures on this page and on page 82?

Do You Know?

1. Why is climate important to farmers?
2. What is the purpose of grain elevators?
3. What happens to wheat when it leaves the grain elevators?
4. How did Cyrus McCormick help make wheat farming easier?

Before You Go On

Learning About Line Graphs

North Vernon is a town in southeastern Indiana. It is one of the largest towns in the surrounding rural area. The graph on the next page shows how the population of North Vernon has changed over the years.

This graph is called a line graph. Line graphs can help you see how things change over time. Reading a line graph is a lot like reading a bar graph. Start by looking at the bottom of the graph. It shows seven years. The first year is 1920. What other years are shown? Now look at the numbers on the left side of the graph. The numbers stand for the number of people living in North Vernon. This graph tells you how many people lived in North Vernon during the years 1920 to 1980.

How many people lived in North Vernon in 1930? Here is how to find out. First, put your finger on the red line above the year 1930. Now slide your finger to the left until you come to the numbers. Your finger should be just below the number 3,000. There were just under 3,000 people living in North Vernon in 1930.

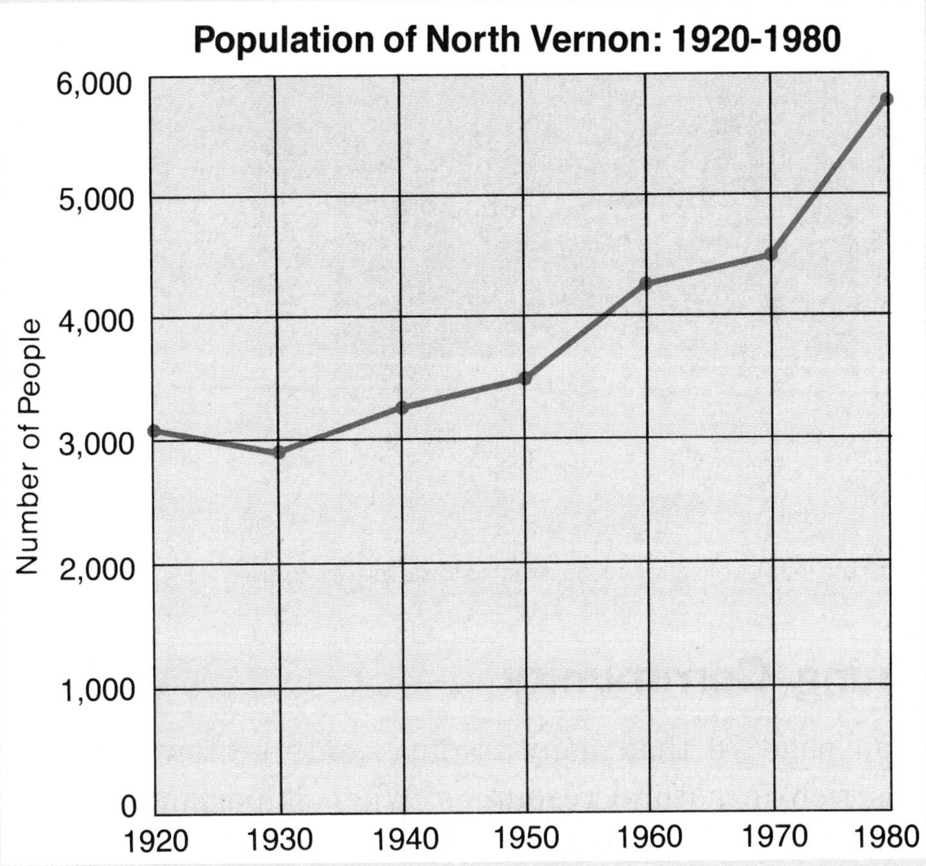

Practicing Your Skills

Use the line graph to answer these questions.

1. About how many people lived in North Vernon in 1920?
2. About how many people lived in North Vernon in 1950?
3. In what year was the population of North Vernon the smallest?
4. Were there more people living in North Vernon in 1960 or in 1970?
5. Did the population of North Vernon go up or down after 1940?

When the gold rush began miners had no time to build places to live.

3 A Mining Community

You read on page 76 that many trading centers grew up in areas rich in natural resources. When important natural resources are discovered, towns sometimes grow up in a hurry. Some of the fastest-growing mining towns were built in California more than 100 years ago.

The California Gold Rush

Mining towns grew up quickly when gold was discovered in California in 1848. News of the gold spread quickly around the world. The news started a gold rush. Thousands of people from many different countries rushed to the new gold mining areas. They hoped to find gold and get rich.

The first gold rush towns were not really towns at all. Miners lived in tents or slept outdoors on the ground. They were too busy to build houses. They looked for gold from morning to night.

In places where a lot of gold was found, a mining town grew up. Houses, streets and sidewalks were built. Not all the miners became rich, but those who did find gold had a lot of money to spend. Many people came to California to sell things to the miners. Soon the towns had stores, restaurants, and hotels.

One example was Columbia, California. Gold was discovered there in 1850. For a while more than $100,000 worth of gold was found near the town each week! But Columbia did not last very long. When the gold ran out, people left. Only empty buildings remained. Today the old mining town is a park. People can visit it and learn about life in the days of the gold rush.

After the California gold rush, gold and other minerals were found in Nevada, Colorado, Idaho, Montana, Alaska, and other western states. With each discovery, large numbers of people rushed to the new mining areas. Mining towns grew up quickly. Many western towns and cities began this way.

Today the old mining town of Columbia is a park. Visitors to the park can see how people lived in the days of the gold rush.

A Mining Community Today

Mining today is very different than it was in the days of the gold rush. Most mining is done by big companies, which can afford to buy the machines that are needed. Miners usually work for the companies that run the mines.

In 1968 two oil companies discovered the biggest oil fields in our country in northern Alaska. Oil is an important fuel (fyo͞o′əl). A fuel is something that is burned to make heat or to provide energy to run machines.

The area in Alaska where oil was found has a very cold climate. The land and water are frozen most of the year and transportation is difficult. A long pipeline (pīp′līn′) was built to carry the oil across Alaska. A pipeline is a long row of metal tubes. The Alaska pipeline stretches 800 miles (1,300 kilometers) across the state and crosses 20 large rivers and 3 mountain ranges. The oil is pumped through this pipeline to the port of Valdez (val dēz′). Then the oil is loaded onto ships.

This map shows the location of the Alaska oil pipeline. Trace the route of the pipeline. In which direction does the pipeline go? Where does it begin? Where does it end?

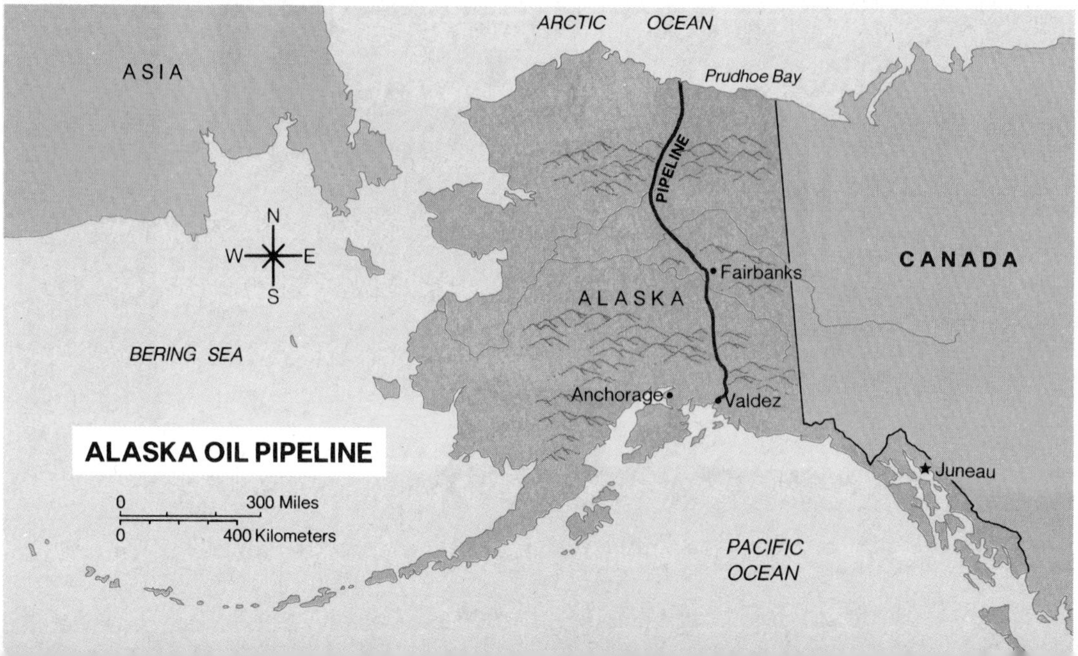

Some people did not want the pipeline to be built. They were afraid it would hurt the plants and animals in the area. Other people thought it was important to build the pipeline. They said that Americans needed the Alaskan oil. Our government decided the pipeline should be built. But before work was started, studies were done to find ways to protect the plants and animals.

The earth is frozen in many parts of Alaska. So the Alaska oil pipeline had to be built above the ground in many places.

Thousands of people moved to Valdez to work on the pipeline. These workers all needed food, tools, and places to live. The town of Valdez grew quickly. While the pipeline was being built, many people and goods arrived in Valdez every day. Now that the pipeline is finished, most of the pipeline workers have left. But Valdez is still a busy port.

Everyone can help in the conservation of our natural resources. These people are collecting old newspapers so the paper can be used again.

Conserving Our Natural Resources

Natural resources are very important in our lives. Coal and oil are used to heat our homes. Trees are used to build houses and to make paper. It is important to use these and other natural resources wisely. We must take care of them so they will not be wasted. Using our natural resources wisely is called conservation (kon′sər vā′shən).

The conservation of our natural resources is a job for everyone. We can all help by not wasting the things we use each day. If we use only what we really need, our natural resources will last a long, long time. They will be there for people to use in the future.

Do You Know?

1. What was the California gold rush?
2. Why was the Alaska pipeline built?
3. Tell why conservation is important.

4 A Tourist Community

The United States is a large and beautiful country. There are high mountains, deep valleys, and wide plains. There are grasslands, forests, and desert areas. There are rivers, lakes, and oceans.

Today much of the land has been changed by people. Cities and suburbs and highways and railroads have been built. Many of the forests have been cut down. Farms, mines, and communities have taken their place. Each year more building goes on. Each year the land is changed a little more.

These pictures show two of the many beautiful places in our country. The picture on the left was taken in Louisiana. The picture below shows part of the coast of Hawaii.

The picture on the left shows Yosemite National Park. The picture below shows Grand Canyon National Park.

National Parks

In the late 1800s a few Americans began to see what was happening. They were afraid that the beautiful places in our country would soon disappear. They said, "We must save some of these lands before they are all gone. Some of the places in our country are especially beautiful. We must make sure that people will be able to enjoy their beauty for a long, long time."

After a while, our country's leaders agreed. They made many of the most beautiful lands into national parks (nash′ən əl pärks). National means belonging to the country. The national parks are for all the people in our country to enjoy.

Many people visit Acadia National Park each year. The park ranger on the right is answering questions about the park.

Acadia National Park

Acadia National Park is located on the eastern coast of Maine. You can see on the map on page 96 that the park is on two islands and a peninsula.

Acadia National Park has a beautiful coast. It has several mountains. There are many things to do in the park. You can go fishing in the ocean, bays, lakes, and streams. You can go swimming or boating. You can see many kinds of birds. Acadia also has trails for hiking, bicycling, and riding horses.

Some people who work in the park are park rangers. They can answer questions visitors have about the park. They can tell visitors about interesting things to see.

A Tourist Town

There are no towns in our national parks. But there are towns nearby where people live and work. Bar Harbor is a town near Acadia National Park. The main business in Bar Harbor is providing services for tourists (toor′ists). Tourists are people who visit a place on vacation. They come to have fun.

Bar Harbor has hotels where tourists can stay. There are stores and restaurants. Many people in the town have jobs in these tourist places. Some have jobs in Acadia National Park.

Protecting the Land

The beauty of the land is an important natural resource. Like all natural resources, it must be used wisely. Making national parks is part of conservation.

Find Bar Harbor on the map. How far is it from Acadia National Park?

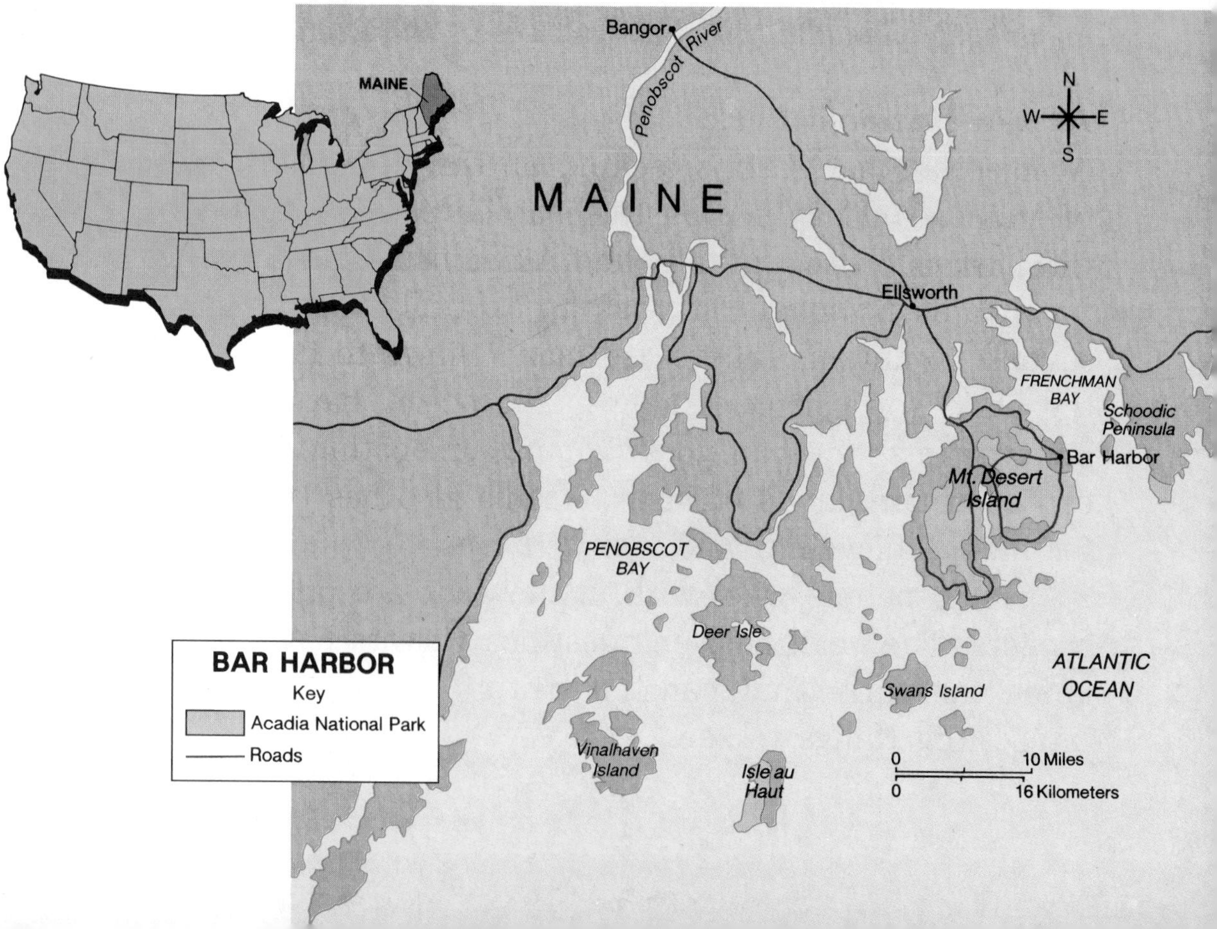

Our national parks must be protected from pollution (pə lo͞o′shən). Pollution is many kinds of dirt and garbage that spoil the land, water, and air. When a lake becomes polluted, it is no longer a beautiful place to swim and enjoy. It is unsafe. Fish can no longer live in it. People cannot swim in the lake or drink the water.

Rachel Carson was a leader in the fight against pollution.

Rachel Carson

People are working to stop pollution. An early leader in the fight against pollution was Rachel Carson.

Rachel Carson wrote a book called *Silent Spring* about pollution. She studied the poisons that were used to kill harmful insects. She showed that these poisons also were killing birds and hurting people. Today, thanks to Rachel Carson and others, people no longer use some of the poisons that pollute our land and water.

Do You Know?

1. What is a national park?
2. Name three jobs in Bar Harbor that provide services for tourists.
3. How does pollution hurt the land?

5 A Village in India

In this unit you have been reading about different kinds of rural communities in the United States. There are rural communities in every country.

Konduru (kon′do͞o ro͞o′) is a rural community in India. India is a large country on the continent of Asia. It has a very large population. The people of India have many different cultures. More than 15 main languages are spoken in the country.

India has some very large and busy cities, but most of the people live in villages in rural areas. Farmers live in villages and walk to their farms each day to work.

Find the village of Konduru. On what river is Konduru located? Find the capital of India. How far is Konduru from the capital?

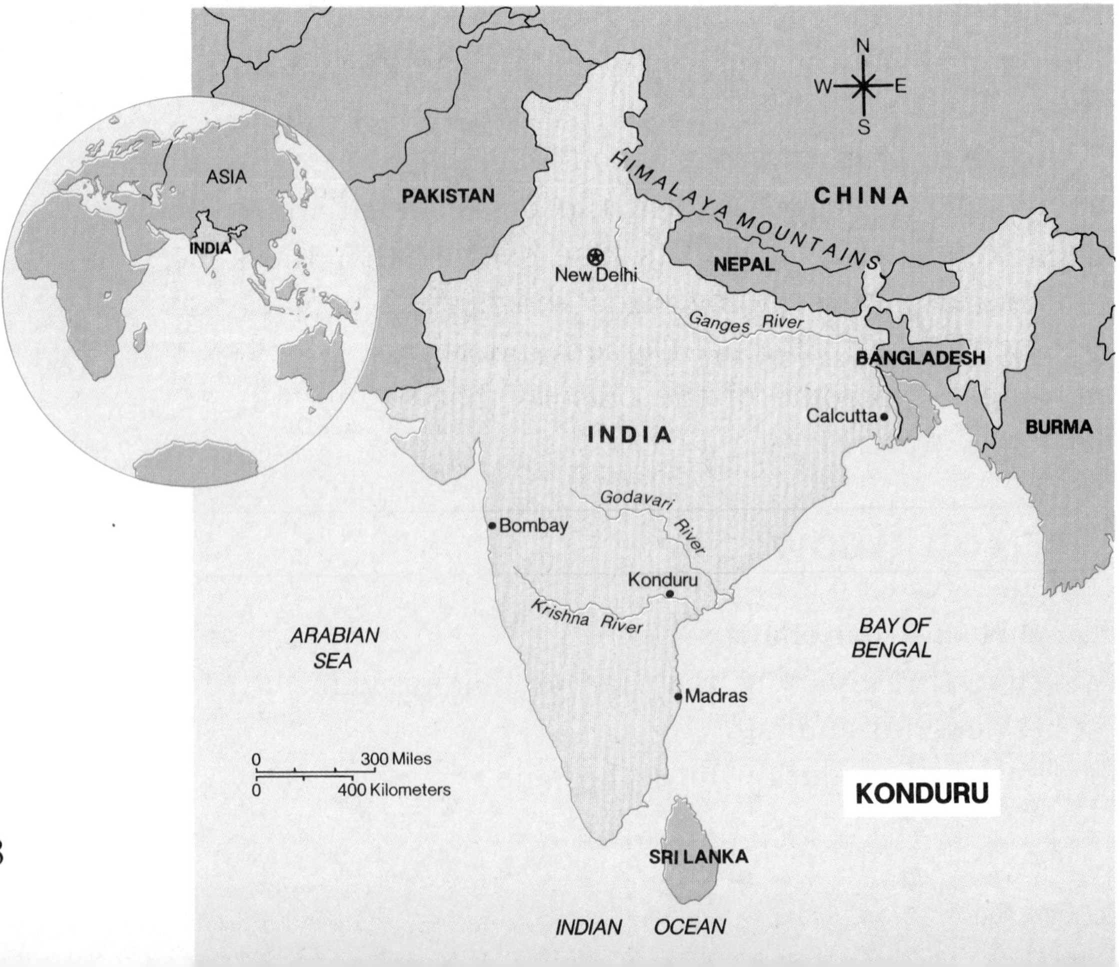

Konduru is one of the larger villages in a farming area of southern India. It is a trading center for the smaller villages and farms nearby. People come to Konduru every Wednesday to sell crops they have grown and to buy things they need. Konduru also is the location of a police station, hospital, and post office.

Market day is a busy time in Konduru and other villages in India. Farmers and their families sell their crops and buy things they need.

Farming Near Konduru

Konduru is located in an area that has three seasons. It has a rainy season, a cold season, and a hot season. The rainy season begins in late May. This is the time for plowing the soil and planting peanuts, cotton, and other early crops. There are many storms. Over and over, heavy rains pour down upon the land.

Rice is the most important crop in India. It is grown in paddies. Water buffalo pull a plow through the paddy. Plowing prepares the soil for planting the rice.

By July the land is very wet. This is rice planting time. Rice is the most important food in India and other countries of Asia. It grows well in warm, wet climate areas.

The rice raised near Konduru grows on land covered with water. It is grown in paddies. A rice paddy is a piece of land with low walls of dirt around it. It is like a pool that gets filled up with rain water.

When the rice plants turn gold in color, they are ready to harvest. This is done by hand. The dried rice will be the main food for the next year.

The cold season begins in November. The days are cool and the nights are cold. During this time the Konduru farmers can still grow some crops.

The people of Konduru and other villages of India work hard planting and harvesting rice. When their work is done they have time for fun with family and friends.

The hot season begins in February. The soil becomes hard and dry and the days are very hot. For the next few months, there will be little farming. This is a time for mending tools. It is a time for holidays, weddings, and visits with family. In the hot season, people come into Konduru from nearby villages. There are fairs, puppet shows, plays, and other special events.

Do You Know?

1. Where is the village of Konduru located?
2. What is the most important food in India?
3. Is rice grown in India during the rainy season, cold season, or hot season?

3 TO HELP YOU LEARN

Using New Words

Read the words in the box. Choose the word that best answers each question below. Write your answers on a sheet of paper.

conservation	mining	climate
national parks	income	tourists
pollution	weather	fuel
pipeline		

1. What is burned to provide energy to run machines?
2. What is the name for people who visit places like Acadia National Park on vacation?
3. What kind of work are people doing when they dig for minerals?
4. What was built to carry oil across Alaska?
5. What are rain and sunshine examples of?
6. Where can people go to see beautiful lands?
7. What can make a lake's water unsafe to drink?
8. What word explains why some foods grow only in certain places?
9. What should people practice in order to save our natural resources?
10. What would you call the money you earned if you helped wash you mother's car?

Finding the Facts

1. Name two ways people in rural areas use towns.
2. Why can some crops be grown only in certain parts of the country?
3. What is the purpose of the Alaska pipeline?
4. What is conservation?
5. Why does our country have national parks?
6. Where is India located?

Using Study Skills

The chart below tells about some well-known national parks in the United States. Use the chart to answer these questions.

1. When was Olympic National Park formed?
2. Where is it located?
3. Which is the oldest national park?
4. Where is it located?
5. Which is the second oldest national park?
6. Which national park is located in Kentucky?

National Parks

Park	Date formed	Location
Everglades	1947	Florida
Mammoth Cave	1936	Kentucky
Olympic	1938	Washington
Shenandoah	1935	Virginia
Yellowstone	1872	Wyoming, Idaho, Montana
Yosemite	1890	California

Things to Think About

1. How do some people in towns depend on nearby natural resources?
2. Why is wheat such an important crop in the United States?
3. How does life in Konduru, India, change as the seasons change?

Things to Do

1. Find out about different ways people in your community try to conserve natural resources.
2. Imagine that you lived during the Gold Rush. You just moved to California to open a store. You plan to sell all the goods that miners might need. Make a list of the goods you would sell in your store.

Learning About Your Own Community

The kinds of crops that can grow in an area depend on the climate. The climate of your community also has a lot to do with the way you live. Describe the climate of your community. Is it hot or cold? How many seasons are there? Do you have a lot of rain or little rain? Does it ever snow?

Learning from Maps

1. Turn to the map on page 98. With your finger point to India on the small map. Point to Konduru on the large map. Which map shows a bigger part of the earth?
2. The product map below shows farm products and natural resources in the southeastern United States. What is the main crop grown in Florida? In which states in coal found? Where is cotton grown? What symbol does the map use to show forests?

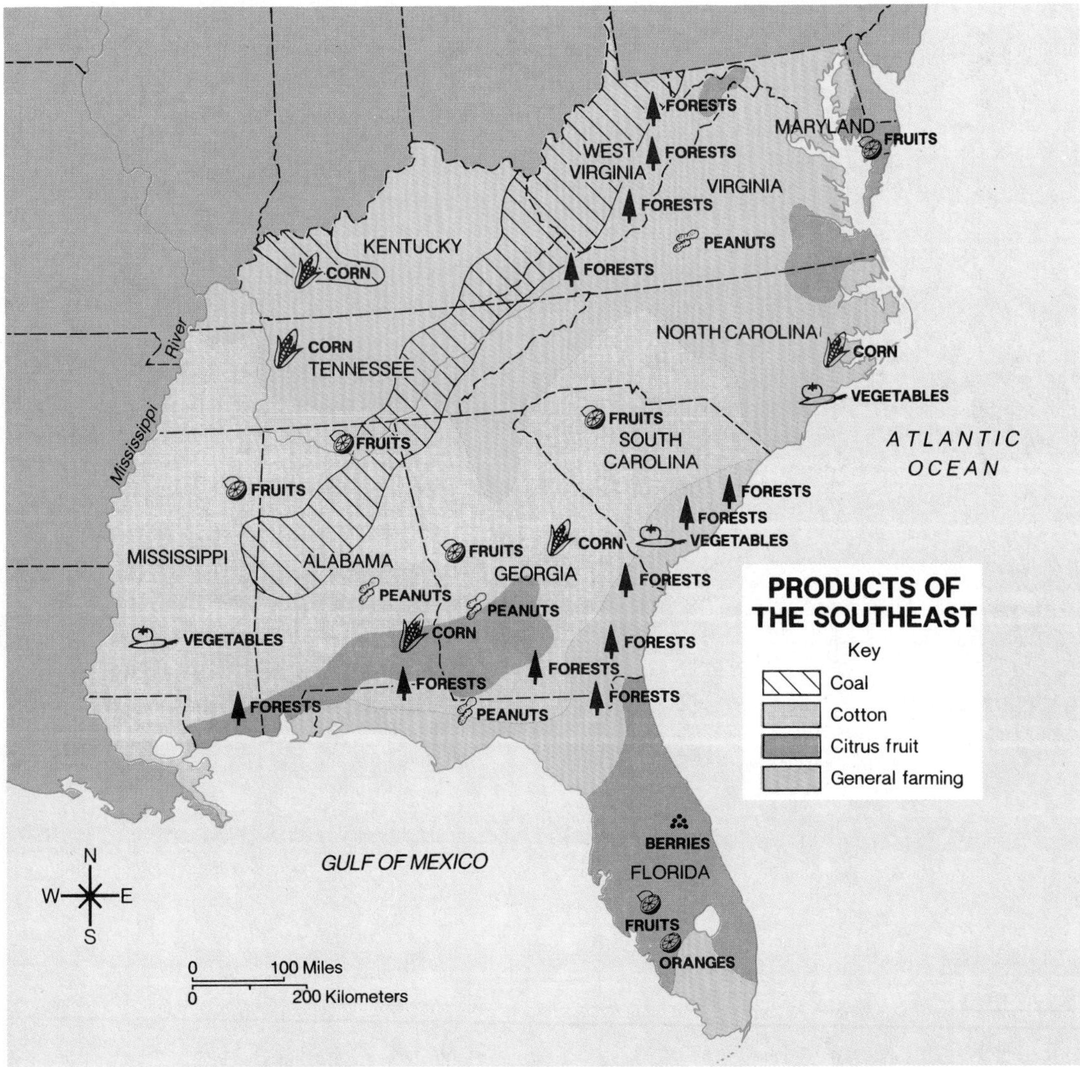

BANK OF AMERICA

4

URBAN COMMUNITIES

Most people in our country live in urban areas. Urban areas are made up of cities and their surrounding suburbs. Urban areas have large populations and tall buildings. People live in many neighborhoods and work in many different kinds of jobs. There are urban communities in all parts of the country.

Looking Ahead

1. This picture shows an urban community. How can you tell that this is an urban area?
2. Which part of the picture shows a city?
3. Which part shows suburbs?

Words to Learn

central business district
industrial area
residential areas
manufacturing
industry
assembly line
ZIP code
mass transit
commuters

1 Living and Working in a City

The bus was filling up with tourists. A young man stood at the door. "Find a seat and get comfortable," he said. "Soon we'll be starting our tour around the city of San Francisco, California. My name is Sam and I'll be your guide today.

"San Francisco is a very beautiful city. It is located on a peninsula. On the west is the Pacific Ocean and on the east is San Francisco Bay. The bay and the ocean are connected by a narrow body of water called the Golden Gate. The city is built on more than 40 hills. Each year more than 2 million tourists visit San Francisco."

This map shows the location of San Francisco and some of its suburbs.

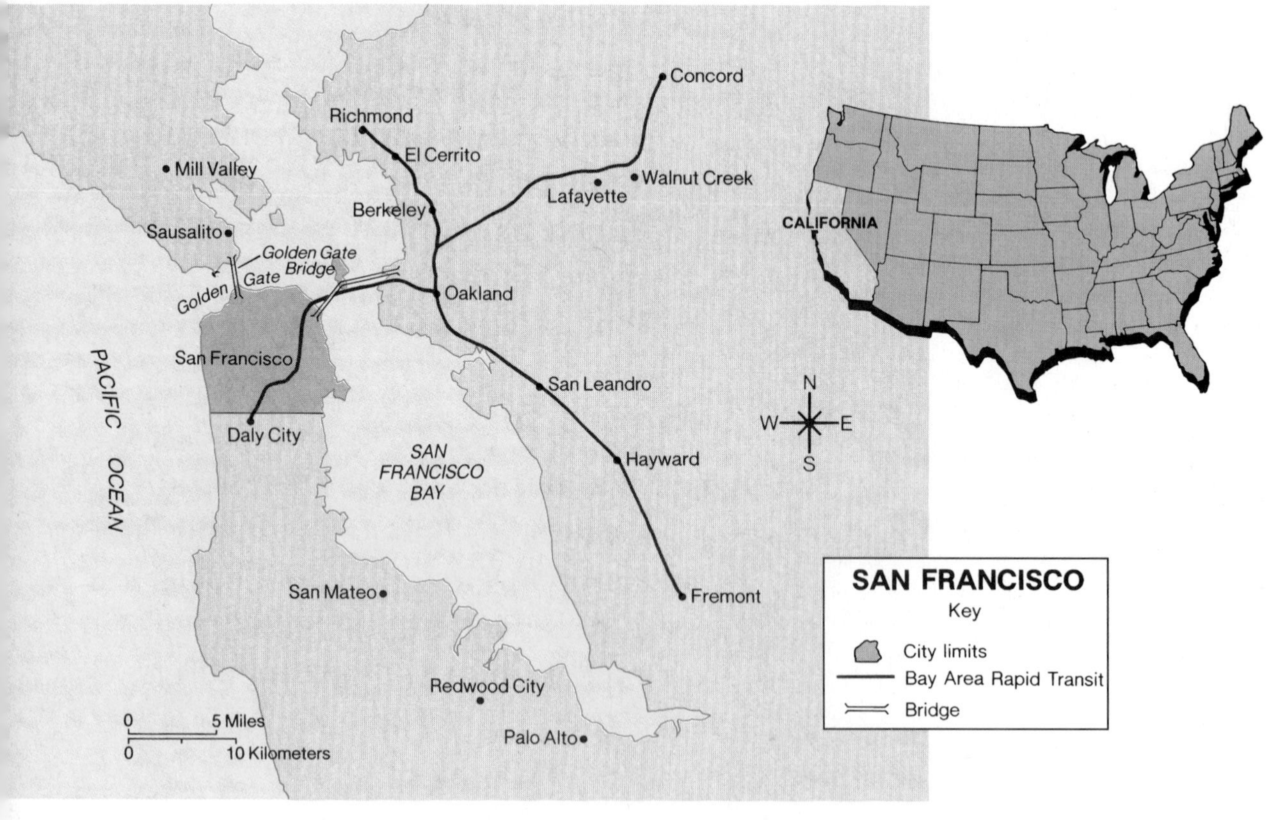

Parts of the City

The bus began traveling down a busy street. "Today we'll look at several parts of the city," Sam said. "This is the downtown area, or the central business district (sen′trəl biz′nis dis′trikt). Every day thousands of people come to the central business district to work and to shop. Businesses have offices in very tall buildings called skyscrapers. People also come downtown to restaurants and theaters.

"Another place where people work is the industrial area (in dus′trē əl er′ē ə). There are many factories in this part of the city. The industrial area of many cities includes a port. The port in San Francisco, called the Embarcadero (em bär′kə der′ō), is on the bay.

"At the northern end of the Embarcadero is Fisherman's Wharf. Here you can see the city's many fishing boats. The wharf, or dock, is famous for its seafood restaurants. Let's stop for lunch."

Sam and the tour group stopped at Fisherman's Wharf for lunch.

After lunch the tour bus traveled through some residential areas (rez′ ə den′shəl er′ē əz) in San Francisco. Residential areas are where people live. Sam explained that there are many residential areas in the city.

"One of the best known neighborhoods is Chinatown. It was started by people who came to California from China during the gold rush. Today Chinatown has many popular shops and restaurants.

"The Mission District is the home of many Spanish-speaking people. All of California was once owned by Spain. In those days, a Spanish priest named Junipero Serra (hoo nē′ perō ser′ə) started many churches in California. He chose the name San Francisco for the church here. That is how the city got its name.

"San Francisco has many other neighborhoods. Some are built on steep hills. They include Nob Hill, Telegraph Hill, and Russian Hill.

Sam pointed out many interesting places in Chinatown.

Cable cars travel on the steepest hills in San Francisco. A ride on a cable car is a good way to see the city.

A Special Kind of Transportation

"Let's stop for a minute at the top of Nob Hill," Sam said, and he pointed out the unusual streetcar that was coming slowly up the steep hill. "This car is pulled by moving cables under the street and runs on rails. It is called a cable car. The cable cars were built in the 1870s. Today people enjoy riding the cable cars to the tops of the city's hills. A ride on a cable car is a great way to see this beautiful city.

"San Francisco also has a new railroad system called the Bay Area Rapid Transit, or BART for short. BART travels both above ground and under the ground. It connects San Francisco with a number of its suburbs."

The City and Its Suburbs

Sam explained that San Francisco has many suburbs. "In many urban areas," he said, "the largest residential areas are in nearby suburbs. The bridge we're crossing now is the Golden Gate Bridge, which connects San Francisco with its northern suburbs.

"Notice how different these communities look from San Francisco," Sam said. "Neighborhoods in the city are crowded and most people live in apartments. There is much more space in suburban communities. Most people here live in houses with yards. There is more space for trees and flowers and grass. There is more space to play outside.

"All this space means that things are farther apart in the suburbs. City neighborhoods often have shops and restaurants right in the residential area. In suburbs, people usually drive to the store. It may be a long distance from where people live to the nearest school or library.

"Many people enjoy living in cities. There are many places to go and many things to do. But cities also can be crowded, polluted, and noisy. Suburbs are cleaner and quieter.

San Francisco has many suburbs. Suburban neighborhoods are less crowded than city neighborhoods.

Before the end of the tour the group stopped to take more pictures. In the background is the Golden Gate Bridge.

"Many people live in the suburbs and work in the city, but there are jobs in the suburbs too. The suburbs, like towns and cities, need police officers, teachers, doctors, nurses, and store clerks. Many businesses have their offices in suburbs."

At last the bus returned to downtown San Francisco. "I hope you enjoyed our tour," said Sam. "There are so many things to see here. Come back again soon."

Do You Know?

1. Tell what people do in the central business district of a city.
2. What is the industrial area of a city?
3. What is the name of the part of a city where people live?
4. Tell two differences between cities and suburbs.

2 Manufacturing in a City

Cities are centers of transportation and trade. They also are centers of business and manufacturing (man′yə fak′chər ing). Manufacturing is the making of large numbers of goods in factories.

Manufacturing Centers
Factories in the United States manufacture many different kinds of goods. They make clothing, furniture, and large machines. Automobiles, airplanes, bicycles, dishes, and many other goods are all manufactured in our country.

The manufacturing of different kinds of goods is important in different cities. For example, the manufacturing of cotton cloth has long been important in cities in the southeastern states. This is because these states are the center of cotton growing in our country.

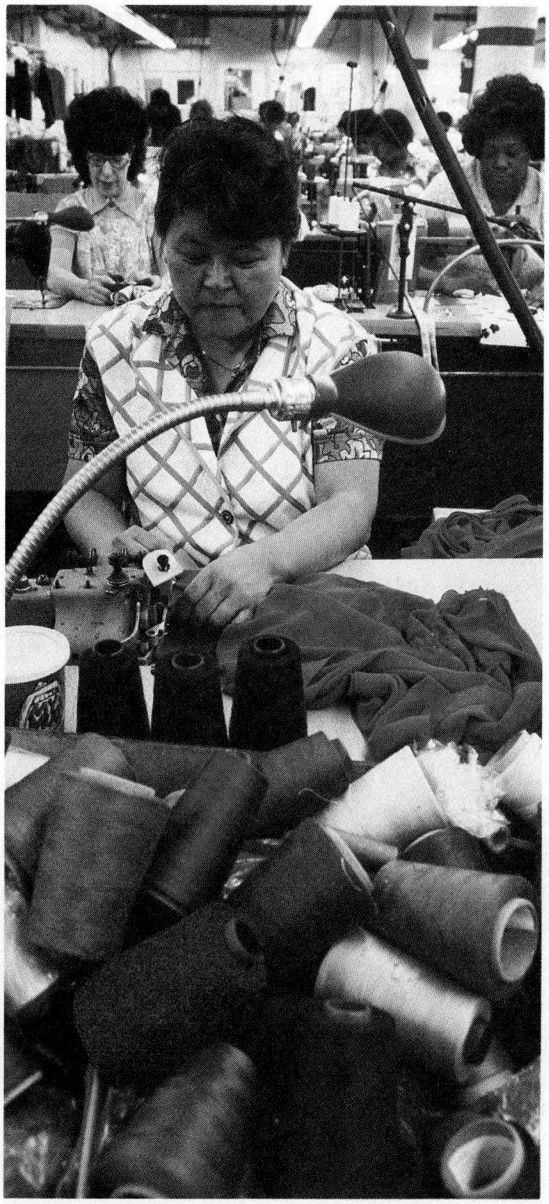

Manufacturing is important in many cities in the United States.

In the urban area of Detroit, Michigan, the most important industry (in′dəs trē) is the manufacturing of automobiles. An industry is the many businesses that make one kind of product. Let's take a look inside one of the automobile factories to see how cars are made.

Manufacturing Automobiles

The first step in manufacturing a car is making all the parts that will be needed. Workers use very large machines to make the doors, roof, and engine, for example. All these parts then are brought to one main factory where the new cars are put together. They are manufactured on an assembly line (ə sem′blē līn). An assembly line is a line of workers who put together a product as it passes by on a slowly moving track.

The workers on an assembly line remain in one place as the cars move slowly through the factory on long tracks. As the cars move, they pass many groups of workers. Each group has a certain job to do. The diagram on the next page shows some of the final steps in assembling a car.

Every worker on an assembly line has a special job to do.

Assembling a Car

This diagram shows some steps on the final assembly line. The parts of the car shown being assembled here were put together on separate assembly lines.

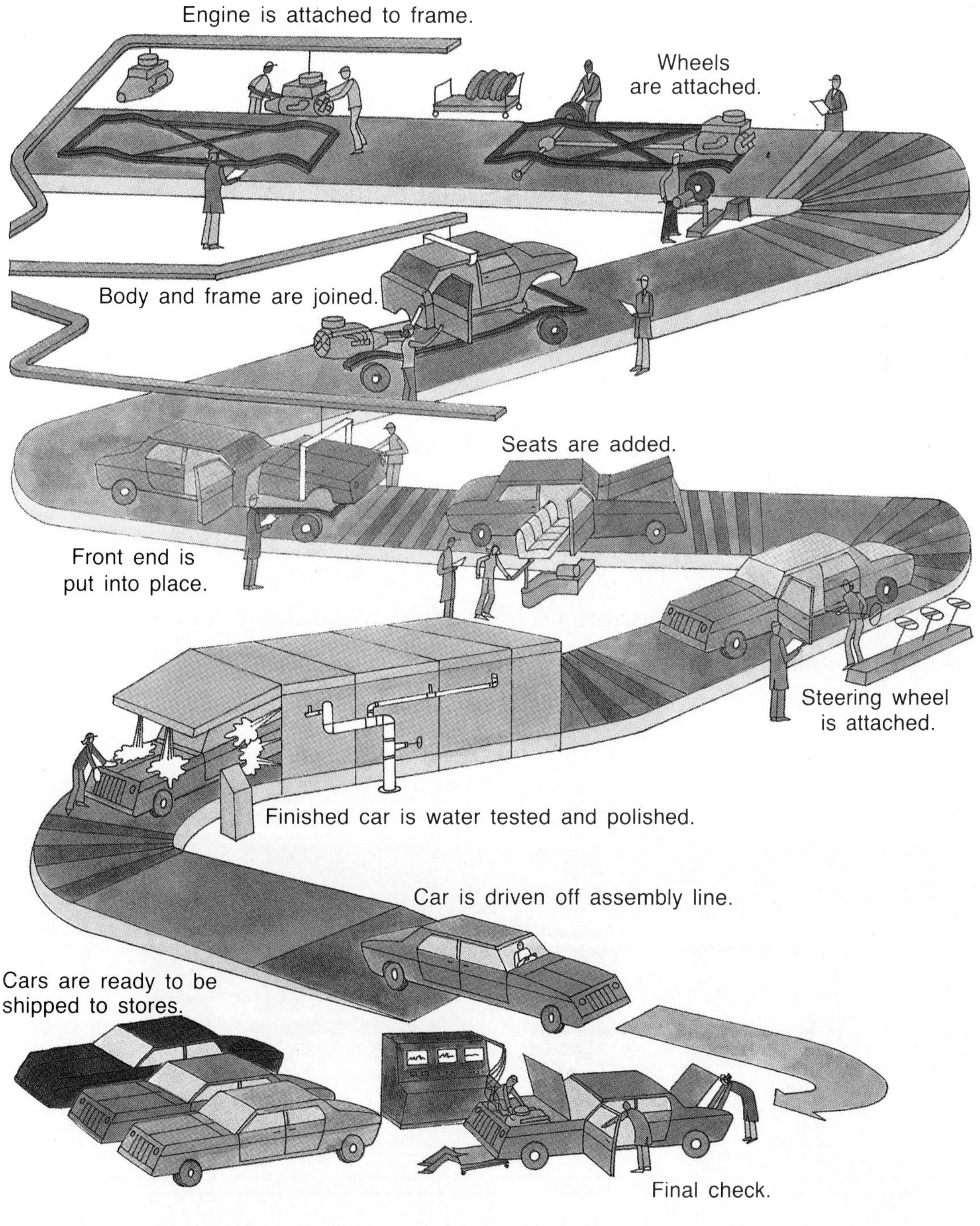
Engine is attached to frame.
Wheels are attached.
Body and frame are joined.
Seats are added.
Front end is put into place.
Steering wheel is attached.
Finished car is water tested and polished.
Car is driven off assembly line.
Cars are ready to be shipped to stores.
Final check.

Henry Ford

In the early days of automobile manufacturing one worker or a small group of workers made the entire car from start to finish. The first person to use assembly lines in manufacturing cars was Henry Ford.

Ford began learning how to make machines when he was a teenager. When he grew up the first cars were being made, but they did not work very well and were very expensive. Henry Ford decided to try to make a car that would work better and cost less. In 1903 he started his own car manufacturing company and in 1913 he began to use an assembly line. His company became one of the biggest in the United States.

Henry Ford's assembly line helped bring about a very important change in manufacturing. Workers on an assembly line made more cars in less time, so Ford could sell his cars for less money. More people could afford to buy them. Before the assembly line was used, workers needed $12\frac{1}{2}$ hours to make a car. The first assembly line workers could make a car in $1\frac{1}{2}$ hours and it was sold for only half the price of a car in 1908.

Henry Ford is standing between two of the cars he built.

Today robots do some of the work on assembly lines.

Changes in Manufacturing

Today many other changes are taking place in manufacturing. For example, work on assembly lines has been speeded up by the use of computers. Computers are machines that help people use information. In factories, computers help people decide how fast the assembly line should move. Some work on assembly lines is being done by robots. A robot is a machine that can do some of the work done by a person.

The use of computers, robots, and other new kinds of machines means that cars now can be made in less time and with less effort. Today cars have many more parts and must pass many more safety checks than ever before. Cars come off the assembly line about one each minute.

Do You Know?

1. What is manufacturing?
2. Tell what happens on an assembly line.
3. Name two changes that are taking place in manufacturing.

Before You Go On

Learning About ZIP Codes

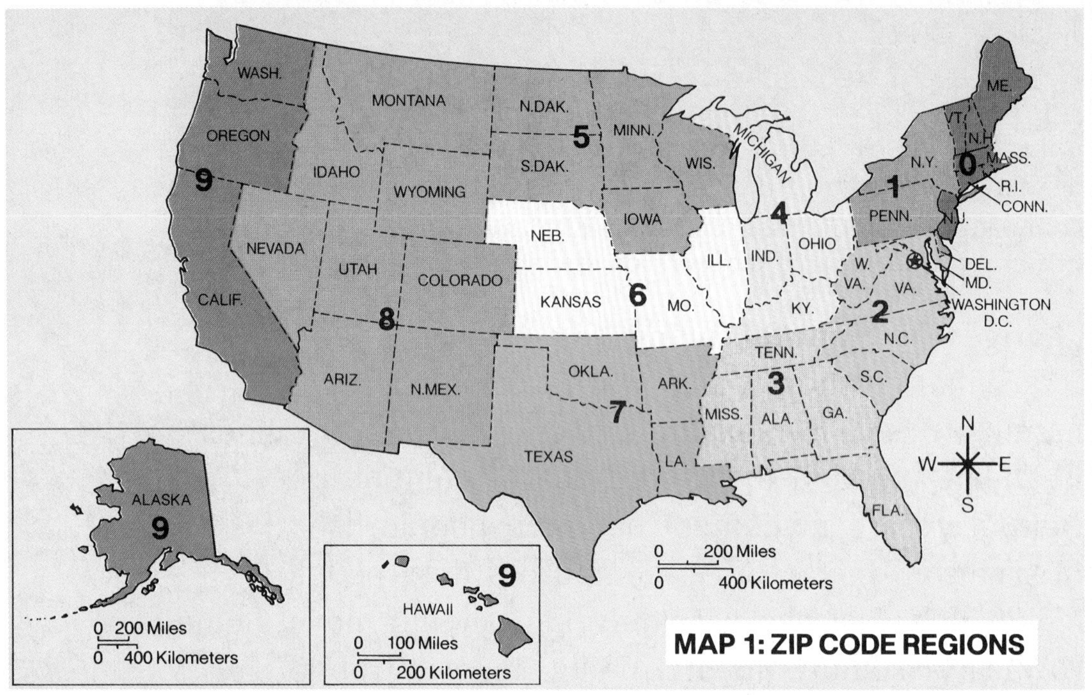

MAP 1: ZIP CODE REGIONS

Suppose you want to send a letter to Rosa Sanchez. This is her address:

Rosa Sanchez
214 Madison Street
Sarasota, Florida 33577

The numbers after the name of the state are the <u>ZIP code</u> (zip kōd). The ZIP code tells the post office where a letter is going.

Each number in the ZIP code is a clue about where the letter should go. The first number stands for the postal region in which each state is located. Rosa Sanchez lives in region 3, which includes Florida. In which region is your community located?

The second and third numbers show the postal areas within each region. These numbers stand for a main post office. Map 2 shows the postal areas in Florida. To find the location of Rosa's postal area, use the first three numbers of her ZIP code.

The last two numbers of the ZIP code stand for the neighborhood post office. Map 3 shows the postal areas in Sarasota.

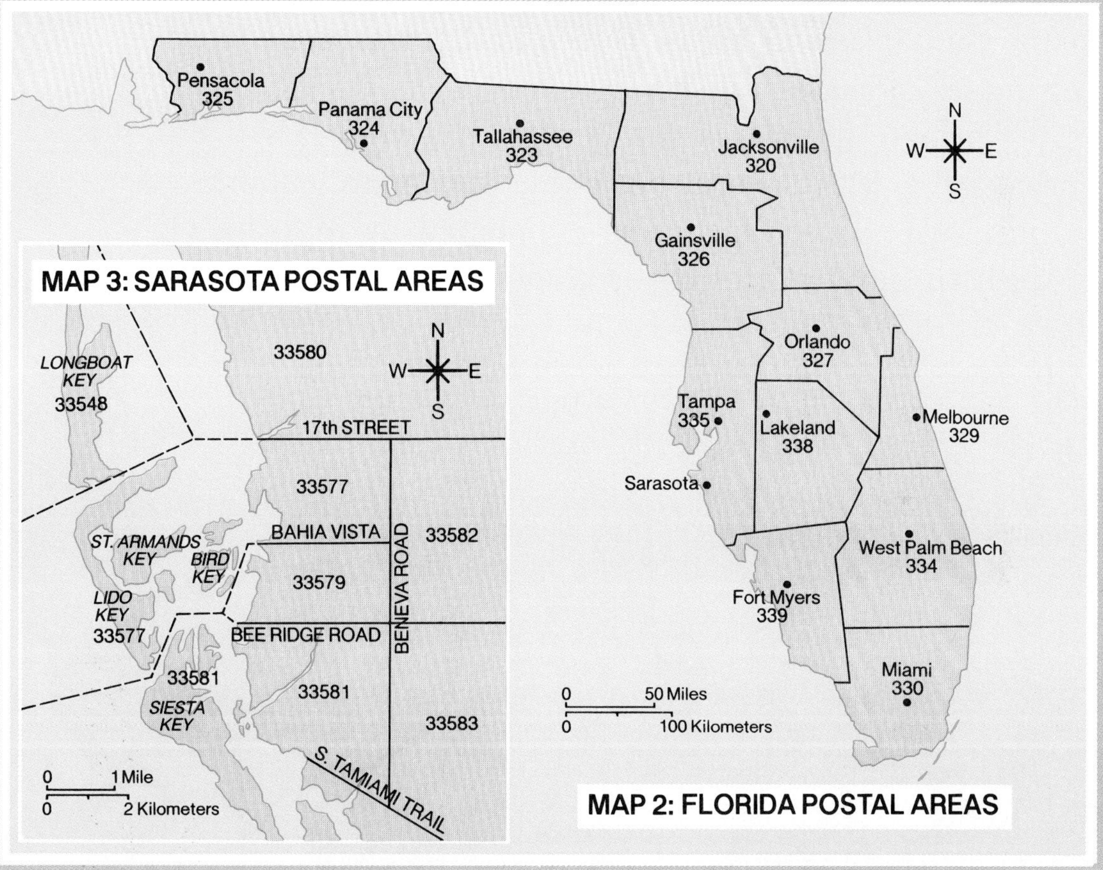

Practicing Your Skills

Use the ZIP code maps to answer these questions.

1. In what region is New York?
2. What states are in region 9?
3. How many postal areas are in Florida?
4. How many ZIP codes does Sarasota have?

3 Getting from Place to Place

Urban areas need good transportation. Large numbers of people must go to work and move from place to place. Goods must move into and out of the city.

Mass Transit

Transportation for large numbers of people is called mass transit (mas tran′sit). Mass transit is very important in urban areas. Buses and trains are examples of mass transit.

Chicago, Illinois, is the center of a very large urban area with several big cities and many suburbs around each one. Chicago is connected by mass transit to most of the other communities nearby.

Mass transit is very important in a large urban area like Chicago. Find three suburbs that are linked by railroad with Chicago.

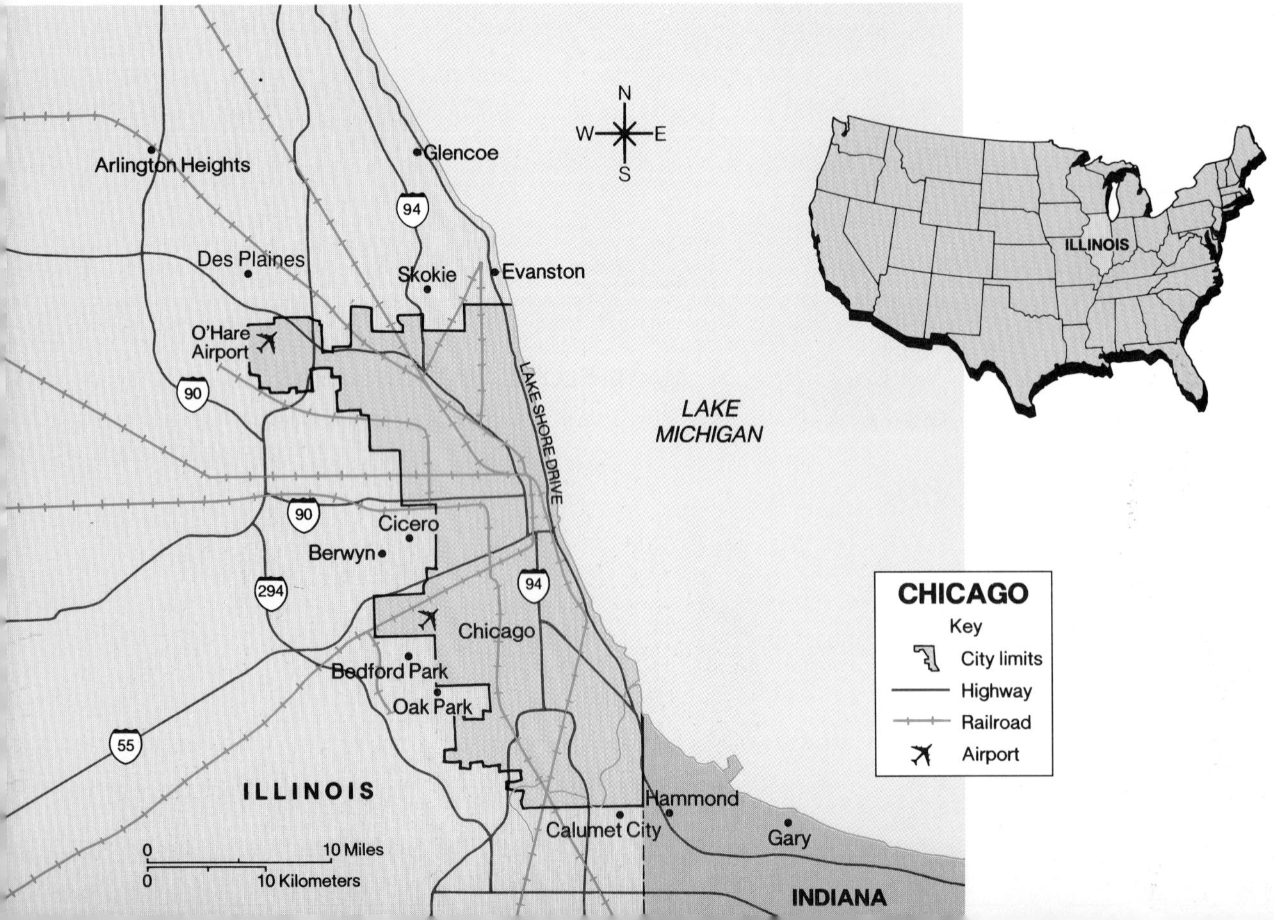

Elevated trains run through most parts of Chicago. When the trains run underground they are called subways.

Downtown Chicago is called the Loop. Trains come into the downtown area, then loop or turn around and go back out again. These trains run on tracks built high above the street. They are called elevated trains, or Els for short. In some places in the city the trains run underground. Then they are called subways.

Like other big cities, Chicago also has buses for mass transit. But the trains usually are faster than the buses because they do not have to wait for traffic.

Traffic is a problem in busy cities. It is especially a problem when people are going to and from their jobs in the morning and evening. These times are called rush hours because people are rushing to and from their jobs. Sometimes during rush hours traffic is so slow that people can walk faster than cars and buses are moving.

Commuters

To get from one place to another in the city of Chicago you can walk, drive a car, ride a bicycle, take a taxi, or use mass transit. But what if you live in the suburbs? How could you get to a job in the city each day?

Many people in the Chicago area travel into the city to work. People who travel from their homes in the suburbs to work in the city are called commuters (kə myo͞ot′ərz). Most commuters drive to Chicago in cars. They use three main highways that lead into the city and many smaller roads. Sometimes workers form a car pool and drive together to their jobs.

Many commuters travel to the city on mass transit. Some commuters use buses or the El. Others ride commuter trains, which make trips every morning and evening during the rush hours.

Many commuters travel from the suburbs to work in Chicago. The city's streets are very crowded during rush hours.

A Busy Transportation Center

You read in Unit 3 that towns are centers of transportation in rural areas. Cities are transportation centers for even larger areas. Trade and transportation are important industries in most big cities.

Chicago is the biggest transportation center in the United States. The city is like the center of a wheel, with different kinds of transportation coming from and going to many places. It is the country's most important railroad center and one of the busiest ports. There are more than 2,000 trucking companies in the city. Chicago's O'Hare International Airport is the busiest airport in the world. Every year more than 40 million passengers use the airport and 1 million planes take off and land there.

Chicago's O'Hare Airport is the busiest airport in the world. Signs tell passengers when planes are landing and taking off.

Every day goods are brought into Chicago from other communities. Goods also are sent from Chicago to communities near and far.

Goods come into Chicago from nearby towns and urban areas. They are sent out on trucks, planes, railroads, or ships to other cities. At the same time, goods come into Chicago from other parts of the country and the world. Some of these goods go to Chicago stores and factories. Others are sent to communities near and far. In Chicago and other urban areas, goods and people are always on the move!

Do You Know?

1. Why is mass transit important in many urban areas?
2. Name the kinds of mass transit in Chicago.
3. What do commuters do each day?

4 A City in Kenya

In this unit you have read about some of the activities that take place in urban areas in the United States. There are urban areas in every country in the world. Some are like those in our country and some are different.

Nairobi (nī rō′bē) is the capital and largest city in Kenya. Kenya is a country on the east coast of the continent of Africa. Most Kenyans live in rural areas and are farmers. Each year more and more people move to Kenya's cities. The country's urban areas, especially Nairobi, are growing rapidly. Like the American cities you have read about, Nairobi is a center of business, transportation, manufacturing, and trade. It is also a tourist center.

Find Nairobi on the map. Name the national parks that are linked by railroad with Nairobi.

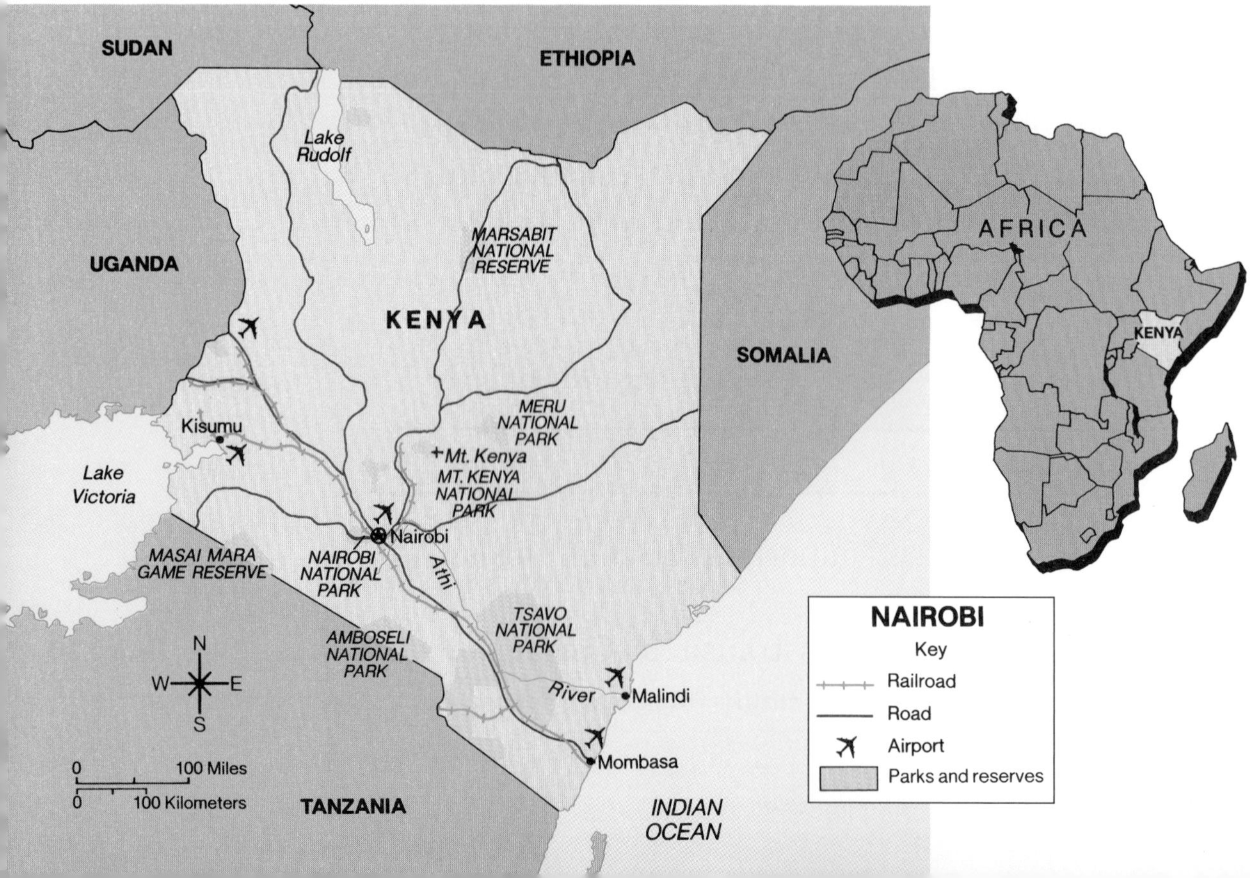

Kenya's national parks were set up to protect its wild animals. Tourists can see many kinds of animals running free in the parks.

Visiting the National Parks

Tourists come to Nairobi from all over the world to see the wild animals in Kenya's national parks. Kenya is famous for its many different kinds of wild animals. In its parks you can see lions, zebras, elephants, and giraffes. You can see many kinds of colorful birds.

These animals are a very special and important natural resource of Kenya. The parks were set up to protect the animals. No hunting is allowed. Visitors travel through the parks in buses or cars, and the animals run free.

Nairobi is the capital and largest city of Kenya.

Visiting Nairobi

Visits to the national parks usually begin with a stop in Nairobi. Tourists fly into Nairobi's busy airport and stay in one of the city's modern hotels. While in the city they can enjoy its restaurants, shops, and theaters. Then they can begin their tour of the national parks. There is even a national park right in Nairobi, just a few minutes from the downtown area.

Jobs in the City

Many people in Nairobi work in the tourist industry. Others have jobs manufacturing shoes, cloth, soap, and cement. Food processing is also an important industry in Nairobi. Making wheat into bread is an

example of food processing. As the capital of Kenya, Nairobi is the place where the country's leaders meet.

Like Chicago, Nairobi is an important railroad center. Railroads link Nairobi with the Indian Ocean port of Mombasa (mäm bäs′ ə) and with other cities in Kenya. Railroads also link Nairobi with other countries in eastern Africa. Nairobi is the most important trading center of eastern Africa.

Do You Know?

1. Where is Nairobi located?
2. Why do many tourists come to Kenya each year?
3. Name three kinds of jobs in Nairobi.

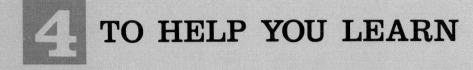

4 TO HELP YOU LEARN

Using New Words

Match each word with its correct meaning. Write each word and its meaning on a sheet of paper.

1. central business district
2. industrial area
3. residential area
4. manufacturing
5. industry
6. assembly line
7. mass transit
8. commuters
9. ZIP code

a. a group of workers putting together a product as it passes by on a slowly moving track
b. part of a city where many factories are located
c. making goods in factories
d. people who travel from the suburbs to work in a city
e. numbers that help the post office deliver mail
f. the downtown area of a city
g. buses and subways are examples of this type of transportation
h. part of a city where most people live
i. all the businesses that make a product

Finding the Facts

1. On what ocean is San Francisco located?
2. What is the central business district of a city?
3. What is an industry?
4. What change did Henry Ford make in the manufacturing of automobiles?
5. Name two kinds of mass transit.
6. Where is Kenya located?

Using Study Skills

The line graph below shows how urban population has changed since 1900. Use the graph to answer these questions.

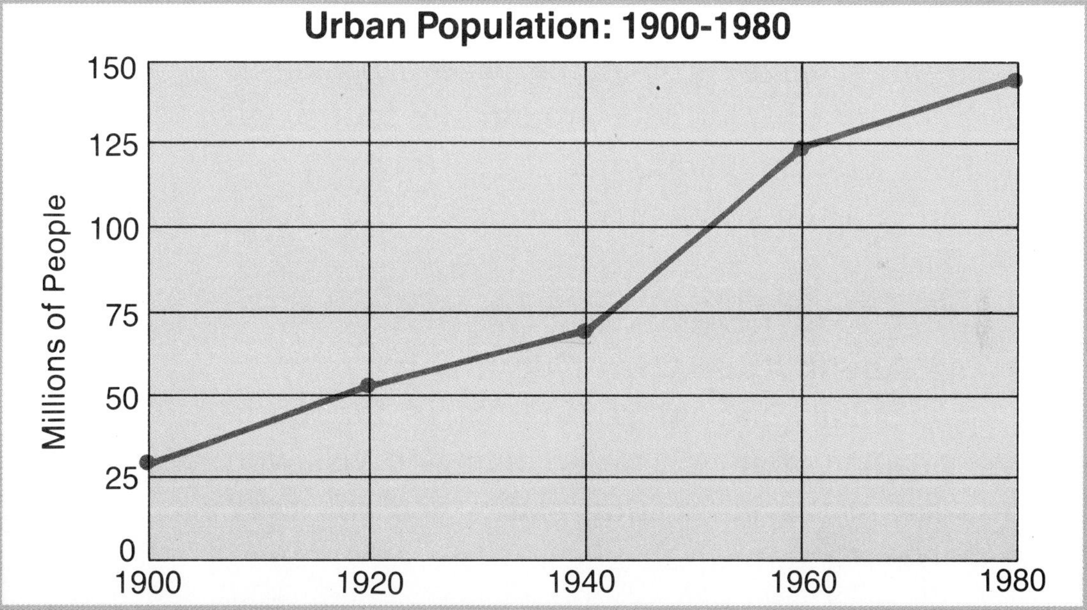

a. About how many people lived in cities in 1900?
b. About how many people lived in cities in 1940?
c. In which year was urban population the highest?
d. In general, has the urban population been going up or down since 1900?

Things to Think About

1. Name two ways in which Chicago and Nairobi are alike. Name two ways in which these cities are different.
2. What types of mass transit do people in your community use? Is mass transit the main type of transportation in your community?

Things to Do

1. Look at the diagram of a car assembly line on page 117. Imagine that cheese sandwiches with lettuce and tomato are made on an assembly line in a factory. Draw a series of pictures showing the steps in making each sandwich.
2. Get a map of your community. Using a red pencil draw a line around the central business district. Draw a blue line around the industrial areas if your community has any. Draw a green line around the residential areas. Do the areas overlap?

Learning About Your Own Community

Every community has interesting places for tourists to see. Imagine your cousin is coming to visit you. Make a list of the interesting places you will take your cousin. Next to each place, write a sentence explaining why you want to take your cousin there.

Learning from Maps

1. Turn the map of San Francisco on page 108. Use the map to answer these questions.
   a. Name one community you could reach by leaving San Francisco on the Golden Gate Bridge.
   b. Which community is farthest south on the BART system?
   c. About how far is Lafayette from Berkeley?
2. The map below shows New Orleans, Louisiana. Use the map to answer these questions.
   a. Name one street in the central business district.
   b. Tell where one industrial area is located.
   c. What color on the map stands for residential areas?

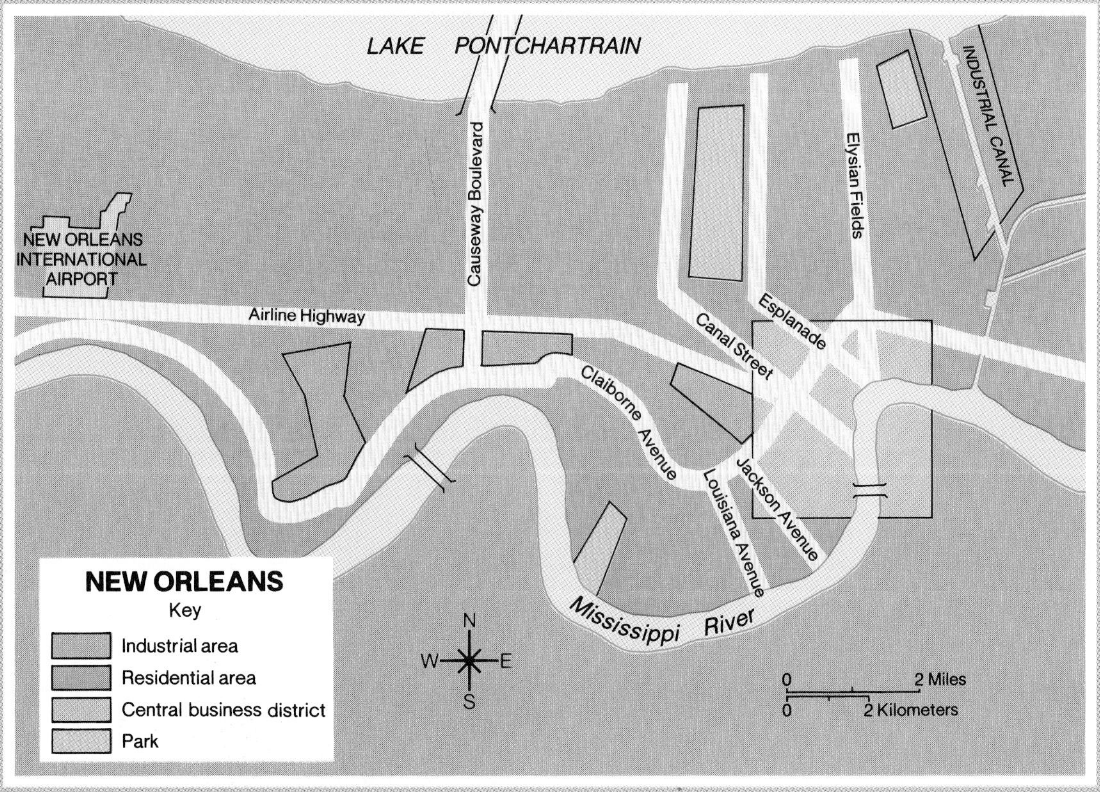

5
COMMUNITIES CHANGE

Communities are always changing. Change happens for many different reasons. New buildings go up and old buildings are torn down. Some communities grow larger and others get smaller. Communities can plan for change.

Looking Ahead

1. This picture shows a changing community. What is happening in this community?
2. What places in your community are changing in this way?
3. What other changes are happening in your community?

Words to Learn

immigrants
desert
irrigation
dam
metropolitan area
communication
invention

1 An Old and New Community

It is hard to believe that the pictures on this page both show the same community, but they do. They show the city of St. Louis, Missouri, at different times in its history.

The history of St. Louis began long ago, before the United States became a country. In those days Indians and explorers traded goods here. Later the city grew up as a busy river port. Today St. Louis is the largest city in Missouri.

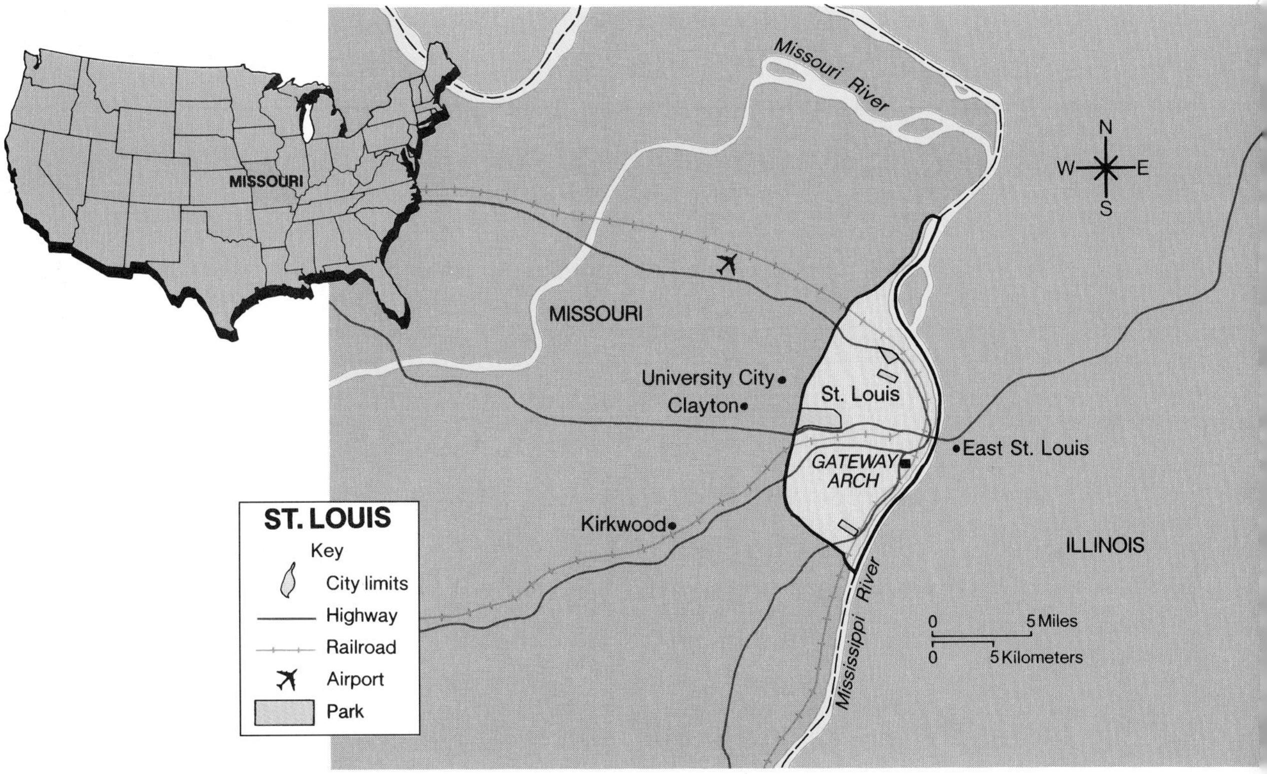

This map shows the location of St. Louis. About how far does the city extend from north to south? What state is east of St. Louis?

Fur Traders

The land where St. Louis now stands was once covered with large forests that were the home of many kinds of animals. For years traders came in search of animal furs. People in Europe wanted the furs to make warm winter clothing. Fur traders brought tools, blankets, and other goods to trade with Indian hunters for furs. Then they sold the furs to make money.

A French fur trader chose the location for St. Louis in 1764. The map can help you see why he chose this spot. St. Louis is located near the place where two of our country's largest rivers—the Mississippi River and the Missouri River—come together. On which river is St. Louis located?

In the early days there were no roads or railroads in this part of the continent. Fur traders usually traveled in canoes on rivers. The rivers were as important as railroads or highways are today. The Missouri River and Mississippi River served as highways to carry people west.

Lewis and Clark

St. Louis became the most important starting place for people traveling west. Two of the most famous early explorers were Meriwether Lewis and William Clark. They were chosen by President Thomas Jefferson to lead a group of explorers into the unknown lands of the west.

Lewis and Clark and their group left St. Louis in 1804. They started up the Missouri River in boats. Then they walked or they traveled by boats on other rivers all the way to the Pacific Ocean and back.

Their trip was long and dangerous, but very successful. Lewis and Clark brought back important information about the land and its resources. They learned about the Indians who lived there.

The explorers Lewis and Clark left St. Louis to travel west. They met many different groups of Indians on their trip.

Gateway to the West

The Lewis and Clark trip helped open the western lands for pioneers. St. Louis became the starting point, or gateway, for pioneers traveling west. Before leaving St. Louis the pioneers bought many of the goods they would need for their trip and to begin their new homes. St. Louis grew rapidly as people moved there to provide goods and services to the pioneers. The city became known as the Gateway to the West.

St. Louis soon became a very important port. Steamboats brought goods and people to the growing city. By the middle of the 1800s railroads linked the city with the eastern and western parts of the country. More and more people moved to St. Louis.

Many of the people who settled in St. Louis in the late 1800s came from other countries. People who come to a new country to live are called immigrants (im′ə grənts). St. Louis became the new home of immigrants from Germany, Ireland, and other countries of Europe. There were many jobs for the immigrants in this rapidly growing city.

St. Louis became an important port on the Mississippi River. Many immigrants came to live in the growing city.

The Modern City

St. Louis continued to grow for many years, but in the 1950s people began leaving the city and moving to new suburbs. Many old neighborhoods in the city became run-down.

People began to worry about what was happening to their city and decided that St. Louis needed to change. It was time, they said, to fix up the older parts of the city.

Many old buildings were torn down and replaced with new office and apartment buildings and stores. Other old buildings were restored, or fixed up so they looked new again. The people of St. Louis wanted to remember their history.

These pictures show the same street in St. Louis. The old buildings were fixed up and made nice places again for people to live in.

The Gateway Arch rises above St. Louis beside the Mississippi River.

St. Louis also built a new park along the Mississippi River to honor the pioneers. The Gateway Arch in the park faces west to remind us that St. Louis was once the gateway to the west. The arch is 630 feet (192 meters) high and visitors can ride to the top for a view of the entire city. Beneath the arch is a museum where people can learn about the history of the west.

Do You Know?

1. Why were the Mississippi River and Missouri River important to fur traders and pioneers?
2. What did President Jefferson ask Lewis and Clark to do?
3. Why was St. Louis called the Gateway to the West?

Before You Go On

Learning About Time Lines

Do you know the year you were born? When did you start the first grade? When did you start the third grade? You can use a time line to see when these things happened. A time line also tells you the order in which they happened.

The time line on this page tells you when some things happened in Dan's life. Read the time line from left to right. It shows you what happened first, what happened next, and what happened last.

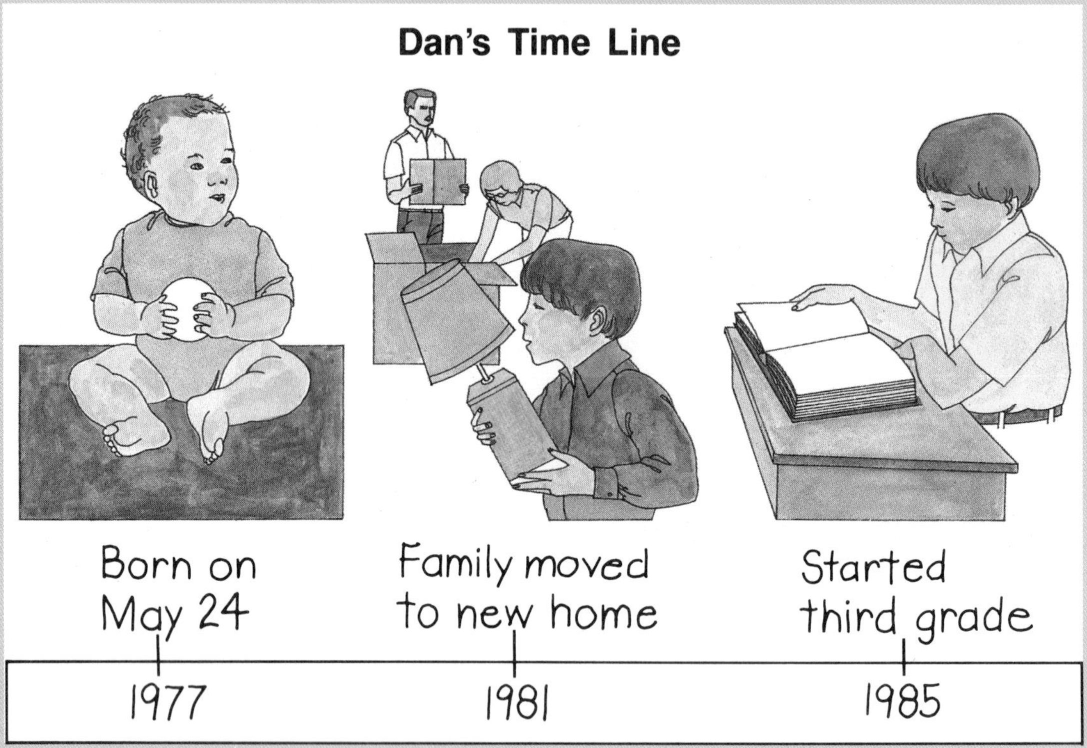

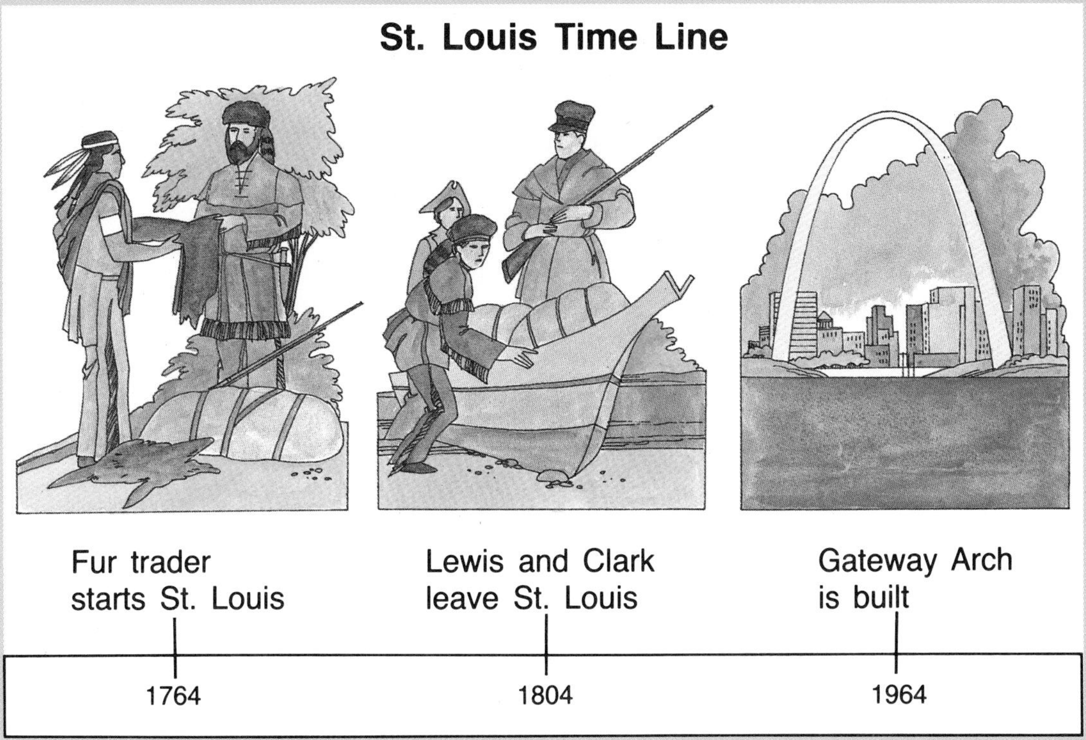

A time line also can show you important events in our country's history. The time line on this page is about St. Louis. It shows three events in the history of the city.

Practicing Your Skills

Use the time line of St. Louis to answer these questions.

1. Which event on the time line happened first?
2. When was the Gateway Arch built?
3. What happened in 1804?
4. Missouri, where St. Louis is located, became a state in 1821. Where would you put this event on the time line?

2 A Fast-Growing Community

Many cities in our country have grown very rapidly in recent years. These cities are mostly in states in the south and the southwest. Large numbers of people have moved to these areas because of their hot, dry climate.

Phoenix, Arizona, for example, is one of the fastest growing cities in the country. Phoenix is located in the Salt River Valley. This is a large, flat area surrounded by mountains. The Salt River Valley is a desert (dez′ərt). A desert is a very dry area where few plants can grow.

A hot, dry climate like the one in Phoenix can be very pleasant. But it also has an important problem. Because there is very little rain, people must get water in another way.

Phoenix is located in a desert. What rivers are near the city? In what direction are the Gila Mountains from Phoenix?

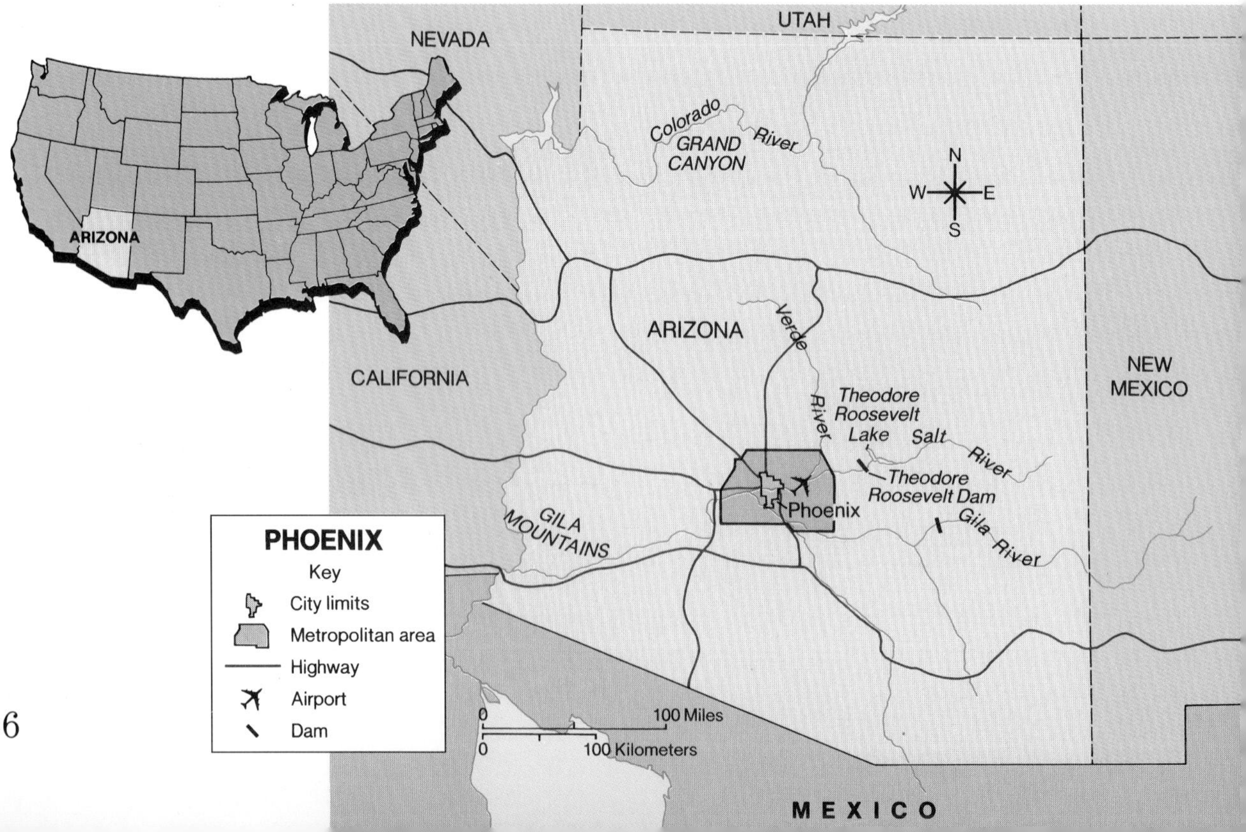

The painting on the left shows the Hohokam using irrigation. The picture on the right shows irrigation today. What is alike in the two pictures? What differences do you see?

The Need for Water

The first people to live in the Salt River Valley were the Hohokam (hō hōk′əm) Indians. They were farmers who used water from the Salt River to grow their crops. But how could they get water from the river to their fields?

The Hohokam used a system of irrigation (ir′ə gā′shən) to bring water from the Salt River to the dry land. They dug long canals, or waterways, to carry water from the river to other parts of the valley. By using irrigation the Hohokam could raise crops in the desert.

In 1867, long after the Hohokam people had left, pioneers arrived in the Salt River Valley and began the city of Phoenix. The pioneers also used irrigation canals to get water from the river to their fields. But the amount of water in the Salt River was not the same all year. Sometimes the river dried up and there was not enough water for irrigation. At other times the river became too full and flooded the land.

Building a Dam

In order for Phoenix to grow, the people had to find a way to prevent floods and make sure there would be enough water all year round. This problem was solved by building a dam (dam) on the Salt River. A dam is a wall built across a river to hold back the water. The water behind the dam forms a lake and can be let out slowly and evenly all during the year. Phoenix now had a steady supply of water.

This is the first dam built on the Salt River. Today there are several dams that provide Phoenix with the water it needs.

The City Grows

Phoenix still had another problem that kept the city from growing. Sometimes its weather gets very, very hot. A way had to be found to keep homes and working places cool. The growing use of air conditioners in the 1950s helped solve this problem.

More and more people began to move to Phoenix. Its population grew from 29,000 in 1920 to more than 700,000 in 1980. Phoenix and its suburbs now fill up most of the Salt River Valley and even cover part of the mountains beyond.

Today Phoenix is the center of a very fast growing metropolitan area (met′rə pol′ə tən er′ē ə). A metropolitan area is a large city and the surrounding suburbs and smaller cities that are linked to it. The Phoenix metropolitan area includes eight cities that are located near Phoenix.

Farming was once the most important activity in the Salt River Valley, but much of the farm land has been used to build new suburbs and cities. Today manufacturing is the leading activity. Two of the main industries are computers and food processing. Many people work in the tourist industry. Large numbers of tourists come to Phoenix to enjoy its climate.

Phoenix is the center of a growing metropolitan area.

A Communication Center

Phoenix, like other large cities, is also a center of communication (kə myo͞o′ni kā′shən). Communication is the exchange of information and ideas. People communicate by talking, listening, writing, reading, and watching. Books, letters, and newspapers are all kinds of communication. So are telephones, radio, and television.

Communication makes it possible for you to know what is happening in your community, state, and country. You can also know almost immediately when something happens anywhere in the world.

Phoenix is a modern communication center. This equipment is used by a local television station to show programs from around the world.

Do You Know?

1. Why has getting enough water been a problem in Phoenix?
2. How did the Hohokam Indians meet their need for water?
3. How did building a dam help Phoenix grow?
4. Name three kinds of communication.

3 Looking to the Future

Communities are always changing. There are many different reasons for these changes. Some changes may happen because a community's population is growing rapidly. Communities also may change if large numbers of people move away.

Sometimes an invention (in ven′chən) brings about changes in a community. An invention is something that has never been made before. The invention of air conditioners, for example, helped Phoenix to grow. Air conditioning meant that people could live comfortably even in a hot climate.

Trains, automobiles, and electric lights are just a few of the many inventions that have changed our communities. How do you think the invention of elevators changed the way communities look?

The invention of elevators made tall buildings possible. How tall do you think buildings could be if people had to walk to the top?

Often the changes in a community are not planned, but sometimes communities can plan for change. People can decide what they want their communities to be like in the future. Let us see how one large community planned for the future.

Planning for the Future

Atlanta is the capital and largest city of Georgia. In the 1950s Atlanta's leaders began talking about an important problem. "More and more people are moving out of the downtown area to the suburbs," they said. "Many stores and businesses are leaving too. Atlanta is losing jobs and income."

Government and business leaders met and made plans for the city's future. They decided to work together to improve the city and bring people and businesses back to the downtown area.

Find the city limits of Atlanta. About how far does Atlanta extend from north to south? Is the airport in the city?

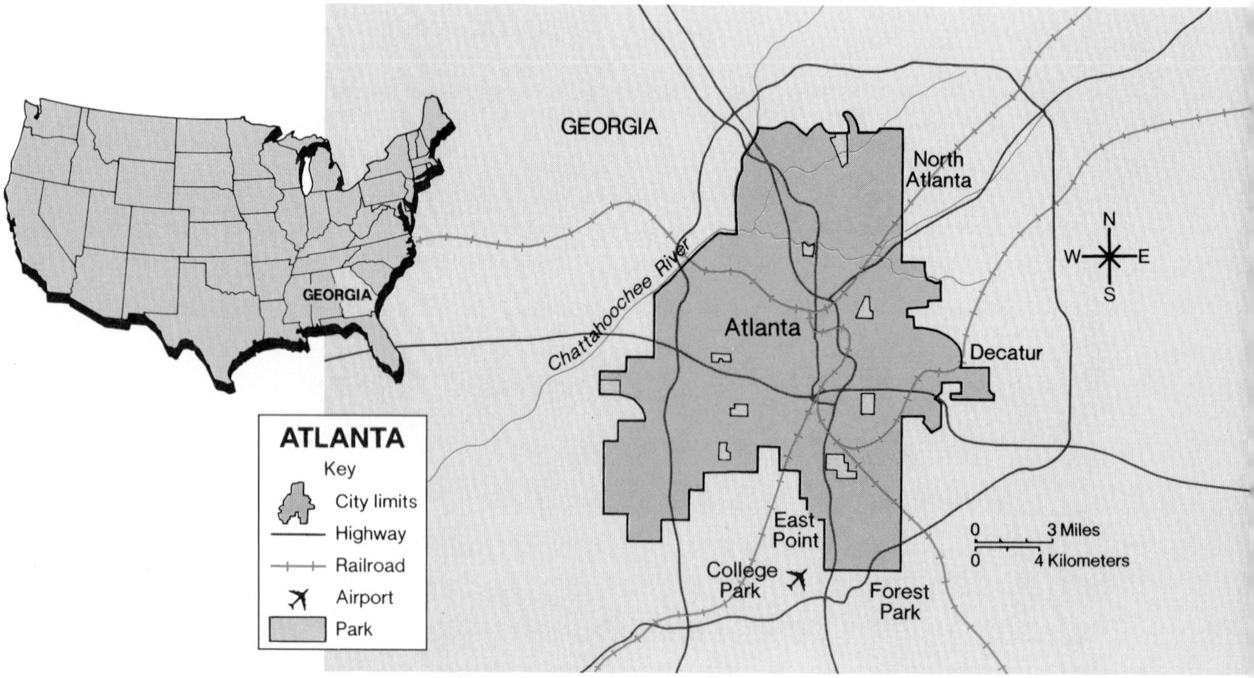

Today Atlanta is a busy and growing city. Its central business district has many tall, modern buildings.

Building and Growing

The plans for improving Atlanta were successful in many ways. Within a few years the city was changing rapidly. The central business district grew up and out. Many tall, modern buildings were put up. There were new offices, apartment buildings, restaurants, theaters, shops, and hotels. Football and baseball teams moved to the city to play in the new Atlanta Stadium.

New highways were built linking Atlanta with its suburbs. The city also started a new railroad system to make getting around Atlanta easier. The airport was rebuilt and today is the second busiest in the country.

Many different kinds of industries moved to Atlanta. Automobiles, clothing, paper, and furniture are some of the goods made in the city. The population grew as many people moved to Atlanta to work in the new jobs being created.

Martin Luther King, Jr.

Dr. Martin Luther King, Jr., was a famous American who was born in Atlanta in 1929. His father and grandfather were both ministers and Martin became a minister too when he grew up.

In those days black children in Atlanta and in many other parts of the country were not allowed to attend the same schools as white children. Black people could not sit in the front of buses or eat in many restaurants. Black people did not have an equal chance to get good jobs.

Martin Luther King, Jr., became a leader of the people working for equal rights for black Americans. He believed that things could be changed peacefully. In 1955, when Dr. King was living in Montgomery, Alabama, he encouraged the black people there to stop riding the city buses. For more than a year the bus company lost money. Finally black people were allowed to sit where they wanted.

Martin Luther King, Jr., worked for equal rights for black Americans. Today black and white children are able to attend the same schools.

In 1963 Martin Luther King, Jr., led a march in Washington, D.C. He told Americans about his dream of equal rights for all people.

Dr. King led marches of black and white people who wanted the black people to have a better life. At a march in Washington, D.C., in 1963 he told the country, "I have a dream." His dream was that all people in our country would have equal rights.

Thanks to the work of Martin Luther King, Jr., and thousands of other Americans, there were important changes in the lives of black people. Today all Americans remember Dr. King in a special way. The third Monday in January was made a national holiday in his honor.

Do You Know?

1. Name two reasons communities change.
2. Why did Atlanta's leaders want to bring people and businesses back to the downtown area?
3. Who was Martin Luther King, Jr.?

4 An Ancient City in Greece

You read in Unit 2 that St. Augustine is the oldest city in our country. It was started more than 400 years ago, but is very new compared to many cities in other countries. Some cities in the world are very old, or ancient. They were built a very long time ago and some are still cities today.

Athens, Greece, for example, is one of the most ancient cities in the world. It has been a city for more than 3,000 years! Today Athens is the capital and largest city of Greece, a country in Europe. Athens is located on a peninsula in southeastern Greece. As you can see on the map, Athens is near a sea. A sea is a large body of water. This sea is called the Mediterranean (med′ə tə rā′nē ən) Sea. Many important cities of ancient times were located around the Mediterranean Sea.

How does the map tell you that Athens is the capital of Greece? What countries are on the northern border of Greece?

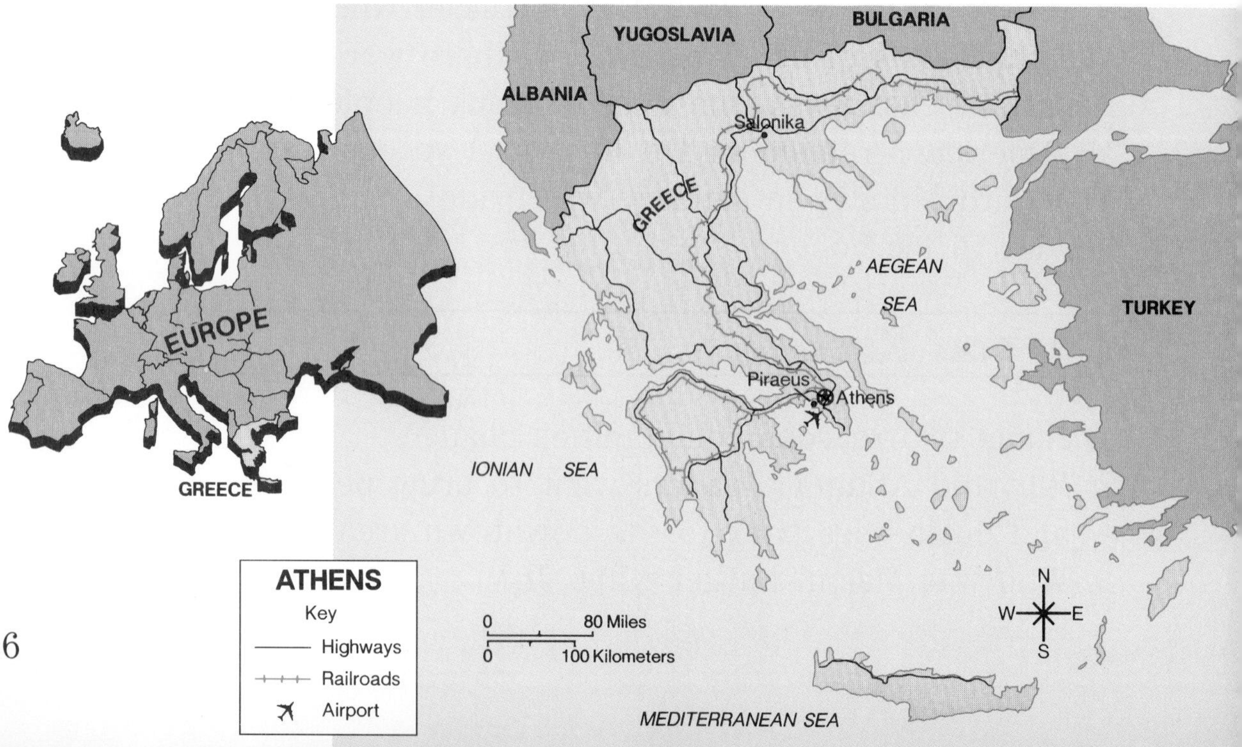

The people of ancient Athens enjoyed plays. Sometimes the audience saw three plays in one day.

Life in Ancient Athens

Athens was one of the most important cities in ancient times. It was a center of trade, learning, art, and government. For many years Athens was the leader of a number of other ancient Greek cities.

Athens became rich and its people wanted to make their city a special place. They built many beautiful buildings. Some of their greatest buildings were on a flat hill called the Acropolis (ə krop′ə lis).

The people of Athens also enjoyed plays. They built a large outdoor theater. Some of the greatest artists, writers, teachers, and thinkers of ancient times lived in Athens. The city became famous for its art, education, and new ideas.

Sports contests had a special place in life in Athens. The very first Olympic games were held in ancient Greece. Athens and the other Greek cities sent their best athletes to the Olympic games. The games were held every four years. They were the start of the Olympic games that are held today.

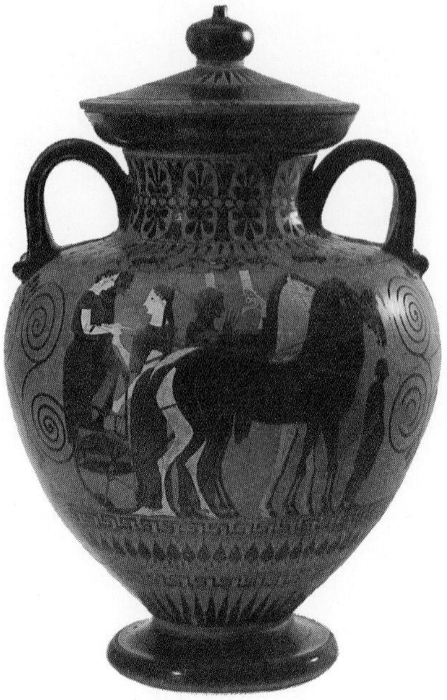

Ancient objects like this plate and vase tell us a lot about how the people of Athens lived long ago.

Learning About Ancient Times

How do we know about things that happened so long ago? We have learned about life in ancient Athens in many ways. We know some things because they were written down. We know about other things because people have found ancient pottery, statues, and other objects. Some of these things had been buried for hundreds of years. These pieces help us learn about the way people lived. Large numbers of these objects are in museums today.

We also have learned about ancient Athens because parts of many of its old buildings are still standing. The most famous ancient building in Athens is called the Parthenon (pär′thə non′). This beautiful building still stands on top of the Acropolis in the middle of the modern city of Athens.

The picture on the left shows the modern city of Athens.
On the right is the port of Piraeus.

The City Changes

During its long history, Athens has changed in many ways. At times the city was very powerful and had many colonies around the Mediterranean Sea. At other times Athens grew weak and was ruled by people in more powerful cities or countries. In 1834 Athens became the capital of the modern country of Greece.

Inventions also have brought changes to Athens. In ancient times messages were carried by runners from one Greek city to another. Today Athens, like other modern cities, is a center of communication, trade, and transportation. Athens has a busy airport and modern mass transit, including buses and a subway. The subway connects Athens with the nearby city of Piraeus (pī rē′əs), which is Greece's largest port. Highways link Athens with all other cities in Greece.

Athens is a popular tourist center. Tourists and the people of Athens like to spend time in the city's many squares.

The modern city of Athens is the business center of Greece. Its factories make clothing, foods, paper, and other goods. Many people work at shipbuilding in Piraeus.

Athens also is an important tourist center. People come to the city from all over the world to learn about its history. Tourists come to see the beautiful ancient buildings and to visit the museums and theaters. Tourists also enjoy relaxing in the city's modern squares, large open areas with restaurants and stores.

Do You Know?

1. Why is Athens called an ancient city?
2. Tell two ways we have learned about life in ancient Athens.
3. Why is Athens an important tourist center?

5 TO HELP YOU LEARN

Using New Words

Read the words in the box. Choose the best word to complete each sentence. Write the completed sentences on a sheet of paper.

metropolitan area	invention	immigrants	dam
communication	desert	irrigation	

1. Something that has never been made before is called an ________.
2. Many ________ have come to live in the United States from other countries.
3. A ________ can be used to keep a river from flooding.
4. Talking to a friend on the telephone is an example of ________.
5. A very dry place is called a ________.
6. A ________ is made up of a large city, its suburbs, and nearby smaller cities.
7. Farmers who live where there is little rain sometimes use ________ to bring water to their crops.

Finding the Facts

1. How was the fur trade important to the beginning of St. Louis?
2. What did the people of St. Louis do to help them remember their past?
3. What changes in Phoenix helped the city to grow?
4. What did Atlanta do to bring people and businesses back to the downtown area?
5. What was Martin Luther King, Jr.'s dream?
6. In what country is Athens located?

Using Study Skills

The bar graph below shows the population of the five largest metropolitan areas in the United States. Use the graph to answer these questions.

1. Which metropolitan area is the largest?
2. About how many people live in the Detroit metropolitan area?
3. Which metropolitan area is larger—Chicago or Detroit?

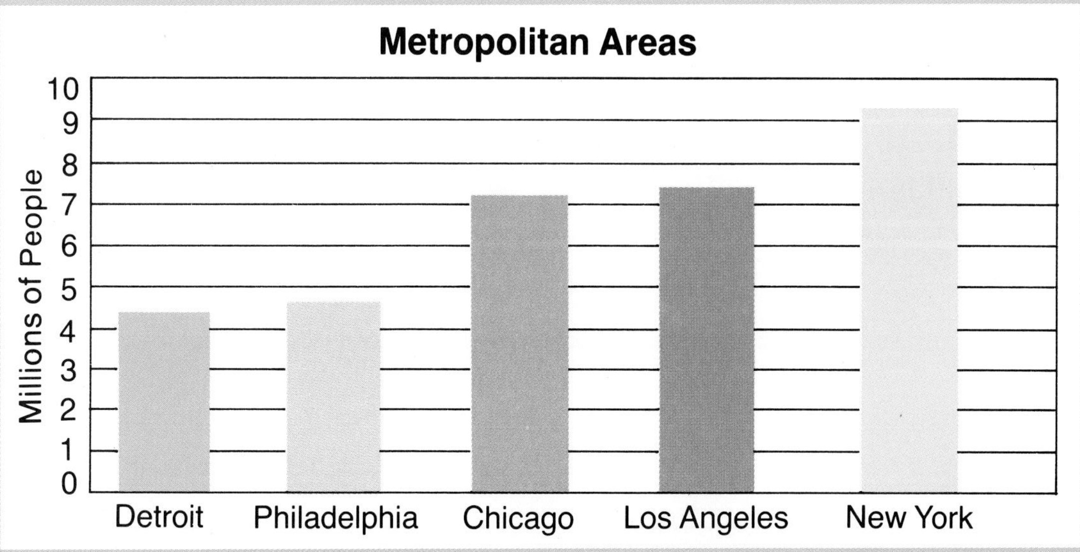

Things to Think About

1. How was climate important to the growth of Phoenix?
2. Is your community part of a metropolitan area? If so, which one? If not, what is the metropolitan area nearest to your community? What are some of the cities and suburbs that make up that metropolitan area?

Things to Do

1. Choose an invention, such as the automobile, airplane, or television. How would your life be different if this thing had never been invented? Make a list of the differences.
2. Speak to someone who has lived in your community for a long time. Ask that person how your community has changed during the time he or she has lived there. Tell the class what you learned.

Learning About Your Own Community

Phoenix is a communication center. It has its own newspapers. It has television and radio stations. What newspapers are there in your community? What radio and television stations can people use to find out about important events?

Learning from Maps

1. Turn to the map of Atlanta on page 152. Use the map to answer these questions.
   a. What is the symbol for a highway on the map?
   b. Name two communities near Atlanta.
   c. In what direction from downtown Atlanta is the airport?
2. The map below shows how Philadelphia has grown since 1800. Use the map to answer these questions.
   a. What color shows the city limits in 1800?
   b. In what general direction did the city grow between 1800 and 1900?
   c. About how far from north to south does the city extend today?

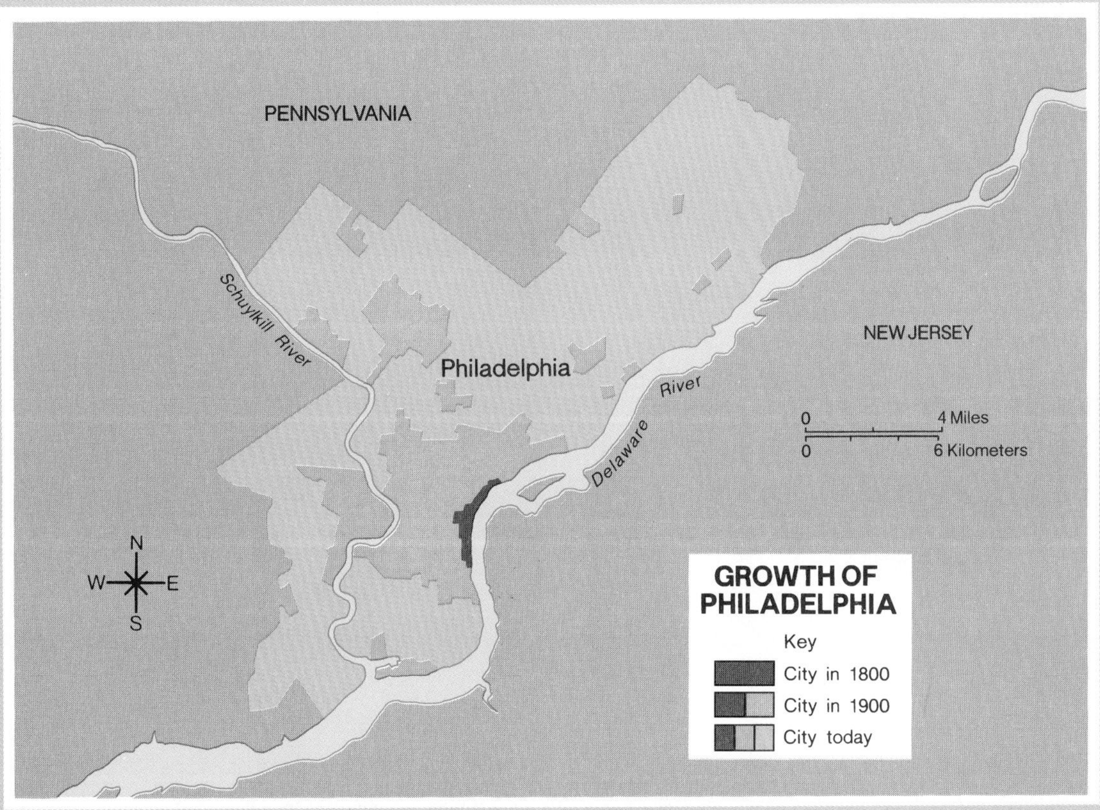

JACKSON SOCCER
JACKSON SOCCER
JACKSON SOCCER

6
COMMUNITIES NEED LAWS

Rules are important in every group. There are rules at home and at school. When you and your friends play a game, you agree on the rules. Rules help people get along with others. Rules are needed to help keep people safe. Rules in the community are called laws. The leaders of the community make the laws and see that they are carried out. Everyone in the community is expected to obey the laws.

Looking Ahead

1. This picture shows a soccer game. Why do games need rules?
2. What do you think the woman with a whistle is doing?
3. What are some of the rules of games you like to play?

Words to Learn

fine	citizens
council	tax
mayor	volunteers
election	petition

1 Laws in Our Community

Suppose that you are a pioneer and have just moved to an area where no one else lives. You build a small house and start a farm. Since there is no one else around, you may do whatever you want. After a short time, other pioneers move nearby. They make a lot of noise at night and you cannot sleep. They dump their trash into the stream and your drinking water becomes polluted. Your horse eats the vegetables in your neighbor's garden.

How could you solve these problems? You and your neighbors might get together and agree on some rules.

- No loud noise after ten o'clock at night.
- No trash may be dumped into the stream.
- Horses must be fenced in.

Pioneers often lived far away from other people. Without nearby neighbors the pioneers needed few rules. Why did community rules become important when more people settled in the area?

What rule is being obeyed in this classroom? Why is this rule important?

Rules at Home and School

Every group needs rules. Rules help people get along with others and help keep people safe. There are rules at home and school and in the community.

Rules at home usually are made by parents. A family may have rules such as:

- Put your toys away.
- Do not play with matches.
- Do your chores before you go outside to play.

Rules in the classroom are made by the teacher. Sometimes students work with the teacher to decide on the rules. Read the rules below. Which of these rules do you have in your classroom? What other rules do you have?

- Raise your hand if you want to speak.
- Do not run in the halls.
- Sit quietly at your desk during study time.
- Help each other.
- Line up quietly.

Communities Have Laws

Our communities have rules too. Community rules are called laws. Everyone in a community must obey the laws. There are laws to protect people and the things they own. There are laws to help keep the community clean and beautiful so that everyone can enjoy it.

Sometimes there are signs to tell you what the laws are. Traffic signs, for example, say STOP, ONE WAY, and NO RIGHT TURNS. In the park there may be signs that say DO NOT LITTER or NO BICYCLE RIDING. Why do you think communities need laws like these?

Signs may use words or pictures to tell their meanings.

Police officers make sure the laws are obeyed. A person who breaks a traffic law may have to pay a fine.

Laws Must Be Obeyed

It is the job of everyone in a community to obey the laws. It is the job of the police to make sure that the laws are obeyed and to protect the people of the community.

What happens if laws are broken? People who break the laws are punished. There are different kinds of punishments for breaking different laws. A driver who does not stop at a red light may have to pay a fine (fīn). A fine is money that must be paid by a person who breaks a law. A person who steals may be sent to jail.

Do You Know?

1. Why are rules needed?
2. What are laws?
3. Tell what happens if laws are broken.

2 Who Makes the Laws?

In pioneer times communities were small and the adults in a community could meet together. They could talk about their needs and help make community decisions. Communities today are much larger. It usually is not possible for everyone to meet together to discuss and decide on community problems. Today laws in most communities are made by the leaders of the community. We choose leaders to speak and act for us, or represent us.

Community Leaders

The leaders in a community are part of the community government. Community leaders make the laws and see that they are carried out.

In many communities the leaders are members of a council (koun'səl). The men and women on the council make the laws for the community. The head of most community governments is the mayor (mā'ər). It is the job of the mayor to see that the laws are carried out. The mayor also works with the council to decide what laws are needed.

Federico Peña was chosen mayor of Denver in 1983. He works with the city council to make the laws for Denver.

There are other kinds of community governments as well. The mayor and council government is the most common. What kind of government does your community have?

Choosing Our Leaders

In the United States we choose our leaders in an election (i lek′shən). In an election people vote for, or choose, the person they want to be their leader. All citizens (sit′ə zəns) have the right to vote in an election when they reach the age of 18. A citizen is a member of a community and a country.

All citizens of the United States have the right to vote in an election when they reach the age of 18.

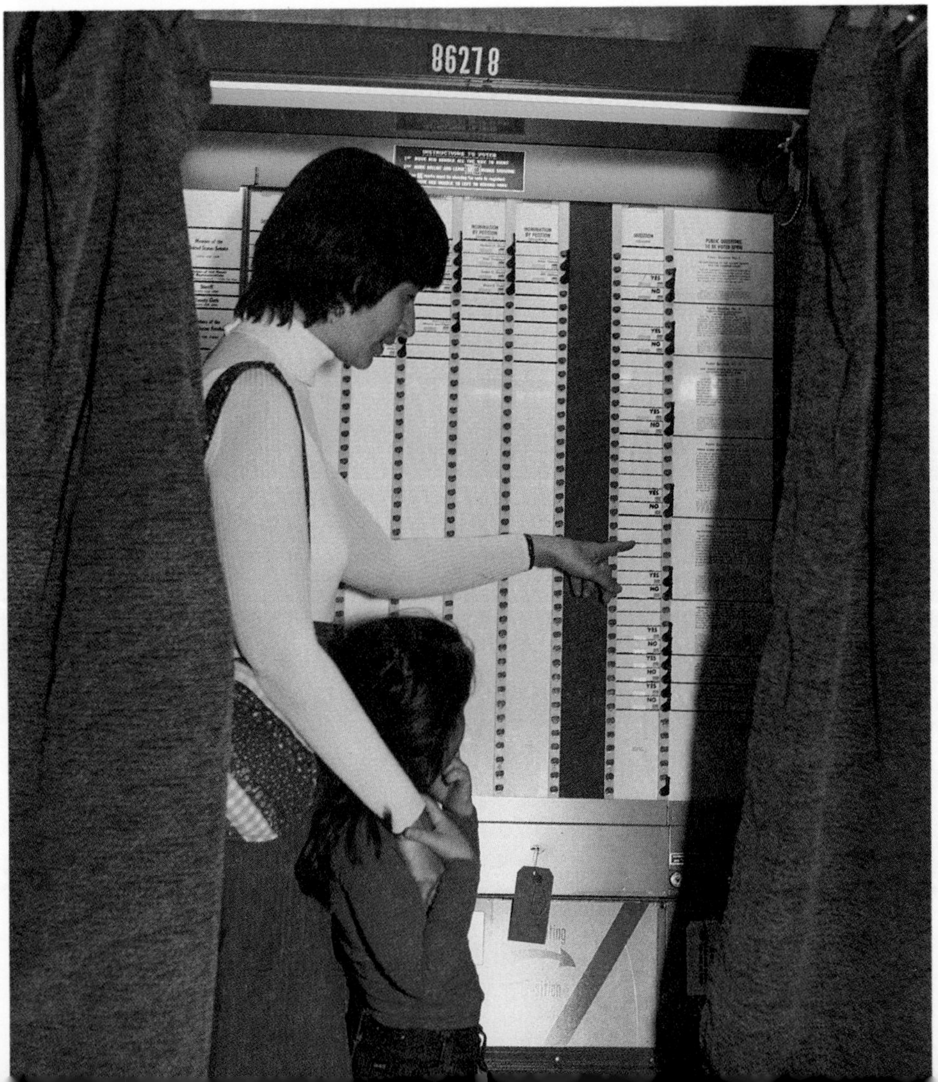

Election time is very special in the United States. This is how an election works. There may be several men and women who want to be one of the leaders in a community. Each person thinks that he or she would do a good job. Each person talks to different groups of people in the community and mails information about his or her ideas.

It is the job of the voters to learn about each person and then make a decision. Voters must decide which person they think will make the best leader.

Every citizen has a responsibility to vote on election day. At the end of election day the votes are counted and the person with the most votes wins the election.

People often wear buttons to show who they support in an election.

Susan B. Anthony

Susan B. Anthony worked all her life for equal rights for women.

For a long time women in our country did not have the same rights as men. Women could not own property or work at many kinds of jobs. They were not allowed to vote. One of the leaders in the work to win equal rights for women was Susan B. Anthony.

Susan B. Anthony was born in 1820. For most of her life she worked to get women the right to vote. She believed that no real changes in women's rights would be possible until women could vote. She wrote books and put out a weekly newspaper. She made many speeches about the need for change. In 1872 she even tried to vote in an election. She was arrested.

The work of Susan B. Anthony and of many other women and men helped bring about changes. Women finally won the right to vote in 1920, 14 years after Susan B. Anthony died.

Do You Know?

1. Who makes the laws in a community?
2. Who may vote in an election?
3. What important right did Susan B. Anthony work for?

3 Communities Provide Services

Every community provides certain kinds of services. Think about some of the services you depend on every day. You need good streets to walk or ride on to school. You need teachers in school to help you learn. You need police officers and firefighters to protect you. The public library has books you may take home to read. You may get your water from a water company run by your community. Traffic lights and traffic signs help keep people safe.

Communities Need Different Services

Different communities have different needs. The services communities provide are different too. Location makes a difference in the services a community provides. Clearing the streets after

Most communities in our country have a public library. Have you ever borrowed books from your library?

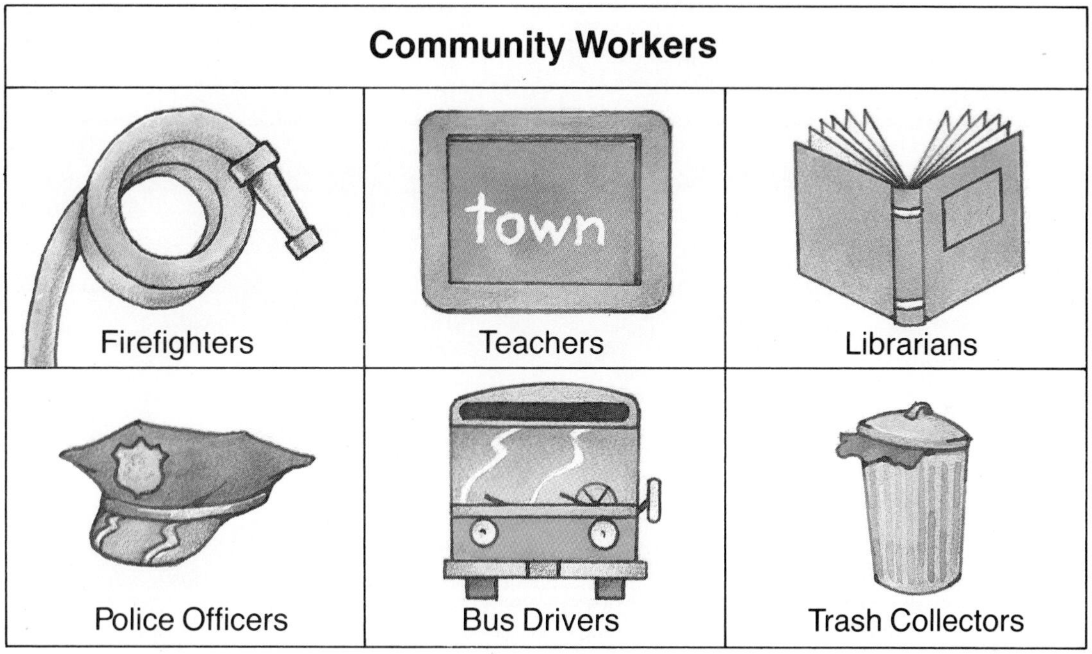

This chart lists some of the workers who provide community services.

a snow storm, for example, is an important service in Bismarck, North Dakota. Why do you think removing snow is not a needed service in Honolulu, Hawaii?

The size of a community also makes a difference in the services a community provides. Large communities usually need more services than small communities. Mass transit is very important in Chicago and other large cities, but not in small towns like Bar Harbor. The city of Houston, Texas, has more than 25 libraries and 50 community swimming pools. There are many parks and museums. Houston offers more services than a smaller community.

Large communities need many workers to provide all the services. They need bus drivers, people to pick up the trash, life guards, and librarians. They need teachers, police officers, firefighters, and people to build and repair roads. What other workers can you name in your community?

In many communities people pay a sales tax when they buy certain goods. Taxes pay for community services.

Paying for Community Services

Communities need a lot of money to provide services. The people who work for the community must be paid. Libraries and schools need money to buy new books. Animals in the zoo must be fed. Fire trucks and police cars have to be repaired and parks have to be kept clean. Who pays for all these services? Everyone who lives in a community helps pay for them.

Money that people must pay to the government is a tax (taks). Taxes are used to pay for community services. There are different kinds of taxes. In many communities you pay a small tax every time you buy certain goods. Suppose you buy a book that costs \$2.00. You may have to pay \$2.10 for the book. The 10¢ is called a sales tax. The store owner pays the 10¢ tax to the community or state. It helps pay for community services.

Volunteers work for free to help others in the community.
Have you ever been a volunteer?

Helping the Community

Sometimes people in a community work without being paid. They are called volunteers (vol′ən tērs′). Volunteers work in their free time to help others in the community. If a community is small, it may not need firefighters very often. So volunteers operate the fire trucks when there is a fire. Volunteers may visit people in hospitals or help in schools and museums. They may help clean up parks. What kinds of work do volunteers do in your community?

Do You Know?

1. Why do communities provide many different kinds of services?
2. Name four kinds of services communities provide.
3. How does a community pay for services?
4. Name two ways volunteers can help a community.

Before You Go On

Learning About Circle Graphs

You have read in this unit that the services a community provides are paid for by taxes. The families and businesses in a community pay money to their town or city government. In return, the government provides services to the people. Communities spend their tax money in different ways. Some communities spend a lot of money for schools. Other communities spend a lot for police and fire protection.

The graph on the next page shows how the small community of New Milford, New Jersey, spends its tax money. This kind of graph is called a circle graph, or pie graph. A circle graph shows how a whole thing is divided into parts. Think of the graph as a pie and its slices. In this graph the whole pie stands for all the tax money that New Milford spends. Each slice stands for one of the ways New Milford spends money.

You can tell by just a quick look at the graph that New Milford does not spend the same amount of money for each service. The graph shows you which services New Milford spends a lot of money for. You also can see which services it spends only a little money for.

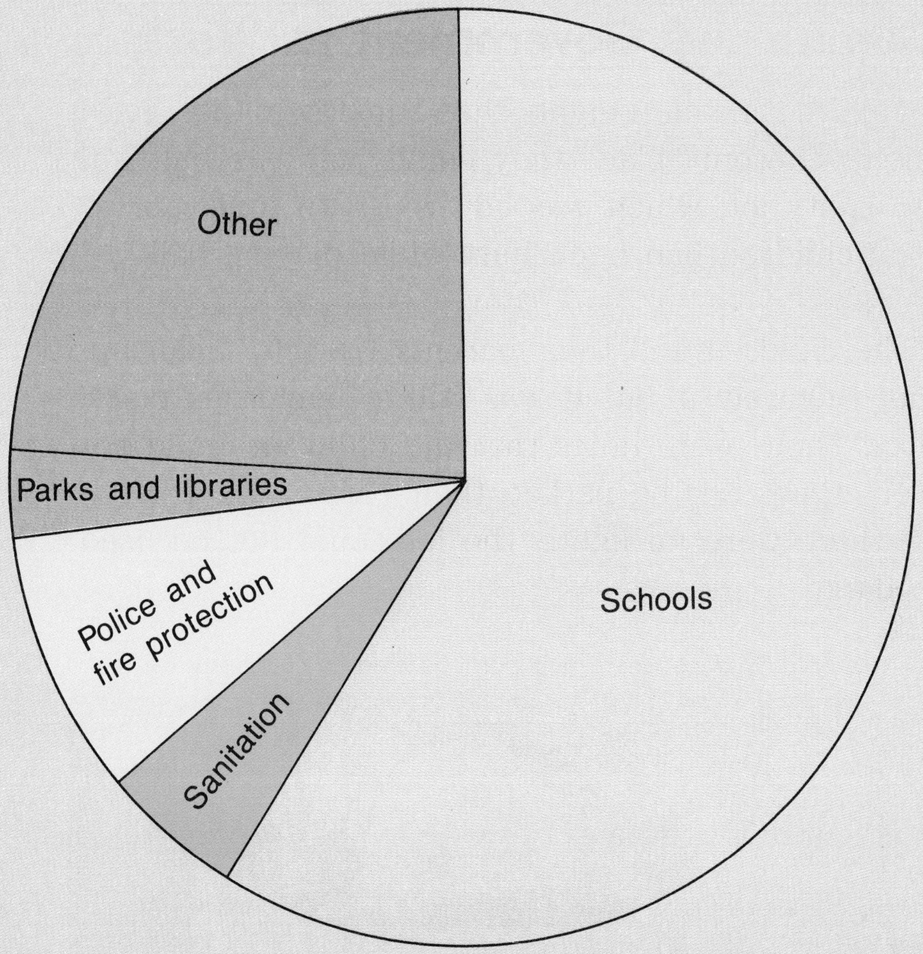

Practicing Your Skills

Use the circle graph to answer these questions.

1. What does New Milford spend the most money for?
2. Does New Milford spend more for police and fire protection or for parks and libraries?
3. Sanitation includes picking up trash and sweeping the streets. Does New Milford spend more for sanitation or for police and fire protection?
4. Name one service that might be included in "Other."

4 Community Government at Work

The children in one neighborhood in River City had a problem. The only place they could play baseball was in an empty lot, which was covered with junk. Several children had been hurt while playing ball there.

The children and their parents tried to clean up the lot themselves, but it was still a dangerous place to play. There were holes that the children could trip in. Sometimes people parked their cars in the lot. Since there were no lights, the lot could not be used after dark.

This lot was the only place where neighborhood children could play ball.

People in the neighborhood held a meeting. They decided to work together to get the city to build a park.

Then Mrs. Kim had an idea. "The city should build a park here," she said. "The whole community would enjoy a park instead of this ugly lot. The children would have a safe place to play. Older people in the neighborhood would have a nice place to talk and exercise. Maybe there could even be a garden."

The people in the neighborhood met to decide what they could do to get the city to build the park. "First we have to find out who owns that land," said Mr. Ross. "Tomorrow I'll go to city hall and look at the records."

At the next meeting, Mr. Ross had good news. "That land is owned by the city," he said. "Our next step is to write a letter to the mayor."

Mrs. Kelly offered to write the letter for the group. You can read her letter on page 184 and the mayor's reply on page 185.

239 Oak Street
River City, Indiana
October 28, 1984

Mayor Carla Smith
City Hall
River City, Indiana 46310

Dear Mayor Smith:

There is an empty city-owned lot at the corner of Oak Street and Maple Road. Since there is no park in our neighborhood, the children play there every day. But the lot is a dangerous place for them to play.

My neighbors and I believe the lot should be made into a park. Everyone in the community could enjoy it.

Please let us know if the city would consider our idea.

Sincerely,
Barbara Kelly
Barbara Kelly

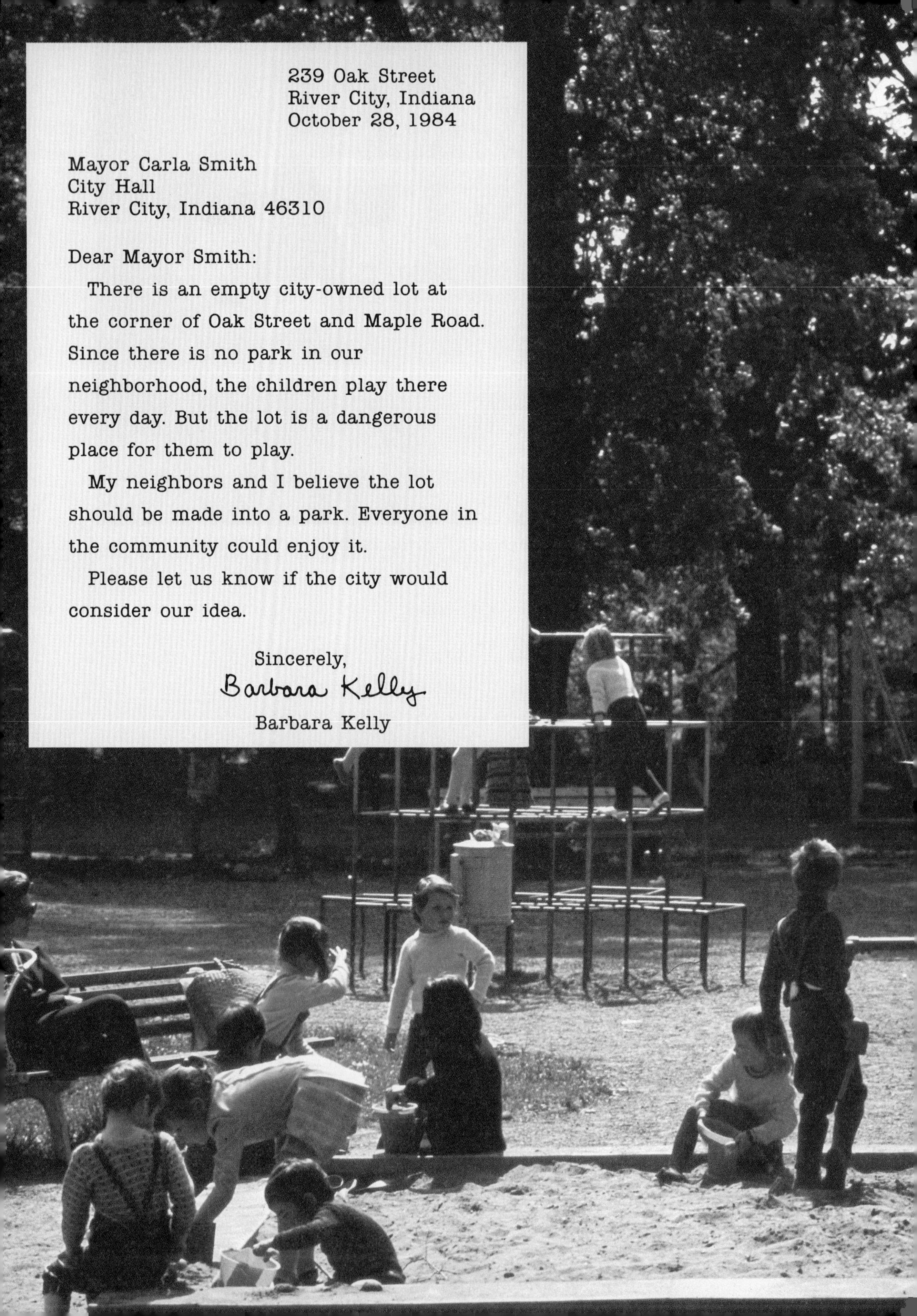

Mayor Carla Smith
City Hall
River City, Indiana 46310

November 4, 1984

Mrs. Barbara Kelly
239 Oak Street
River City, Indiana 46310

Dear Mrs. Kelly:

I am writing in answer to your letter about the city-owned land on the corner of Oak Street and Maple Road. The city government does not have any money for making parks this year. But the city council will be meeting soon to make plans for next year. I suggest you attend that meeting and tell the council members about your idea.

Sincerely,

Carla Smith

Carla Smith
Mayor

Messages to the City Council

When Mrs. Kelly received the mayor's letter the neighbors met again. They knew that the city council would have many difficult decisions to make.

"There are many things our leaders would like to do for the city," said Mr. Clark. "But there is not enough tax money to pay for everything people want. The council will have to decide which things are most important. We have to show that this park is needed by all the people in the neighborhood."

The group decided to ask their friends and neighbors to write letters to members of the city council. Mr. Clark wrote a petition (pə tish′ən) to the mayor and members of the council explaining why the park was needed. A petition is a written request made to a leader. Everyone agreed to take a copy of the petition around and ask people to sign it.

Everyone in the neighborhood wanted the park to be built. The petition to the city council was signed by many people.

The city council agreed to build a park for the neighborhood. Now the park is enjoyed by everyone in the community.

The City Council Decides

One of the children spoke at the city council meeting. Joe Martin told the council members why his neighborhood needed the park. "We have no place to play," he said. "The empty lot is dangerous. Some children have been hurt while playing there. After it rains the lot turns into mud. It's a mess. Please build a park for our neighborhood."

The council members discussed the park and voted. They agreed to use the city's tax money to build the new park next year.

Do You Know?

1. Why did the people in the neighborhood want a park?
2. Name two things the people did to try to get the city to build a park.
3. Why did the city council have to decide which things were most important?

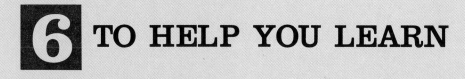

6 TO HELP YOU LEARN

Using New Words

Read the sentences below. Choose the word in the box that answers each question. Write your answers on a sheet of paper.

volunteers	election	council
petition	tax	mayor
fine	citizens	

1. Who is the community leader whose job it is to see that the laws are carried out?
2. If you break a traffic law, what might you have to pay?
3. What is the name for people who help others in a community without being paid?
4. If you wanted a new street light near your home, what might you send to your community leaders?
5. What do we call the members of a nation?
6. How are most government leaders in the United States chosen?
7. What is the name for money that people must pay to the government?
8. What group makes the laws in most communities?

Finding the Facts

1. Give two examples of laws in a community.
2. What is the job of the mayor?
3. Who can vote in an election?
4. How do the size and location of communities make a difference in the services they provide?
5. What are taxes used for?

Using Study Skills

The circle graph below shows how Terry spends the hours of her day. Use the graph to answer these questions.

a. What does Terry spend the most time doing?
b. Does Terry spend more time playing or doing chores?
c. Does Terry spend more time at school or doing homework?
d. Name one thing that might be included under "Other."

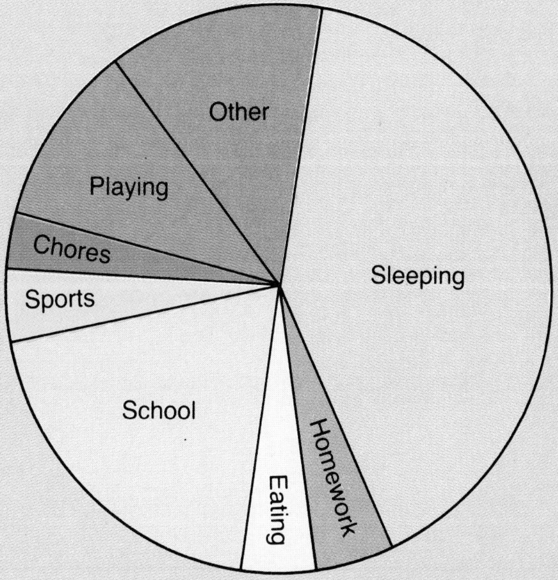

Things to Think About

1. What happens during an election?
2. Suppose you wanted your community leaders to pass a certain law. What actions could you take to try to get them to pass the law?

Things to Do

1. Draw or find pictures in magazines that show services provided by community governments. Use the pictures to make a bulletin board display about community services.
2. The place where people go to vote in elections is called a polling place. Find out from your parents the location of the polling place where they vote. Is it the same for everyone in the class? Why or why not?

Learning About Your Own Community

Many community governments are made up of a mayor and council. What kind of government does your community have? What are the names of your community's leaders?

Learning From Maps

The map below shows landforms in Oregon. Use the map to answer these questions.

1. What kind of land covers most of the state?
2. Which color shows mountains?
3. What kind of land is farthest west?
4. In which part of the state are plains located?
5. Are the mountains east or west of the plateaus?

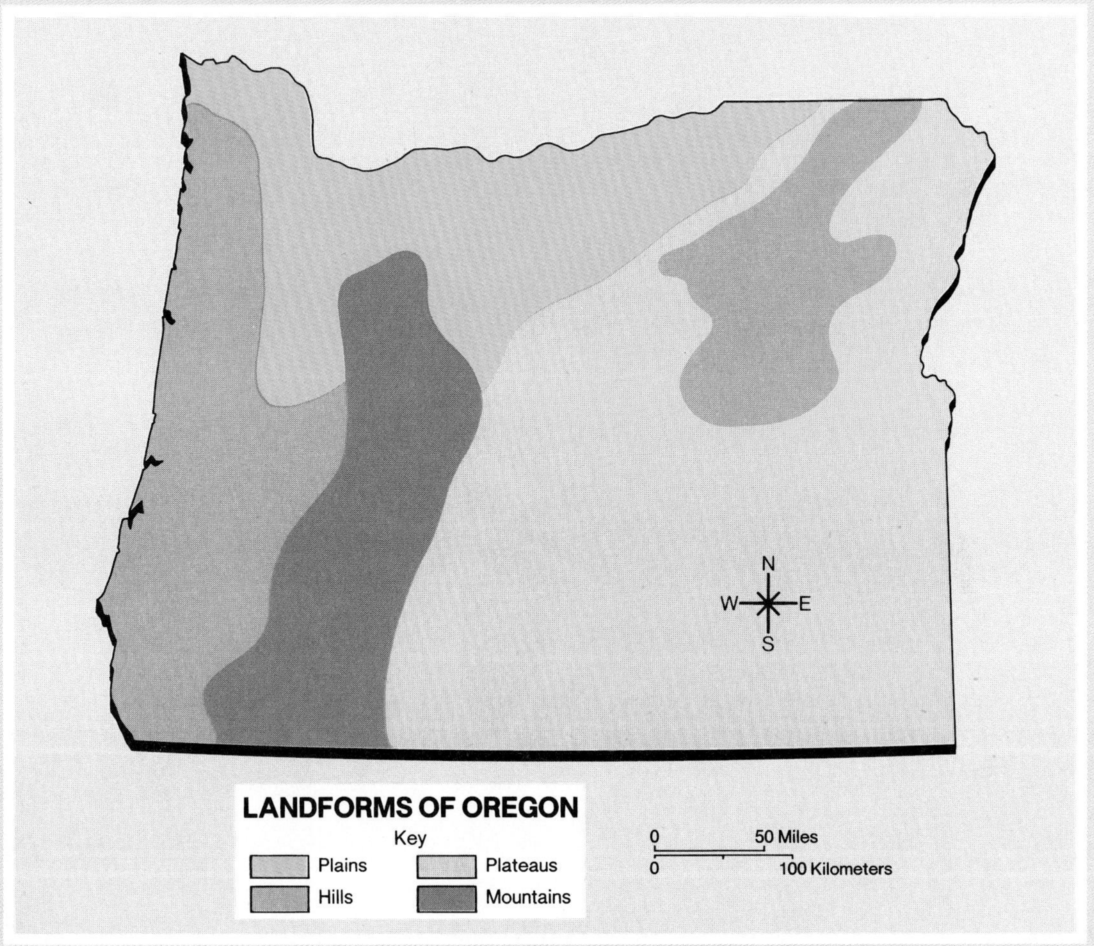

7

WASHINGTON, D.C.

The capital city of the United States is Washington, D.C. This is where our country's government meets and works. Our government moved to the new capital city in 1800. Since then our country and its government have grown much larger. Washington, D.C., is now a busy and beautiful city. Each year millions of tourists visit the city to see its many famous places.

Looking Ahead

1. This picture shows one of the most popular places in Washington, D.C. What might be the reason for the fireworks?
2. Washington, D.C., is the capital of our country. What is the capital of your state?

Words to Learn

Capitol
Congress
White House
monuments
memorial
pages
diplomats

1 Planning Our Capital City

Our leaders were meeting in Philadelphia when they declared our country's independence in 1776. For the next several years the capital of the new United States was moved to a number of different cities. The government met for a short time in Baltimore, Princeton, Trenton, New York, and other cities as well. Finally our leaders decided the country should build a new city to be the capital.

Choosing a location for the new capital city was not easy. The people of each state wanted the capital to be in their state. In 1790 the leaders decided to build the capital on land given to the United States by Virginia and Maryland. The location was about halfway between the northern and southern borders of the new country. George Washington, our country's first President, chose the exact place along the Potomac (pə tō′mək) River.

This historical map shows the first 13 states of the United States. Washington, D.C., was built in the middle of the country.

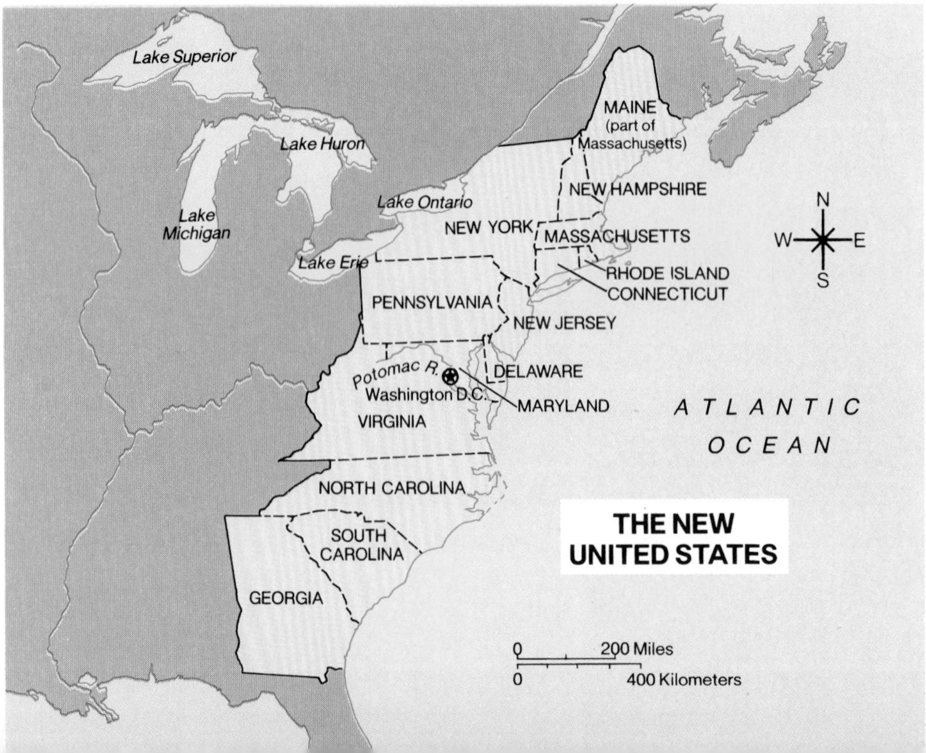

President Washington chose this place to build the country's capital.

Choosing a Name

As you read in Unit 1, Washington, D.C., is not part of any state. It was named for President George Washington. The "D.C." in the city's name stands for District of Columbia. It was named for the famous explorer Christopher Columbus.

Making a Plan

The location chosen for the new capital was a muddy piece of land with a few homes and shops nearby. It would take a long time to build a beautiful capital for the United States.

Our leaders decided that the new capital should be carefully planned. They chose a Frenchman named Pierre L'Enfant (pē er′ län fän′) to plan the city and decide where the streets, buildings, and parks should be located. Two Americans named Benjamin Banneker and Andrew Ellicott helped L'Enfant draw up plans and maps for the new city.

President Washington and Pierre L'Enfant met often to plan the capital.

L'Enfant thought about the new country and the new capital city. He wanted Washington, D.C., to be beautiful, with large buildings and wide streets. He wanted the city to have many green parks. The most important place, he decided, would be the building where our leaders would meet to make the laws. "This building," he said, "should be like the center of a wheel, with main streets leading out from it in many directions."

L'Enfant wanted to make it easy for people to travel in the city. He planned streets running north and south and streets running east and west. Streets running north and south were given numbers for names. Streets running east and west were given letters for names. Avenues running northeast and southwest and northwest and southeast were named for states. You can see the street names on the map on pages 202-203.

Before building began, L'Enfant argued with the city's leaders and left. He took all his plans and maps with him. No one knew what would happen now, but Benjamin Banneker came to the rescue. He remembered L'Enfant's plans and was able to draw the map for Washington, D.C., again. Now work on the city could begin.

Benjamin Banneker remembered L'Enfant's map for the new capital.

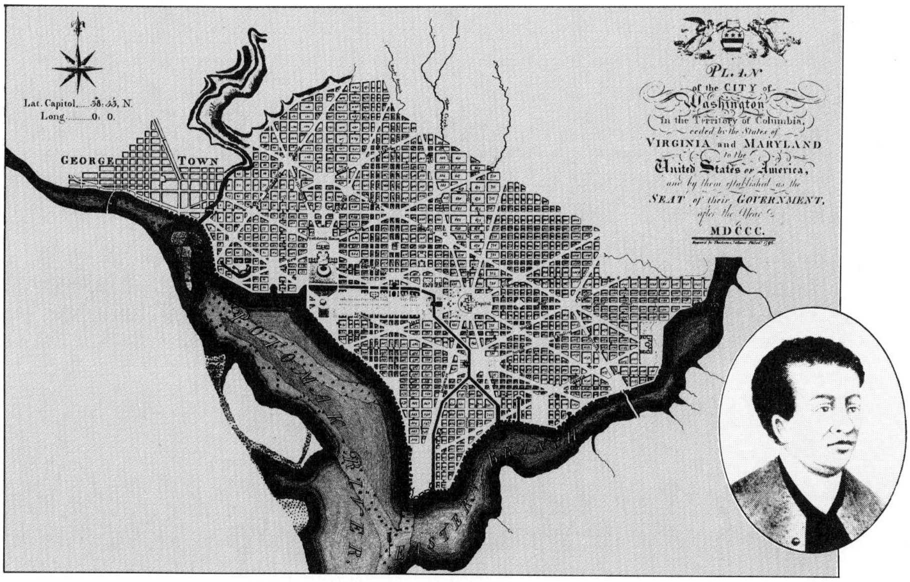

The New Capital

The government of the United States moved to Washington, D.C., in 1800. Now the government had a city of its own. Washington, D.C., became the capital of the whole country.

The leaders of our government traveled to the new capital by boat, wagon, and stagecoach. They found a city that was still being built. Work was going very slowly. Most government buildings still were not finished. At this time only 8,000 people lived in Washington, D.C., and the surrounding area.

Abigail Adams was the wife of President John Adams. Abigail and John Adams were two of the most famous people in American history.

Abigail Adams

The first President to live in Washington, D.C., was John Adams. He and his wife, Abigail Adams, moved to the capital in November 1800. John Adams was the second President of the United States. He had been an important leader in our country's fight for independence. Abigail Adams was one of the most important women of the time. Abigail and John Adams worked closely together and shared their views on many subjects. John Adams often asked his wife for advice about problems that were facing the country.

Abigail Adams was a great letter writer. In letters to her husband, she described what was happening in their community in Massachusetts. She wrote her opinions about events that were taking place in the country. In one letter she asked John Adams to "remember the ladies" when making laws for the new country.

Abigail Adams described the new capital city in a letter to her sister in 1800. Washington, D.C., was like a new country, she wrote. It had many trees and stumps and muddy paths instead of streets. There were only a few houses anywhere in the city. But she also wrote that the location chosen for the city was beautiful. "The more I view it," she said, "the more I am delighted with it."

Abigail Adams wrote letters throughout her life. They have been printed in many books. Today her letters continue to provide a fascinating picture of the way people of her time lived and what they believed.

Abigail Adams described the new capital city in her letters. This painting shows Washington, D.C., soon after she lived there.

Today Washington, D.C., is a large, modern city. It has many offices and government buildings.

The City Grows

The United States had grown to 16 states when Washington, D.C., became the capital in 1800. Since then our country has grown to 50 states. The government has grown too. More and more people moved to Washington, D.C., to work for the government. Today Washington, D.C., is a busy and beautiful city.

Do You Know?

1. Why was it difficult to choose a location for the new capital city?
2. Tell how Washington, D.C., got its name.
3. Why is Washington, D.C., called a planned city?

2 A Tour of Washington, D.C.

Washington, D.C., is the center of our country's government. It is also an important tourist center. Each year millions of people from all over the United States and from other countries visit Washington, D.C. They come to see the city's many famous places.

The map on pages 202-203 shows the location of some of the best-known places in the capital. You will read about these places on pages 204-211. As you read about each place, find it on the map.

This is a special bus for tourists. It goes to many of the famous places in Washington, D.C.

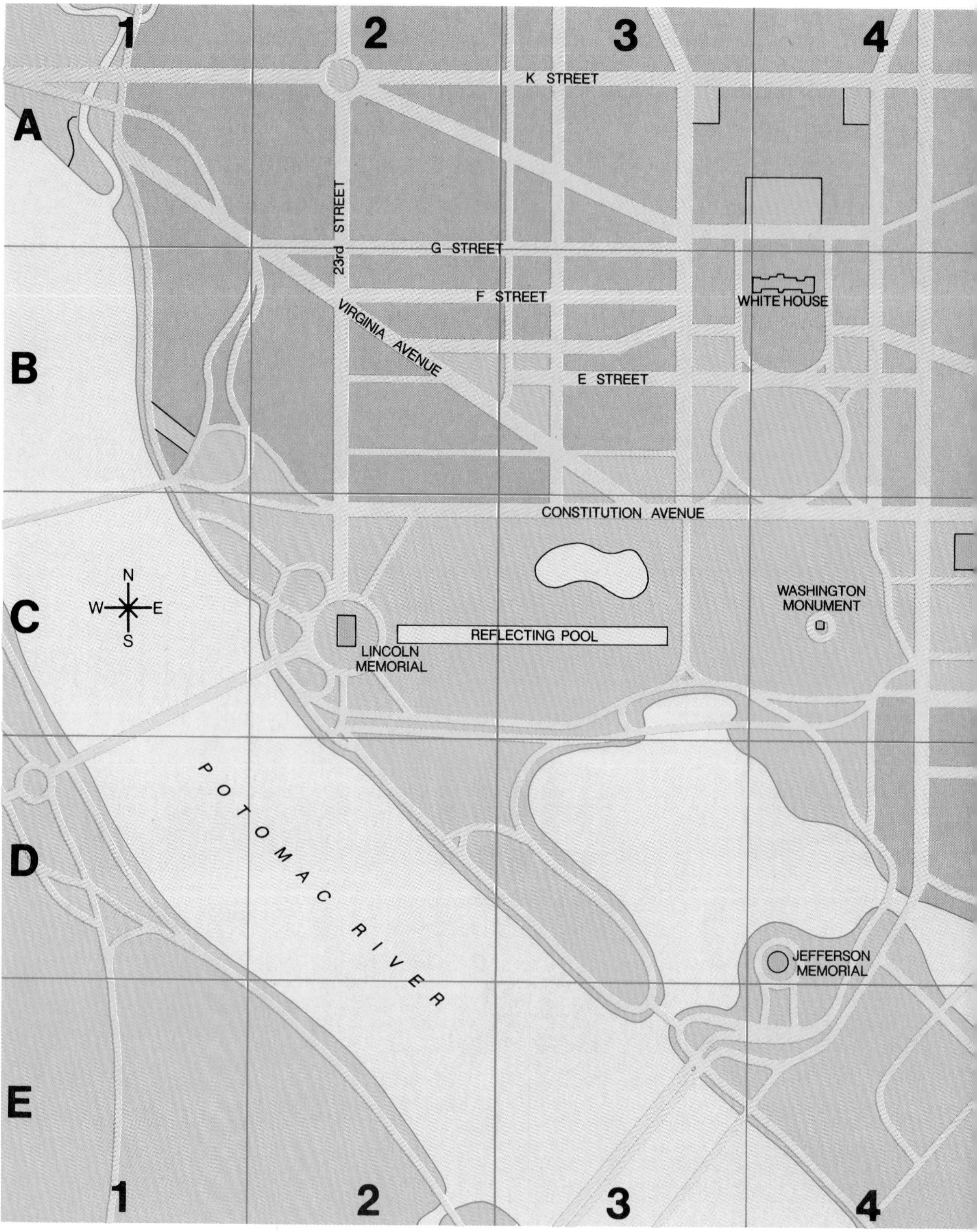
1
2
3
4
A
B
C
D
E
K STREET
23rd STREET
G STREET
F STREET
VIRGINIA AVENUE
E STREET
WHITE HOUSE
CONSTITUTION AVENUE
N
W
E
S
WASHINGTON MONUMENT
REFLECTING POOL
LINCOLN MEMORIAL
POTOMAC RIVER
JEFFERSON MEMORIAL

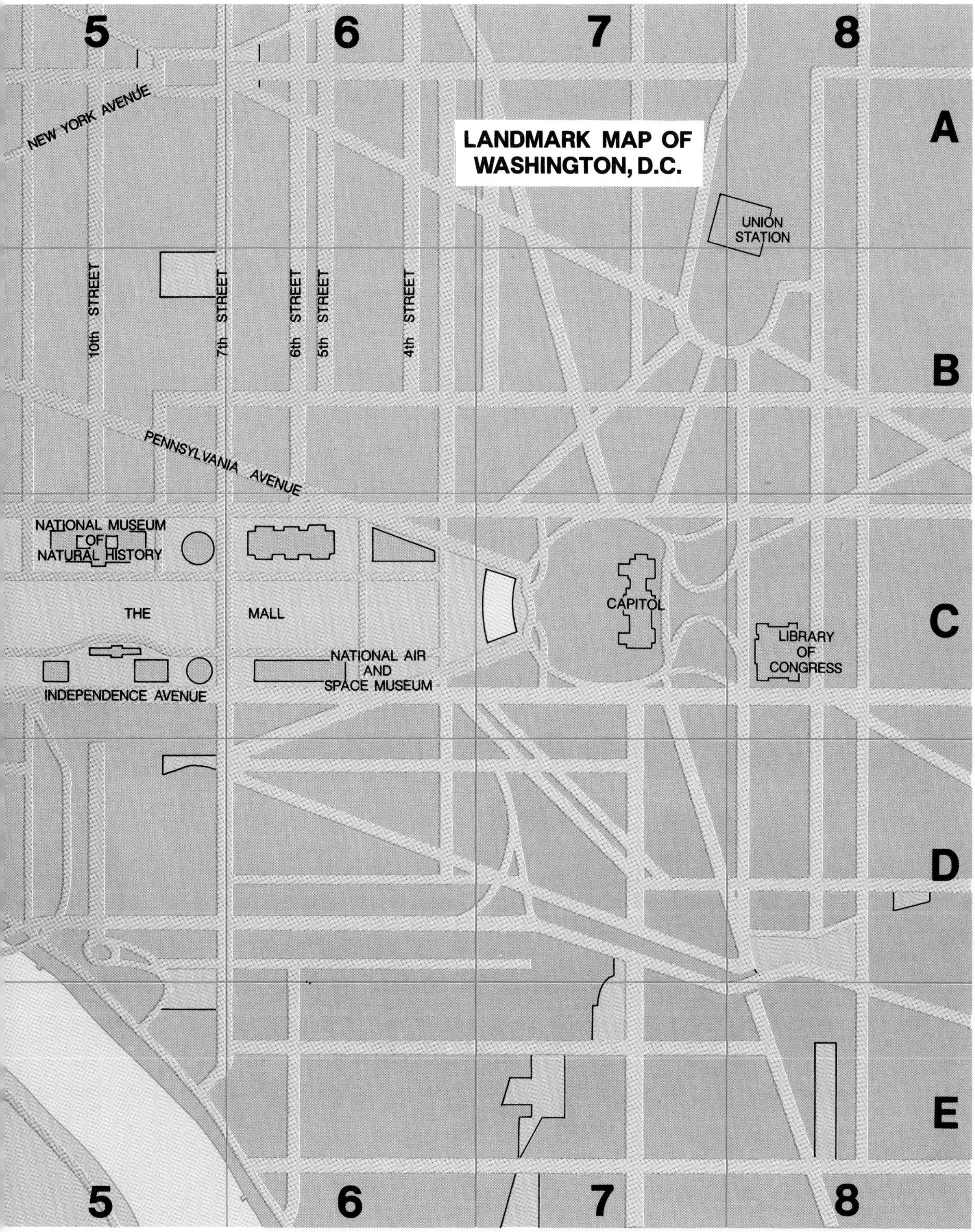
LANDMARK MAP OF
WASHINGTON, D.C.
5
6
7
8
A
B
C
D
E
NEW YORK AVENUE
UNION
STATION
10th STREET
7th STREET
6th STREET
5th STREET
4th STREET
PENNSYLVANIA AVENUE
NATIONAL MUSEUM
OF
NATURAL HISTORY
THE
MALL
CAPITOL
LIBRARY
OF
CONGRESS
NATIONAL AIR
AND
SPACE MUSEUM
INDEPENDENCE AVENUE

The Capitol

Under L'Enfant's plans, the most important place in Washington, D.C., was to be the building where our leaders meet and make laws. The name of this building is the Capitol (kap′it əl). "Capitol," the word for the building, sounds just like "capital," the word for the city. But the words are spelled differently.

The Capitol is on a hill in the center of the city. It is the meeting place of Congress (kong′gris). Congress is the group of men and women who are elected to make the laws for the United States.

You can visit the members of Congress if you go to Washington, D.C. Their offices are in buildings right next to the Capitol. You also can attend meetings of Congress. You can see members of Congress discuss and vote on new laws.

The Capitol is where members of Congress meet and make laws for the United States.

The White House is where the President of our country lives and works. The picture on the right shows the Green Room. It is one of the five rooms open to tourists.

The White House

The White House (hwīt hous) has been the home and office of every American President since John Adams. The President is the leader of the United States. It is the job of the President to see that the laws of our country are carried out.

The White House is a beautiful, large building with 132 rooms. Tourists cannot visit the rooms where the President lives and works. But five rooms are open to the public. These are the rooms where the President entertains guests.

The picture on the left shows the Jefferson Memorial. On the right is the Washington Monument.

Monuments to Famous Presidents

Washington, D.C., has monuments (mon′yə mənts) that honor several of our country's most famous Presidents. A monument is something built to remember a person or an event. Monuments to three Presidents—George Washington, Abraham Lincoln, and Thomas Jefferson—are among the most popular sights in the city.

The Washington Monument was built to remind people of George Washington, our first President. The monument is 555 feet (169 meters) tall and you can walk or ride an elevator to the top. From there you have a beautiful view of the city.

A memorial (mə môr′ē əl), like a monument, is built to honor a person or an event. The Jefferson Memorial reminds us of Thomas Jefferson, the third

Inside the Lincoln Memorial is a huge statue of Abraham Lincoln. Parts of his speeches are carved into the walls.

President of the United States. Thomas Jefferson wrote the Declaration of Independence in 1776. This famous paper told the reasons the colonies were declaring their independence. It also stated the belief that the purpose of government is to protect the rights of the people.

The Lincoln Memorial honors Abraham Lincoln, our 16th President. Abraham Lincoln was President from 1861 to 1865. When Lincoln became President most black people in the United States were slaves. A slave is a person owned by another person. The black slaves had no rights. They had to work on large farms, called plantations, in the South. President Lincoln did not believe in slavery. He helped to free the slaves. Today people often speak out for the rights of Americans at the Lincoln Memorial.

The City's Museums

Washington, D.C, has some of the most famous museums in our country. It has so many museums it would take weeks and weeks to explore them all. Many of the city's museums are part of the Smithsonian (smith sō′nē ən) Institution. The Smithsonian Institution is the part of our government that runs the largest group of museums in the world. Some of the museums have famous paintings from all over the world. Others are science and history museums. Even the large zoo in Washington is part of the Smithsonian!

One of the most popular museums is the National Air and Space Museum. Here you can see the airplane flown by the Wright Brothers in 1903. It was the first plane to fly. Another popular plane in the museum is the *Spirit of St. Louis*. In this plane Charles Lindbergh (lind′burg′) became the first

Visitors can see many old planes in the National Air and Space Museum.

person to fly alone across the Atlantic Ocean in 1927. The museum also has many new things to see. Some of the spacecraft that have been used to travel in outer space are here. There also are rocks you can touch that were brought back from the moon.

Another popular museum is the National Museum of Natural History. Here you can learn about the way of life of many kinds of animals. You can see stuffed animals and some of the largest dinosaur skeletons ever discovered. The museum also has minerals and rocks from earth and from outer space.

The National Museum of Natural History has some of the world's largest dinosaur skeletons. Visitors can see how these huge animals once lived.

A Special Library

The Library of Congress is one of the largest libraries in the world. It has more than 77 million books, maps, photographs, records, and other items. Some of its books were printed just after the invention of the printing press in the middle 1400s.

The main job of the Library of Congress is to provide information to members of Congress to help them make the country's laws. The library also is open to the public. People from all parts of the country and the world come to the library to study. Another service the library provides is books in braille (brāl) for blind readers. Braille is a way of writing and printing for the blind that uses raised dots. A blind person can read the braille alphabet by touching the dots.

Each day hundreds of people use the Library of Congress.

The Mall

One of the best-known areas in Washington, D.C., is a long, narrow park called the Mall (môl). The Mall connects some of the most famous places in the city. At the eastern end of the Mall is the Capitol and at the western end is the Lincoln Memorial. Between the Capitol and the Lincoln Memorial is the Washington Monument.

The Mall extends from the Capitol to the Lincoln Memorial. What is the name of the monument that rises in the middle of the Mall?

The Mall is one of the most popular tourist places in the capital. There are museums on each side of the Mall. People often stop on the Mall to rest between visits to the museums. Sometimes people gather on the mall to express their opinions. They come to show that they agree or do not agree with what their government is doing.

Do You Know?

1. What is the difference between the Capitol and the capital?
2. What is the Congress?
3. Where does the President live and work?
4. What is the purpose of a monument?

Before You Go On

Learning About Timetables

Mary Cohen and her family are going to Washington, D.C., for a vacation. They plan to travel by train on Friday afternoon from their home in New York City. The Cohens need to find out what time trains leave New York City for Washington, D.C. They also need to know what time the trains arrive in Washington, D.C. A train timetable will give them this information.

The timetable on the next page will help the Cohens plan their trip. It is set up like a chart. On the left are the cities on the train route between New York City and Washington, D.C. On the right are the times when the train will arrive in those cities.

Suppose the Cohens want to leave New York City at 2:00. When will they arrive in Washington, D.C.? To find out, start by locating New York City on the timetable. Now slide your finger to the right until you come to 2:00. Then read down the list of times until you come to the last time. Washington, D.C., is the last stop. So the last time on the list tells when the train will arrive in Washington, D.C. The 2:00 train from New York City will arrive in Washington, D.C., at 4:55.

Train Schedule New York City to Washington, D.C.						
Train Number	**283**	**117**	**285**	**121**	**123**	**125**
New York, N.Y.	Noon	2:00	3:00	4:00	5:00	6:00
Philadelphia, PENN.	1:08	3:08	4:08	5:08	6:08	7:08
Wilmington, DEL.	1:30	3:30	4:30	5:30	6:30	7:30
Baltimore, MD.	2:16	4:16	5:16	6:16	7:16	8:16
Washington, D.C.	2:49	4:55	5:49	6:55	7:55	8:55

Practicing Your Skills

Use the timetable to answer these questions.

1. Where do the trains stop between New York City and Washington, D.C.?
2. At what time does the 6:00 train arrive in Washington, D.C.?
3. When does the 5:00 train stop in Baltimore?
4. Which train arrives in Washington, D.C., at 6:55?

3 Living and Working in the Capital

Imagine that you are flying over Washington, D.C., in a helicopter. It is 8:00 on a Monday morning. You see thousands of commuters on their way to work. You see lots of cars and buses coming into the city from its suburbs. You see other cars, buses, and taxis going from one part of the city to another. You see many, many, people walking. You do not see them, but there also are many people moving across the city on the subway.

Each day thousands of commuters travel to work in Washington, D.C.

Working in the Capital

You know that the President of the United States and the members of Congress work in our country's capital. But that is just the beginning! Most of the people who work in Washington, D.C., have jobs with the government. Government workers include secretaries, librarians, scientists, planners, writers, printers, and many, many more.

This picture shows pages with leaders of Congress outside the Capitol.

There is a special group of workers in the capital called pages (pā′jiz). Pages are high school students who help members of Congress by running errands. Pages go to a special high school in the Library of Congress.

Diplomats (dip′lə mats′) from many countries also work in Washington, D.C. A diplomat is a person who represents his or her country. Diplomats meet with the President and with other government leaders.

Like other cities, Washington, D.C., has workers who provide goods and services for the people who live here. They also serve the many tourists who visit the city. There are many hotels, restaurants, and shops.

Transportation and Communication

Washington, D.C., is a major center of transportation. The city is served by three airports, two in Virginia and one in Maryland. Washington National Airport, just across the Potomac River in Virginia, is one of the country's busiest airports. Passenger trains also connect Washington, D.C., with other parts of the country. The railroad station, called Union Station, is located just north of the Capitol.

Our capital city is one of the most important communication centers in the world. All the leading newspapers, magazines, and radio and television stations send reporters to the city. They gather and report information about our government for Americans and people all over the world. People need to know what our government is doing.

President Ronald Reagan meets with reporters in the garden of the White House. Reporters come to the city from all over the world.

Georgetown is one of the city's residential areas. It has beautiful old homes and many popular stores and restaurants.

Living in the Metropolitan Area

Washington D.C., is a large city with a population of more than 600,000 people. The city's residential neighborhoods have mainly one-family and two-family houses and small apartment buildings. Unlike most large cities, Washington, D.C., does not have any skyscrapers. A law limits the height of buildings. This is so the Capitol and the Washington Monument will remain the city's highest buildings. They can be seen from many parts of the city.

Today Washington, D.C., is the center of a large metropolitan area with more than 3 million people. The city has suburbs in both Maryland and Virginia. Some parts of the government have offices in the suburbs, but most people who live in the suburbs work in Washington, D.C.

You read on page 214 that one way people travel to work in Washington, D.C., is on the subway. The city's subway is called the Metro. It links the downtown area with suburban communities in Maryland and Virginia. The Metro began operating in 1976 and is still being built. The map on the opposite page shows the Metro's routes.

The Washington, D.C., Metro connects the downtown area with suburbs in Maryland and Virginia. Many commuters ride the Metro to work.

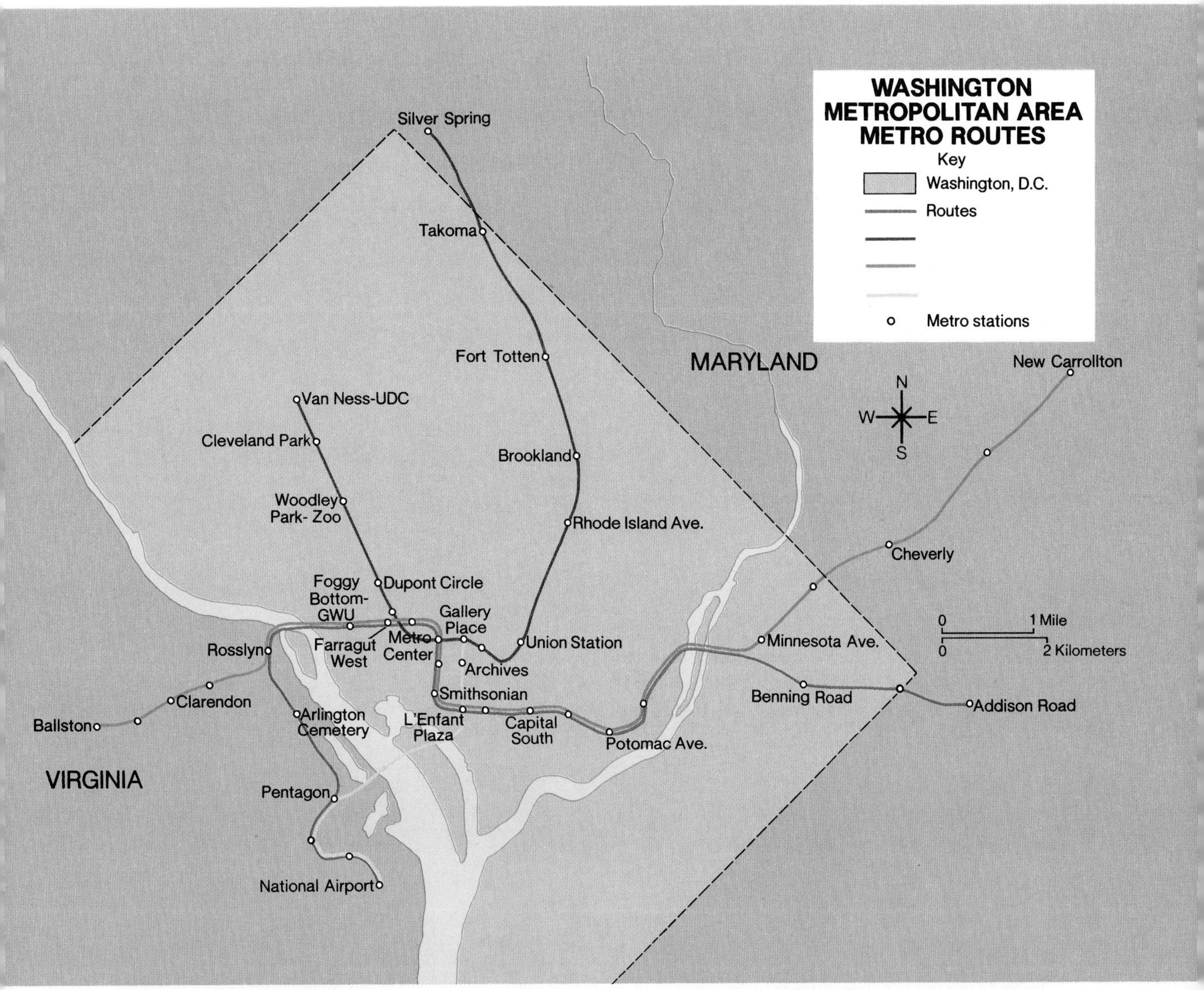

This map can help you travel on the Metro. How many routes does the Metro have? Which routes meet at Metro Center? Which route would you take to go from Metro Center to Union Station?

Do You Know?

1. For whom do the largest number of people work in Washington, D.C.?
2. Why are there no skyscrapers in Washington, D.C.?
3. Where are the capital's suburbs located?

4 Our Country Is Special

Washington, D.C., is the capital for all the people in the United States. Our capital is a special place for Americans. It is the center of our country's government. Many places in the city remind us of our history. Our country was started because the colonists wanted to be free. Today Americans still share a belief in freedom.

It Is Our Government

We live in a free country. Our rights, or freedoms, cannot be taken away from us by the government. The government of the United States belongs to all American citizens. It was formed to help protect our rights.

At least once a year the President goes to the Capitol to speak to members of Congress. Everyone can watch the speech on television.

All American citizens have a responsibility to vote when they become 18. These teenagers are signing up to vote for the first time.

All Americans have rights. We also have responsibilities. When something belongs to you, it is your responsibility to take care of it. All Americans have a responsibility to take part in our government. We must obey the laws. When we become 18 years old, it is our responsibility to vote.

This Land Is Your Land

Americans share rights and responsibilities. We also share the beauty of our country. We appreciate its great size and variety. There are mountains and valleys. There are rivers and deserts. There are forests, farm land, minerals, and other natural resources.

This Land Is Your Land

Words and Music by Woody Guthrie

REFRAIN
C
G
This land is your land, This land is my land
D7
G
From Cal - i - for - nia to the New York is - land;
C
G
From the red-wood for - est to the Gulf Stream wa - ters;
D7
G
Fine
This land was made for you and me.

VERSE
C
G
1. As I was walk - ing ___ that rib - bon of high - way, ___
2. I've roamed and ram - bled ___ and I fol - lowed my foot - steps ___
D7
G
1. I saw a - bove me ___ that end - less sky - way. ___
2. To the spark - ling sands of her dia - mond de - serts, ___
C
G
1. I saw be - low me ___ that gold - en val - ley, ___
2. And all a - round me ___ a voice was sound - ing, ___
D.C. al Fine
D7
G
1. This land was made for you and me. ___
2. This land was made for you and me. ___

Many Special Places

Americans also share an interest in the history of our country. You have read about the monuments in Washington, D.C., that remind us of some of our Presidents. There also are special places in all parts of the United States that help us remember our country's history. Look at the pictures on this page and the next. They show you two of the many special places in the history of the United States.

The Declaration of Independence was signed in Independence Hall in Philadelphia. Visitors can see where our country's history began.

The Statue of Liberty is a symbol of our free country for all Americans.

In this book you have read about communities in our country. They are similar in many ways. They have many differences. But the people who live in our communities are all Americans. We are all proud of our country.

Do You Know?

1. Why is Washington, D.C., a special place for all Americans?
2. Name two responsibilities of American citizens.
3. What are two things that Americans share?

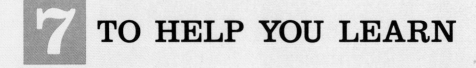

7 TO HELP YOU LEARN

Using New Words

Read the words in the box. Choose the best word to complete each sentence. Write the completed sentences on a sheet of paper.

White House	diplomats	Congress
monuments	Capitol	pages
memorial		

1. The members of ________ make laws for the people of the United States.
2. The ________ from Greece and Kenya met with the President.
3. The President lives and works in the ________.
4. One of the most famous ________ in Washington, D.C., was built to honor George Washington.
5. High school students called ________ help members of Congress by running errands for them.
6. Congress meets in the ________ building.
7. A ________ in Washington, D.C., was built to help us remember President Abraham Lincoln.

Finding the Facts

1. Who chose the exact place along the Potomac River for the country's new capital?
2. Who was Abigail Adams?
3. What is the Capitol? What is the capital of the United States?
4. How does the Library of Congress help Congress and the public?
5. What is the Washington, D.C., Metro?

Using Study Skills

The time line below shows when four states became part of the United States. Use the time line to answer these questions.

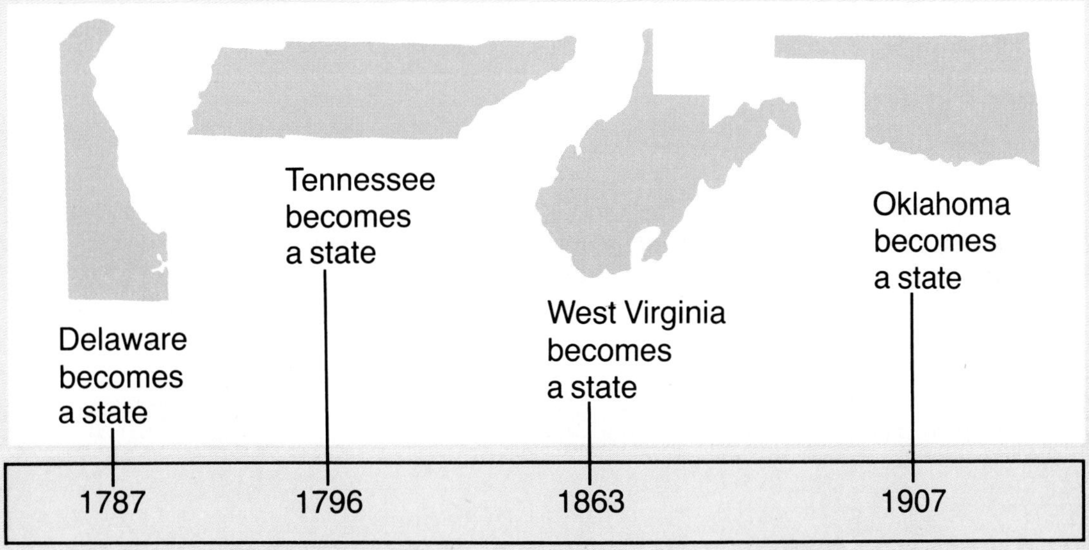

1. Which was the first state to become part of the United States?
2. Which state became part of the United States first—Tennessee or West Virginia?
3. When did Oklahoma become a state? When did Delaware become a state?

Things to Think About

1. Why is Washington, D.C., a special place for all Americans?
2. Name some things all Americans share.

Things to Do

Look at a road map of the United States. Plan a trip by car from your home to Washington, D.C. Through what states would you travel? Through what cities would you pass? Mark your route on the map.

Learning About Your Own Community

Members of Congress make laws for all the people of the United States. Who makes the laws for your state? What is the capital of your state?

Learning from Maps

Use the landmark map of Washington, D.C., on pages 202–203 to answer these questions.

1. In what square is the Library of Congress?
2. In what square is the Lincoln Memorial?
3. In what squares is the Mall?
4. In what direction would you travel to go from the Capitol to the White House?

Learning About Maps and Globes

Maps and globes are special tools. They help us to understand the earth and the people, places, and things on it. Maps and globes are useful tools only if we know how to use them. The lessons in this section will help you improve your skills in using maps and globes.

Words to Learn

axis
cardinal directions
compass rose
hemisphere
intermediate directions
interstate highways
scale

1 Reviewing Globes and Maps

Globes and maps help you understand what the earth is like. They show the land and water areas of the earth. They also can show such features as deserts, mountains, countries, and cities.

A globe is round like the earth. It is a model, or small copy, of the earth. A globe shows the true shapes, sizes, and positions of the earth's land and water areas.

Look at the pictures of the globe below. Each picture shows only half of the globe. Now study your classroom globe. Can you ever see more than half of a globe at one time?

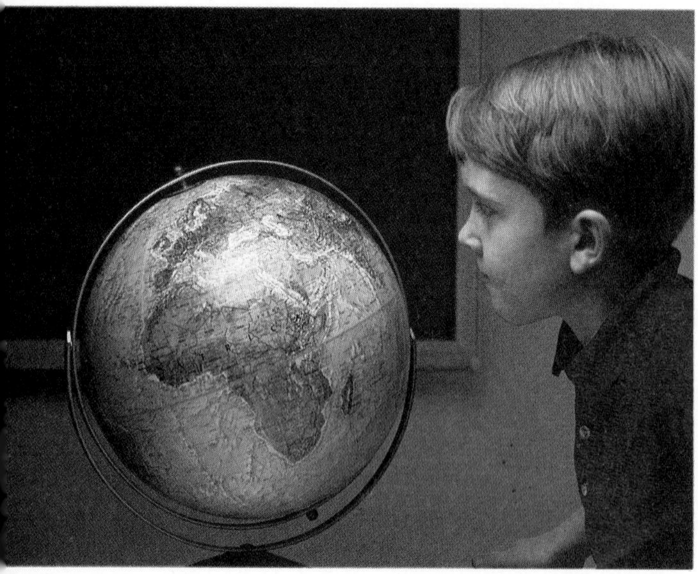

A map is a flat drawing of the earth or part of the earth. Maps are very useful. They can easily be folded and carried. They can be printed in books.

There are many different kinds of maps. Some maps show only part of the world. They can tell you many things about the part of the earth that they show. A world map shows the whole world in one view. On a world map you can compare different parts of the world at the same time. Use the map on this page to tell whether South America is larger or smaller than Africa.

Map of the World

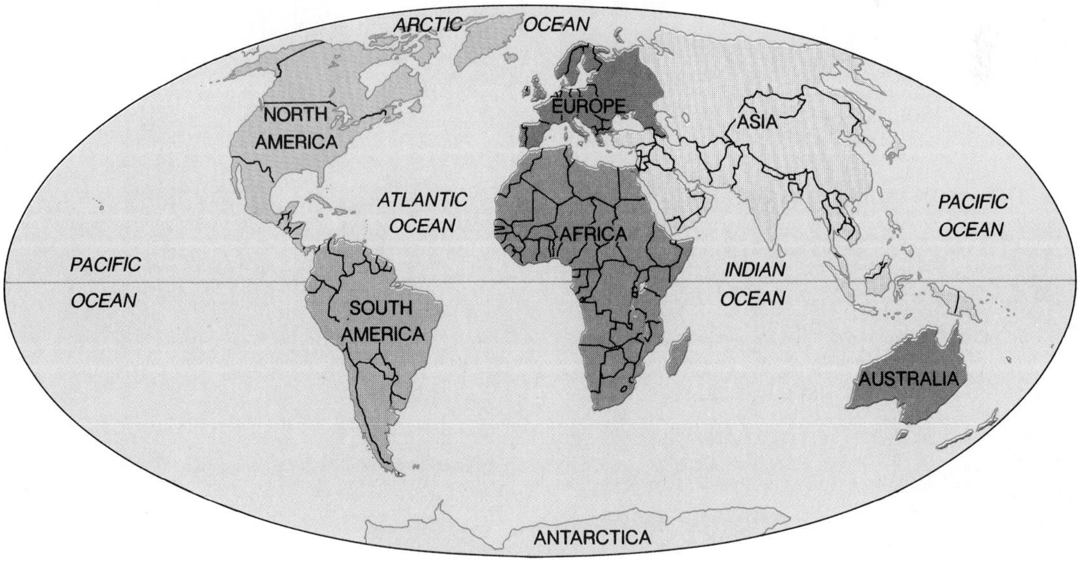

2 Finding Directions on a Map

Knowing directions helps you find places more easily. You know that north is the direction toward the North Pole. When you face north, east is to your right. West is to your left, and south is behind you. North, east, south, and west are the four main directions. They are known as cardinal directions (kärd′ə nəl di rek′shənz).

A compass also helps you find directions. When a compass is held flat, its needle points north.

A compass rose (kum′pəs rōz) can help you find directions on a map. A compass rose is a circle design showing directions. Find the compass rose on the map on the next page. How are north, east, south, and west marked?

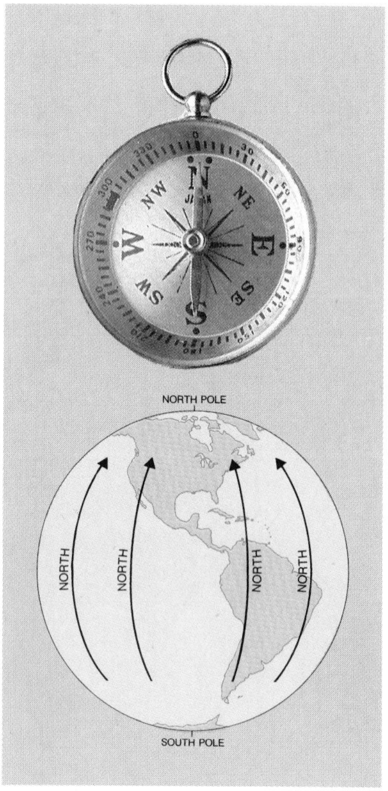

A compass rose also shows the intermediate (in′tər mē′dē it) directions. The intermediate directions are halfway between the cardinal directions. What intermediate direction does NE stand for? SE? SW? NW?

Study the compass rose and the map of the United States on this page. What country is north of the United States? In what direction is Mexico from the United States? What state is just west of Colorado? In what direction is Wisconsin from Texas?

In what direction would you travel to go from Washington to Florida in the most direct way? Through what states would you pass if you traveled directly west from central Kansas to the Pacific Ocean?

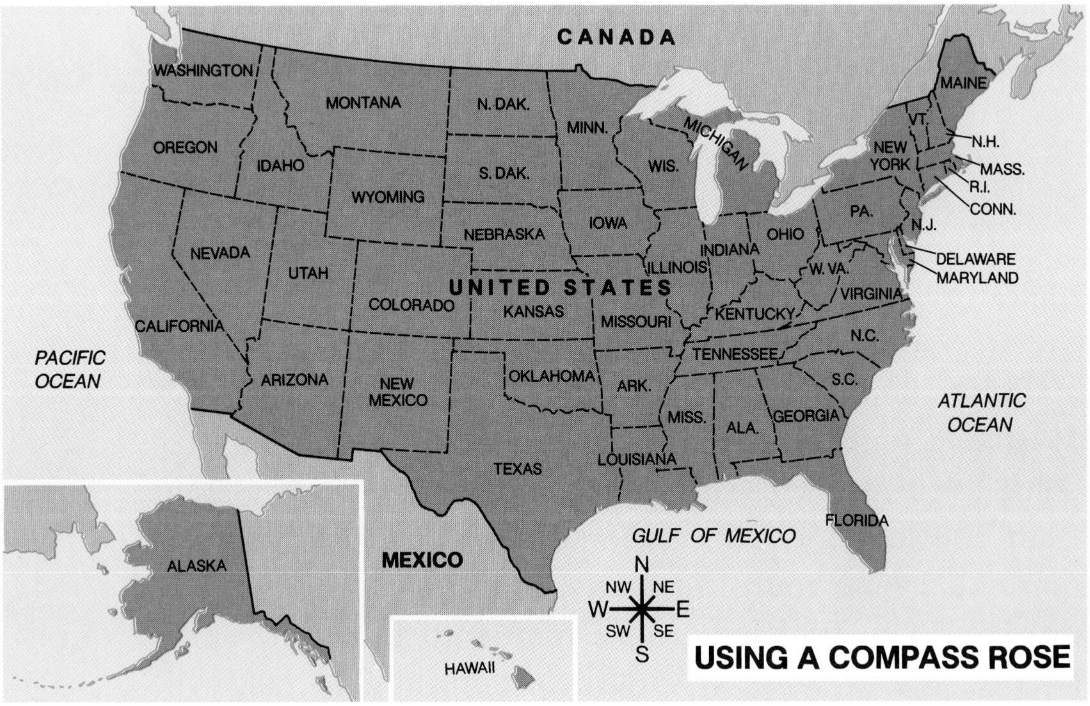

USING A COMPASS ROSE

3 Using a Road Map

A road map is a special kind of map that shows you how to travel from one place to another. The road map of Wyoming on the next page shows some of the cities of Wyoming and the main roads that connect them.

Two different symbols are used for roads on this map. The heavy purple line shows interstate highways (in′tər stāt′hī′wāz′). Interstate means "between or among two or more states." The United States has a system of interstate highways that cross the country to connect many important cities. Most interstate highways have four lanes and are very good roads. What are the numbers of the interstate highways that cross Wyoming?

The red lines on the map show other important roads. Some are federal highways and others are state highways. How do you know which are federal highways and which are state highways?

If you study the map, you will see that most even-numbered roads run generally east and west. Most odd-numbered roads run generally north and south. You also will see that some roads have more than one number. The reason is that they are part of more than one route. At some point, such roads divide. If you traveled from Douglas to Lusk on routes 18 and 20, and wanted to continue on route 18, in what direction would you turn at Lusk?

Many road maps show distances in miles or kilometers between certain points. On this map, the red numbers tell the distance in miles between the red dots.

In what direction from Thermopolis is Riverton? What routes would you follow to travel from Thermopolis to Riverton? How far is it between the two cities? If you traveled 55 miles an hour, about how many hours would it take to go from Rawlins to Rock Springs on Interstate Highway 80?

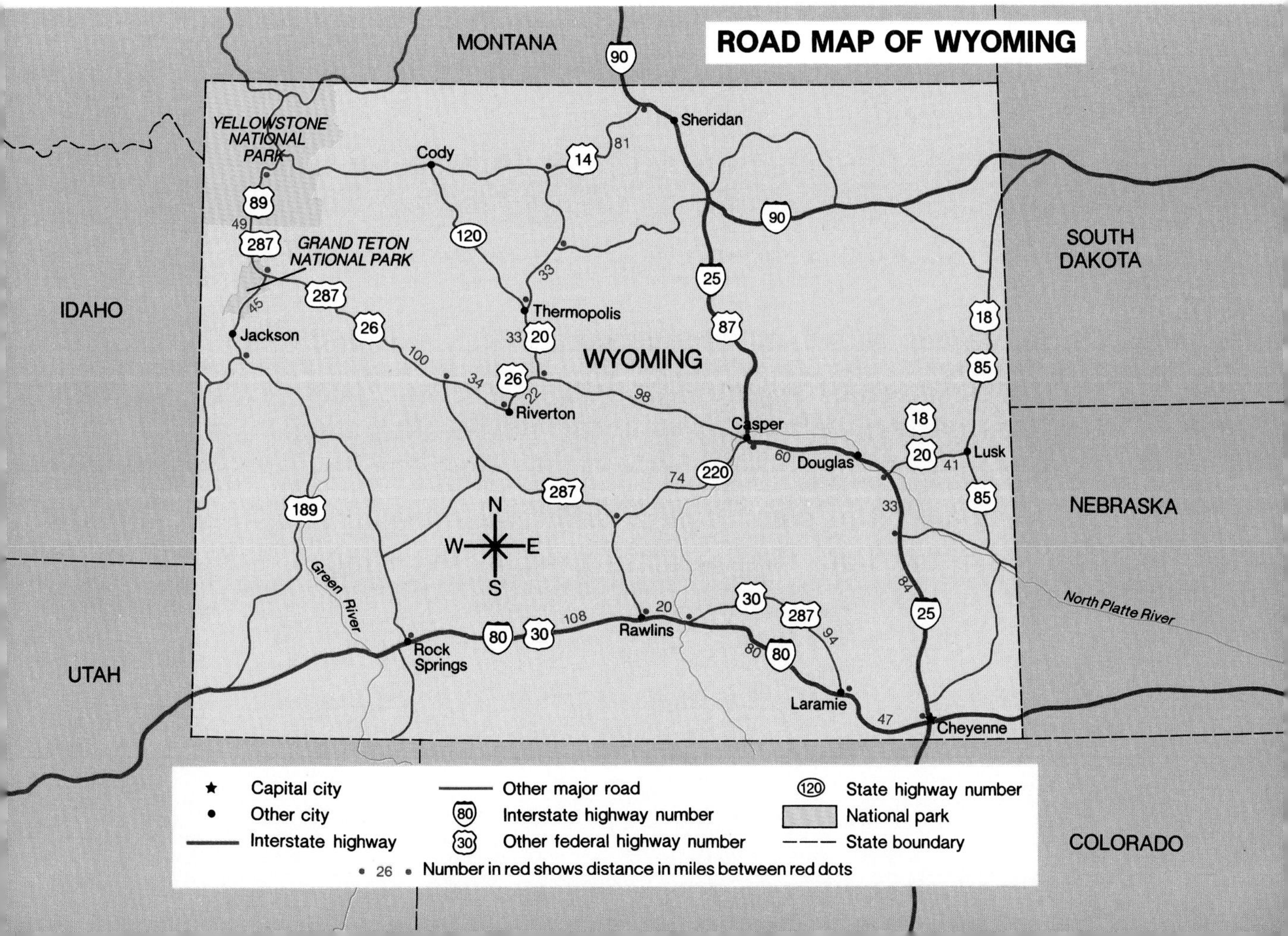

4 Using a Land Use Map

A map can show how people use the land to make a living. The map on the next page is a land use map of the United States. The colors on the map show how the land is used for different kinds of work. Use the key to name the kinds of jobs shown.

The map cannot show all the millions of different jobs. It shows only the general kinds of work people do in our country. For example, there are many jobs that have to do with farming. Can you name some?

Study the patterns shown on the map. Compare the areas used for farming with those used for ranching. Is farming more important in the eastern part of the United States or in the western part? Where is ranching more important?

What are the important kinds of land use in Hawaii? What kinds of jobs do people have in Colorado? In what areas is fishing an important kind of work?

The areas shown in orange come closely together in the northeastern part of the United States. What does this pattern tell you about the northeastern part of our country?

What does the color yellow show on the map? Where is there land that is little used in the United States?

LAND USE IN THE UNITED STATES
WASHINGTON
OREGON
IDAHO
MONTANA
NORTH DAKOTA
SOUTH DAKOTA
WYOMING
NEBRASKA
NEVADA
UTAH
COLORADO
CALIFORNIA
ARIZONA
NEW MEXICO
KANSAS
OKLAHOMA
TEXAS
MINN.
IOWA
MISSOURI
ARKANSAS
LOUISIANA
WISC.
MICHIGAN
ILLINOIS
INDIANA
OHIO
KENTUCKY
TENNESSEE
MISS.
ALA.
GEORGIA
FLORIDA
SOUTH CAROLINA
NORTH CAROLINA
VIRGINIA
W.VA.
PENN.
NEW YORK
MAINE
VT.
N.H.
MASS.
R.I.
CONN.
NEW JERSEY
DELAWARE
MARYLAND
PACIFIC OCEAN
ATLANTIC OCEAN
GULF OF MEXICO
N
W
E
S
ALASKA
PACIFIC OCEAN
HAWAII
PACIFIC OCEAN
Key
Farming
Ranching
Lumbering
Fishing
Mining
Manufacturing and Trade
Land that is little used

5 Using a Landform Map

There are four main kinds of landforms on the earth's surface. They are plains, hills, plateaus, and mountains.

Plains are flat or almost flat lands.

Hills are rounded and raised lands.

Plateaus are flat lands with steep sides, raised above the surrounding land.

Mountains are high lands with steep sides and rounded or pointed tops. Mountains are higher than hills.

A landform map can help you understand how the earth's surface looks. On the map below, colors show the different kinds of landforms. What landform is shown by green? What color shows mountains?

What states have mountains? Hills? Plateaus? Plains? What city is located on a plain? Where is there a plateau? In what kind of landform region is Aspen located? Describe the location of Denver.

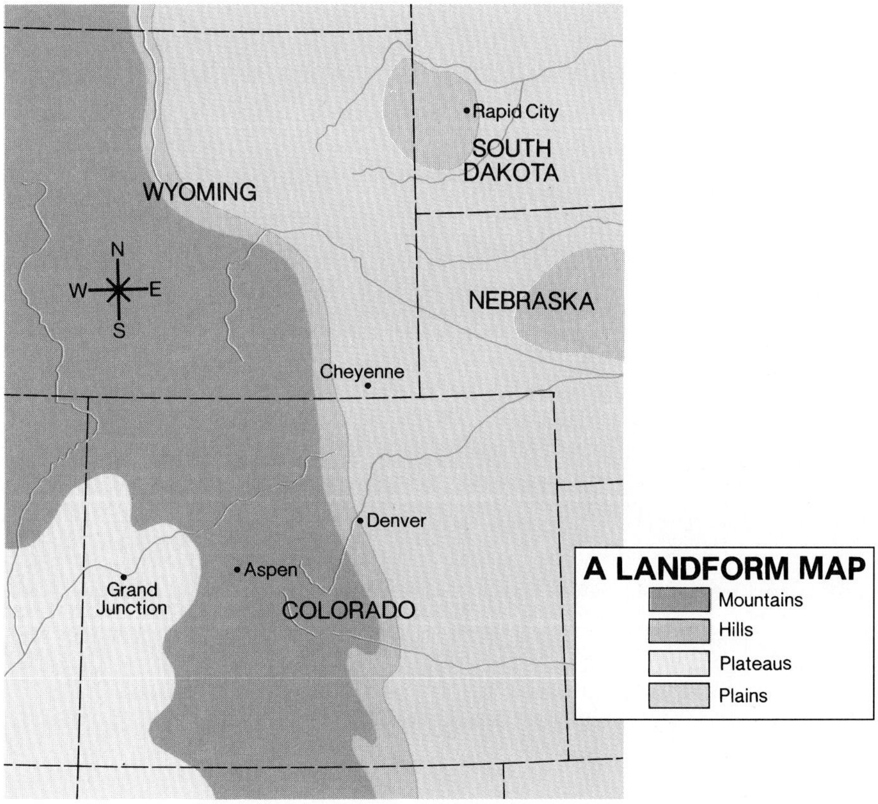

6 Understanding Map Scales

Sometimes you want to know the distance between places. A map scale (skāl) helps you find distances. A scale tells how many miles or kilometers on the earth a certain space shows on a map.

Map A below has a bar scale. It tells how many miles on the earth's surface are shown by one inch on the map. It also tells how many kilometers are shown by two centimeters. How many miles does one inch show? How many kilometers are shown by two centimeters?

To use the bar scale, take a strip of paper and lay it against the bar scale. Slide the paper along to mark it as shown below.

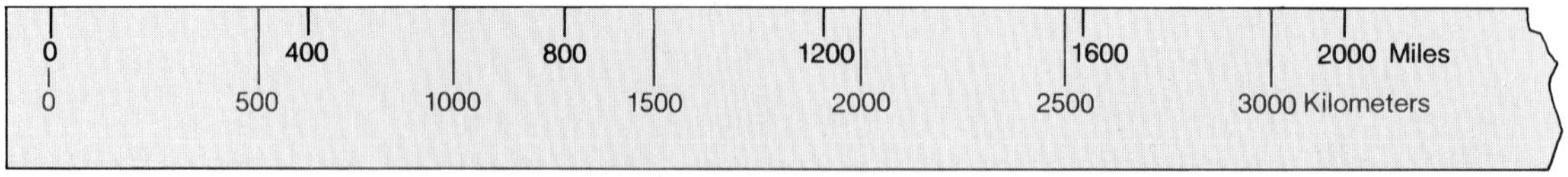

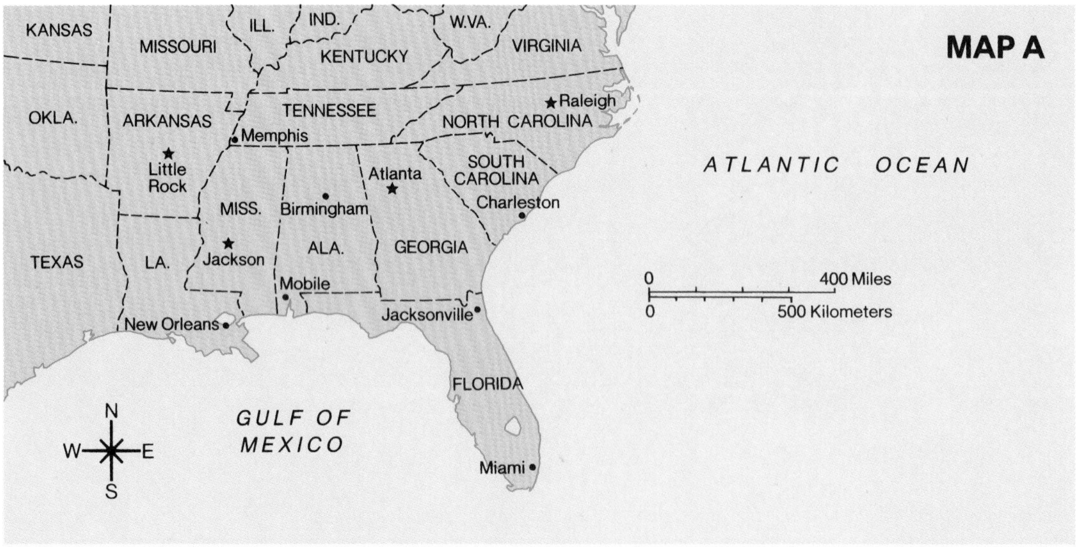

Now use the bar scale you have made to find the distance from New Orleans to Jacksonville on **Map A.** Lay the strip of paper on the map with the edge just below the dots for the two cities. Place the "**0**" on New Orleans. How many miles is it from New Orleans to Jacksonville? What is the distance in kilometers from Memphis to Atlanta?

Map B below shows a smaller part of the earth than **Map A. Map B** has a different scale. Does an inch on **Map B** show a greater distance or a smaller distance than it does on **Map A**?

Maps can have different scales, but distances on the earth remain the same. You can check this by finding the distance from New Orleans to Jacksonville on **Map B.** Mark a strip of paper and measure as you did before.

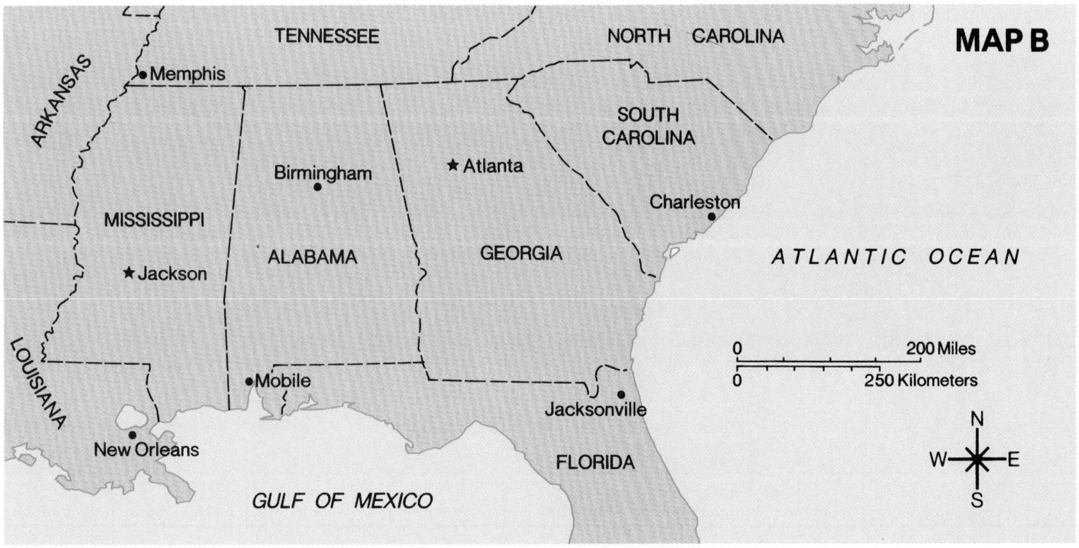

7 Understanding Day and Night

You know that the earth has a North Pole and a South Pole. The earth also has an axis (ak′sis). The axis is an imaginary line that runs through the center of the earth from the North Pole to the South Pole. The earth rotates, or turns, on its axis. Once a day, or once every 24 hours, the earth turns completely around on its axis. This turning, or rotation, of the earth causes night and day.

The arrows show the direction in which the earth rotates. Can you tell whether the earth rotates from east to west or from west to east?

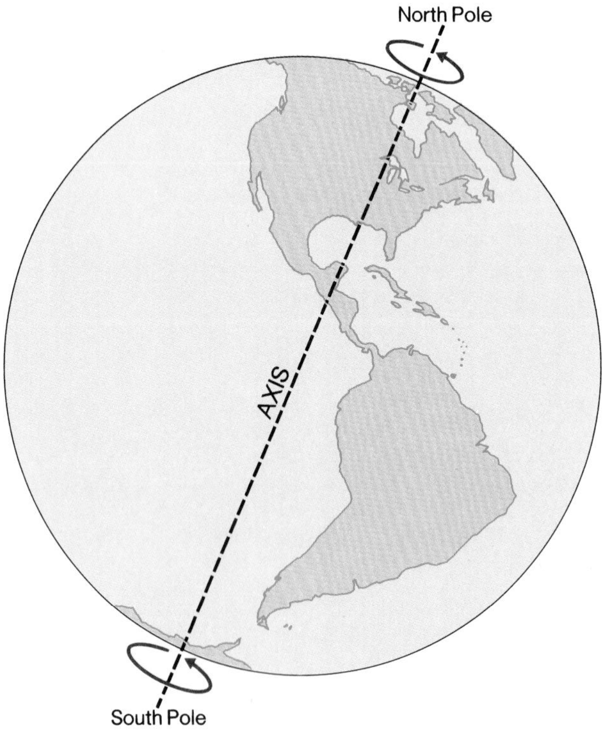

The sun's rays shine on only one side of the earth. It is day on the side of the earth facing the sun. It is night on the side of the earth turned away from the sun. Look at the drawing on the right. Is it day or night in the United States?

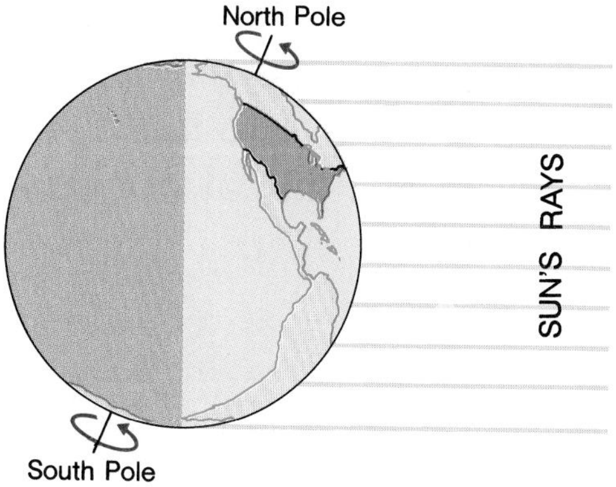

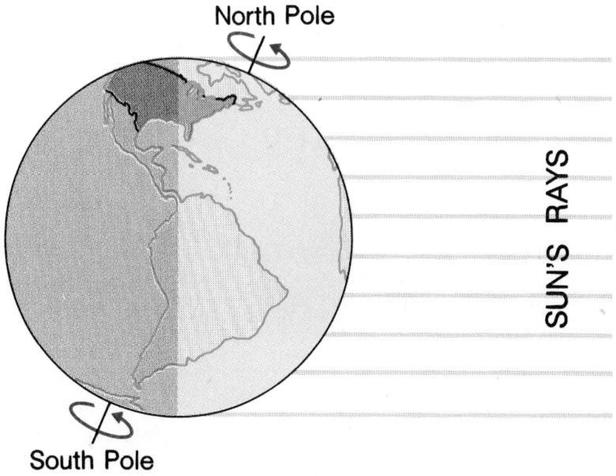

The earth never stops turning. As the earth rotates, the side toward the sun changes. Look at the drawing on the left. Is it day or night in the United States?

8 Understanding Hemispheres

A sphere (sfēr) is a round body. A ball, the earth, and a globe are all spheres. No matter how you look, you can see only half a sphere at one time. Check this by looking at your classroom globe. Half a sphere is called a hemisphere (hem′ə sfēr). Hemi means "half."

The earth can be divided into hemispheres. The maps on the top of the next page show you how the earth is divided into the Western Hemisphere and the Eastern Hemisphere. The maps on the bottom of the page show how the earth is divided into the Northern Hemisphere and the Southern Hemisphere. The equator divides the Northern Hemisphere from the Southern Hemisphere.

In what hemispheres is North America? Is South America in the Eastern Hemisphere or the Western Hemisphere? What continents are entirely in the Southern Hemisphere? What continents are partly in the Northern Hemisphere and partly in the Southern Hemisphere?

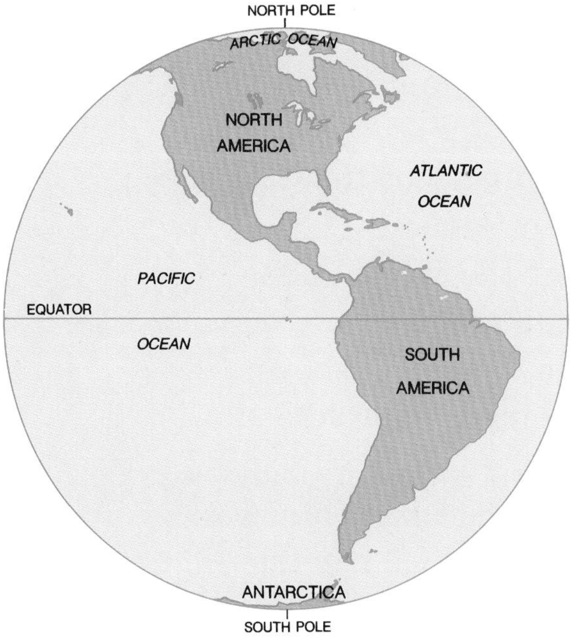

WESTERN HEMISPHERE

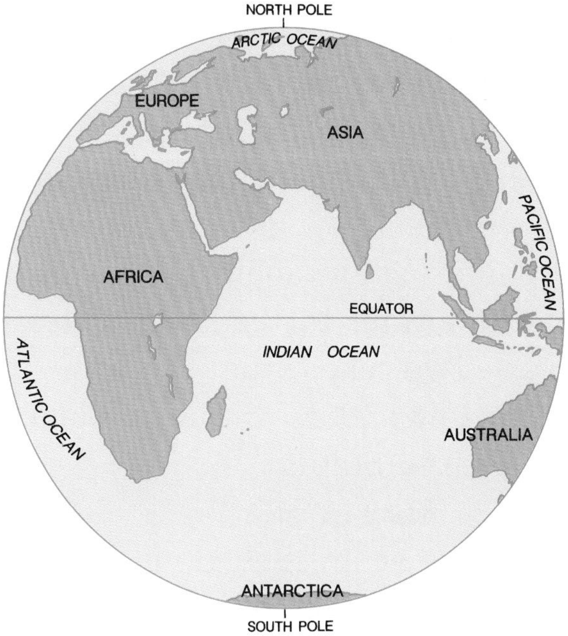

EASTERN HEMISPHERE

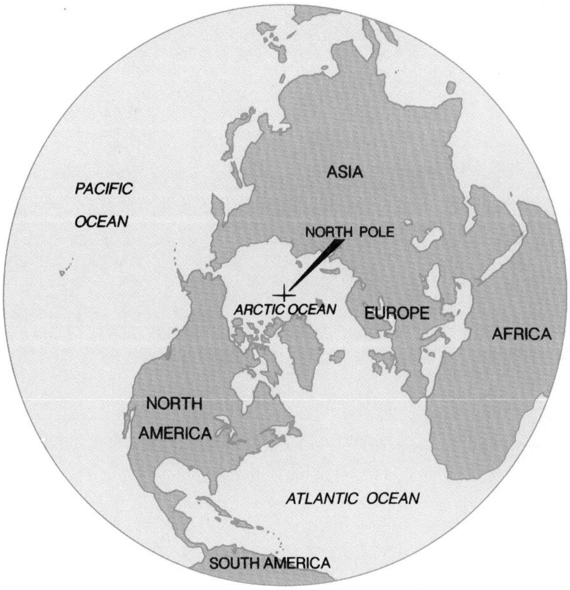

NORTHERN HEMISPHERE

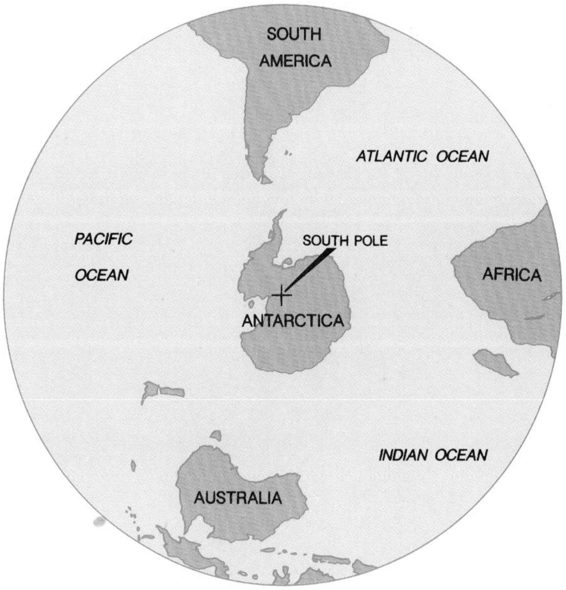

SOUTHERN HEMISPHERE

9 Using an Atlas

A book of maps is called an atlas. Your book has a special section called an atlas. Use the table of contents to find the atlas in your book.

Atlas maps may show different parts of the world. They also may show different kinds of information about the same part of the world. It is important to read map titles carefully.

Two maps from the atlas in your book are shown below and on the next page. Both maps show the United States.

Map A is a political (pə lit′i kəl) map. Political maps show such things as countries, states, capital cities, and other cities. What does the symbol ★ stand for on this map?

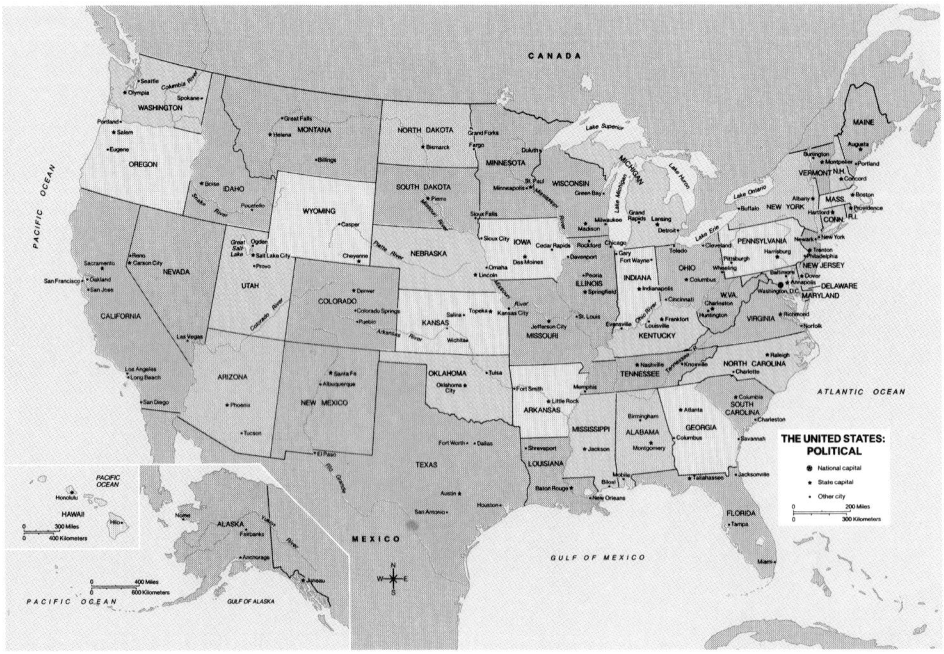

Map B is a physical (fiz′i kəl) map. Physical maps show landforms such as mountains, valleys, and rivers. They help you understand what the land looks like. What color shows mountains on **Map B?**

Political maps and physical maps are two kinds of maps often found in atlases. Political maps usually show some physical features. Most physical maps show some political features.

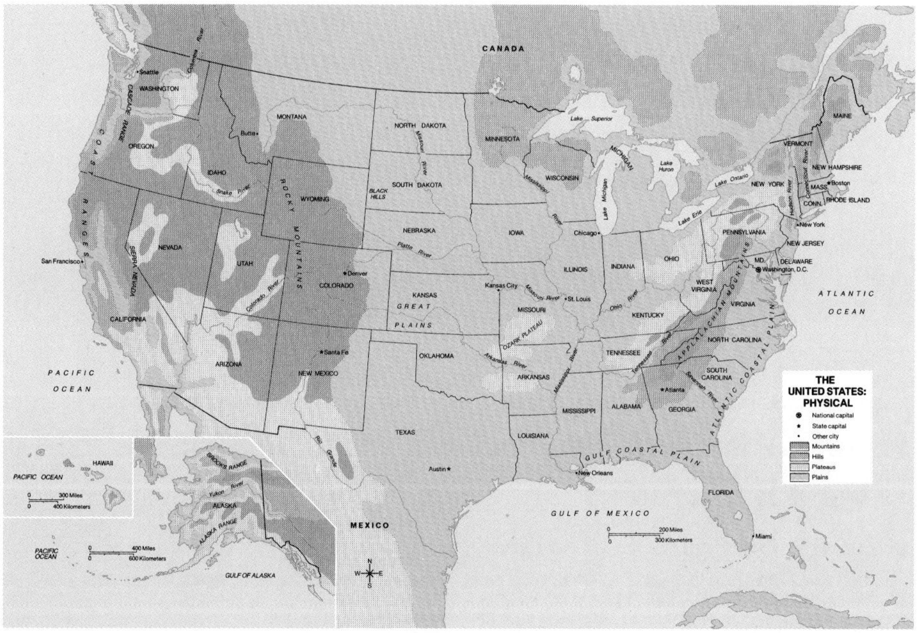

Now turn to pages 10–11 in your atlas. The four maps on these pages give you special information about the United States. What do these four maps show? It is important to use the keys on these maps to learn what the color symbols stand for.

Enrichment 250

UNIT 4

UNIT 5

UNIT 6

UNIT 7

This chart shows how some businesses help the people in a community meet their needs. Use the chart to answer the questions below. Write your answers on a piece of paper.

Businesses	Employees	Goods	Services
Telephone Company	786	Telephones	Phone calls; repairs
Power Company	1,009		Electricity and gas
Shoe Store	532	Shoes and boots	
Clothing Store	24	Clothing	
Supermarkets	1,112	Food	
Dairy Farms	342	Milk	
Construction Company	844	Housing	
Bus Company	203		Transportation

1. Which business has the greatest number of employees?
2. What services does the Power Company provide?
3. Which business repairs telephones?
4. Which business helps the people meet their need for shelter?
5. Which two businesses help the people meet their need for clothing?
6. Which two businesses help the people meet their need for food?
7. Which business helps the people go from one place to another?

Looking at Communities

To follow page 21

Look at the pictures. Then on a piece of paper write two sentences that describe each picture. Include the words in the box.

city	town	suburb

1.

2.

3.

Using a State Map

To follow page 30

Here is a map of New Mexico. Use the map and the map key to answer the questions below. Write your answers on a piece of paper.

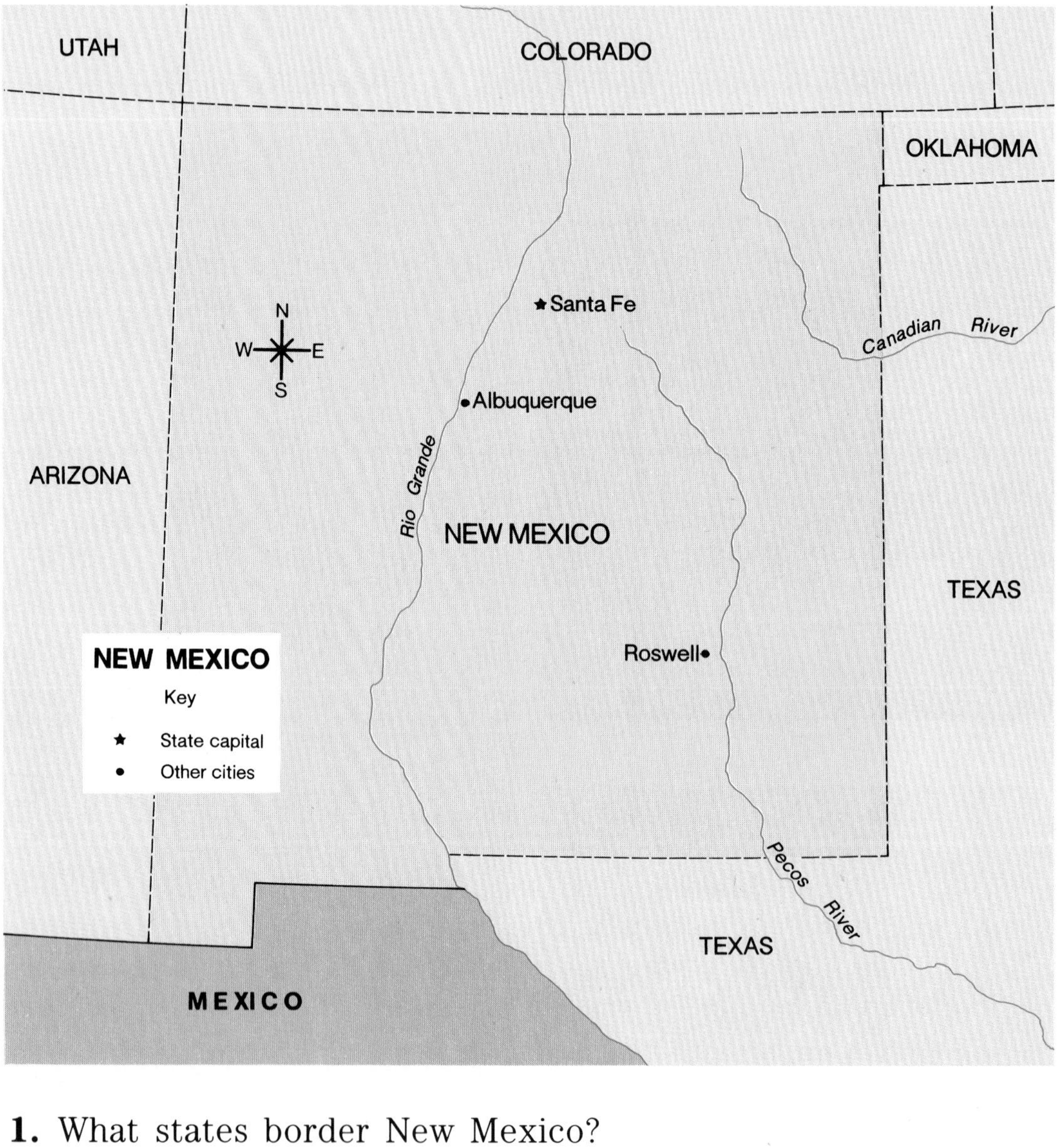

1. What states border New Mexico?
2. What country shares a border with New Mexico?
3. What is the capital of New Mexico?
4. How many rivers are shown on the map?

Using a Picture Graph

To follow page 42

Beth makes and sells hand-painted mirrors. This picture graph shows how many mirrors Beth made between September and February. Use the graph to answer the questions below. Write your answers on a piece of paper.

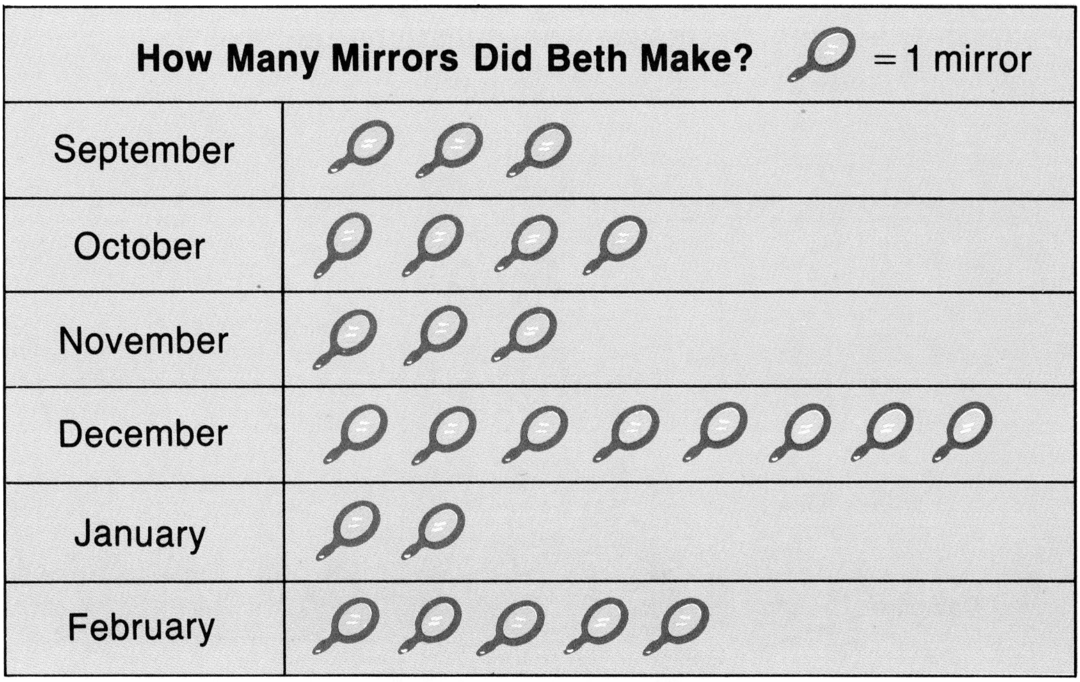

1. How many mirrors did Beth make in September?
2. How many mirrors did she make in February?
3. In what month did Beth make four mirrors?
4. In what two months did Beth make the same number of mirrors?
5. In what month did Beth make the most mirrors?
6. In what month did she make the fewest mirrors?
7. How many mirrors did Beth make from September to February?
8. Beth was paid $5.00 for each mirror she made. How much money did she earn in January?

Understanding a Diagram

To follow page 53

The Plains Indians lived in a kind of shelter called a tepee. This diagram shows some parts of a tepee.

The frame for the tepee was made by putting long poles into the shape of a cone. The poles were tied together at the top. Then buffalo hides were stretched over the frame.

Use the diagram to answer the questions below. Write your answers on a piece of paper.

Plains Indians Tepee

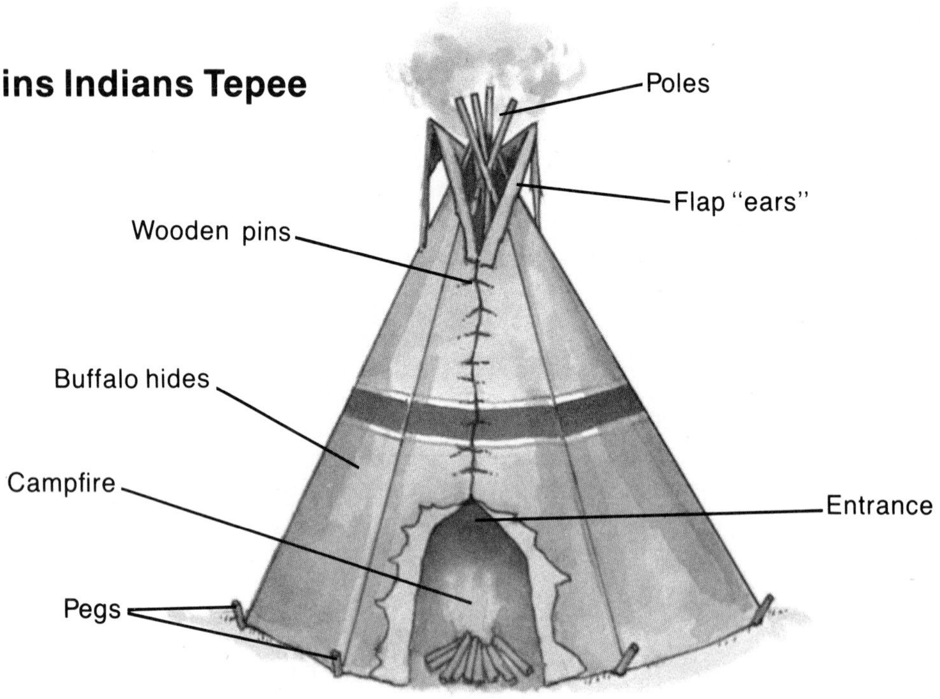

1. What are the openings at the top of the tepee called? Why do you think the tepee had openings at the top?
2. What material was used to cover the tepee?
3. What holds the buffalo hides together above the entrance?
4. What was used to hold the hides to the ground?
5. Where was the campfire?

Using a Historical Map

To follow page 57

This is a map of the 13 colonies. It shows the first community in each colony and the date it was settled. Use the map to answer the questions below. Write your answers on a piece of paper.

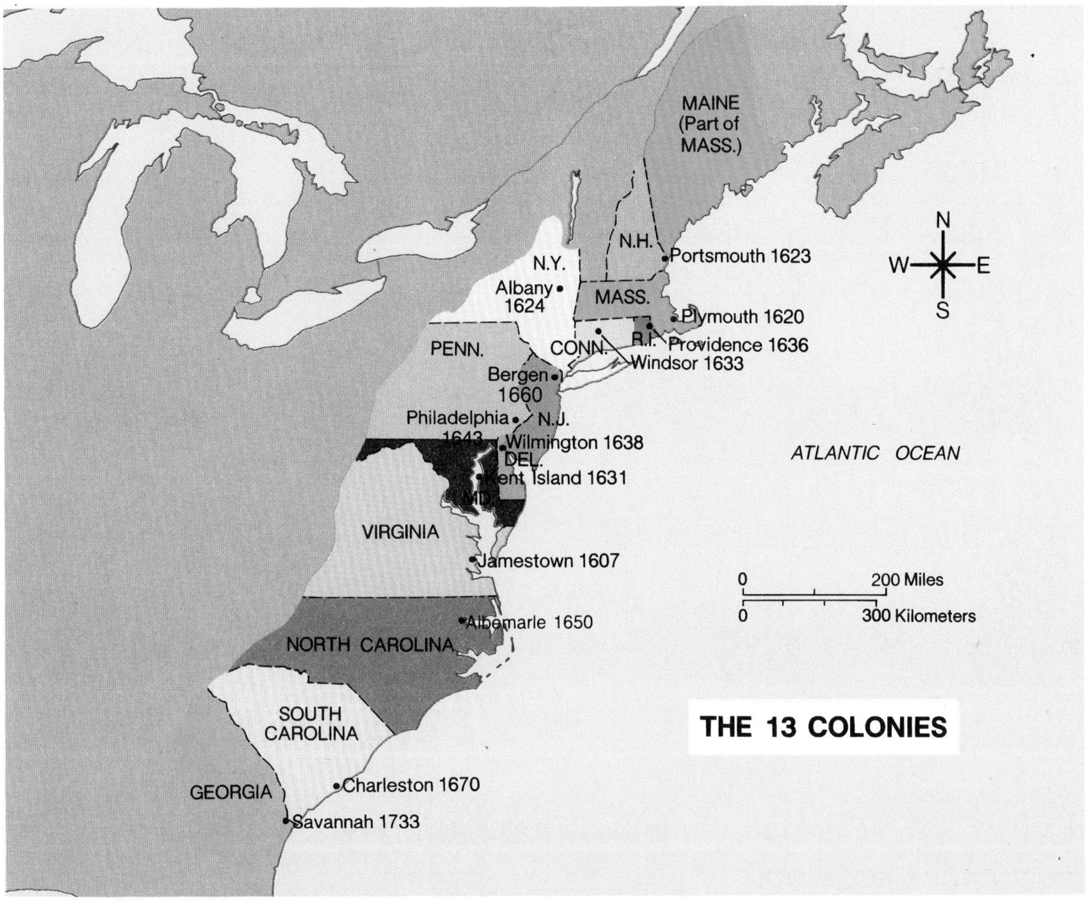

1. The first community was in Virginia. What is the name of the community?
2. In what year was it settled?
3. Was Plymouth settled before or after Philadelphia?
4. Was Albany settled before or after Bergen?
5. What was the first community in Rhode Island?
6. When was the last community settled?

Using a Bar Graph

To follow page 59

This bar graph shows the number of people who lived in Cincinnati, Ohio, from 1850 to 1980. Use the graph to answer the questions below. Write your answers on a piece of paper.

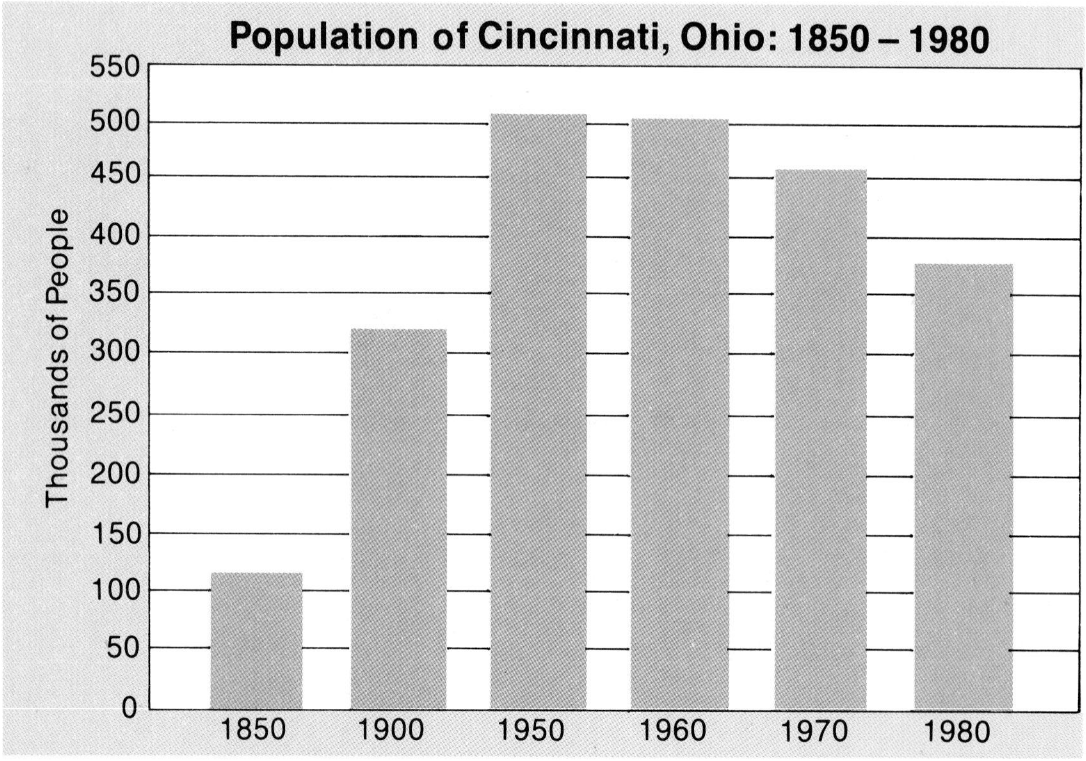

1. In what year did Cincinnati have the fewest number of people?
2. In what year did Cincinnati have the greatest number of people?
3. Did the number of people living in Cincinnati go up or down between 1900 and 1950?
4. Did the number of people go up or down between 1970 and 1980?
5. Between which two years did the number of people stay almost the same?

Putting Sentences in Order To follow page 64

These pictures show how the pioneers crossed a river with their wagons. Number a paper from **1** through **4**. After each number, write the sentence that tells what is happening. Use the sentences at the bottom of the page.

1.

2.

3.

4.

The pioneers guided the raft
across the river.
The pioneers took their wagon apart.
The pioneers tied the wagon and
wheels to the raft.
The pioneers took the wagon off the
raft and put it back together.

Using a Route Map

To follow page 69

The railroads were important to the growth of the United States. This map shows the routes of four major railroads in the 1800s. Use the map and the map key to answer the questions below. Write your answers on a piece of paper.

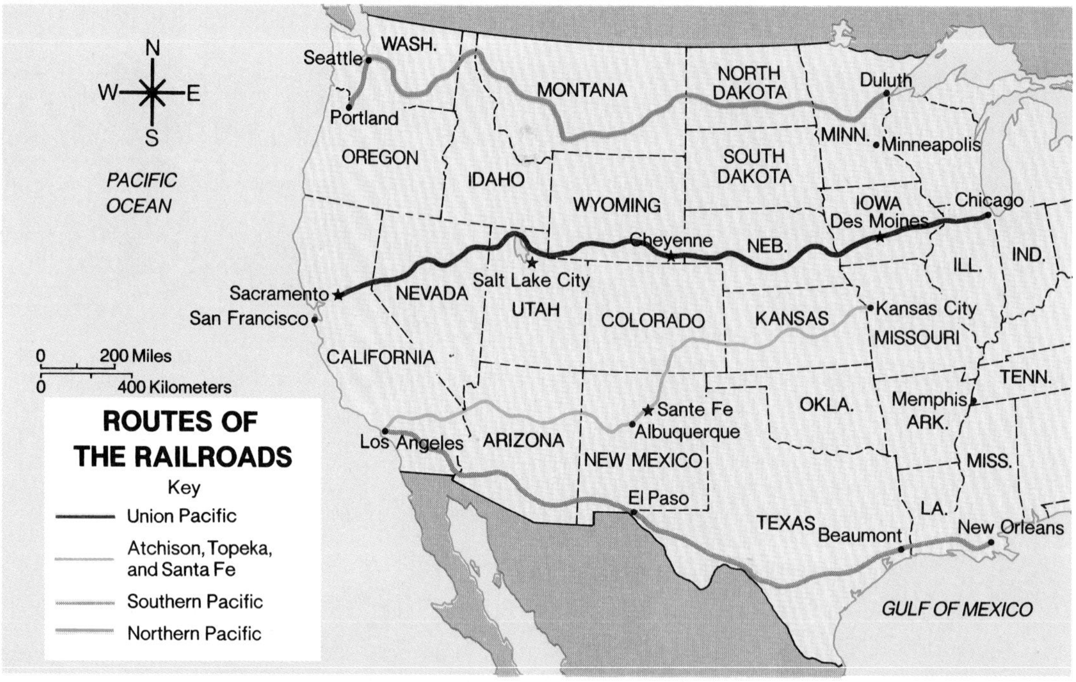

1. Which railroad line is blue on the map?
2. In which direction would a person travel to get from Cheyenne to Chicago?
3. Which railroad line connected Albuquerque, New Mexico and Kansas City, Missouri?
4. Name two cities that the Southern Pacific Railroad passed through going from Los Angeles to New Orleans.
5. Did the Union Pacific Railroad run north or south of Salt Lake City?
6. Which two railroads went through Arizona?

Using a Product Map

To follow page 79

This map shows some of the products grown or made in Washington. Use the map to answer the questions below. Write your answers on a piece of paper.

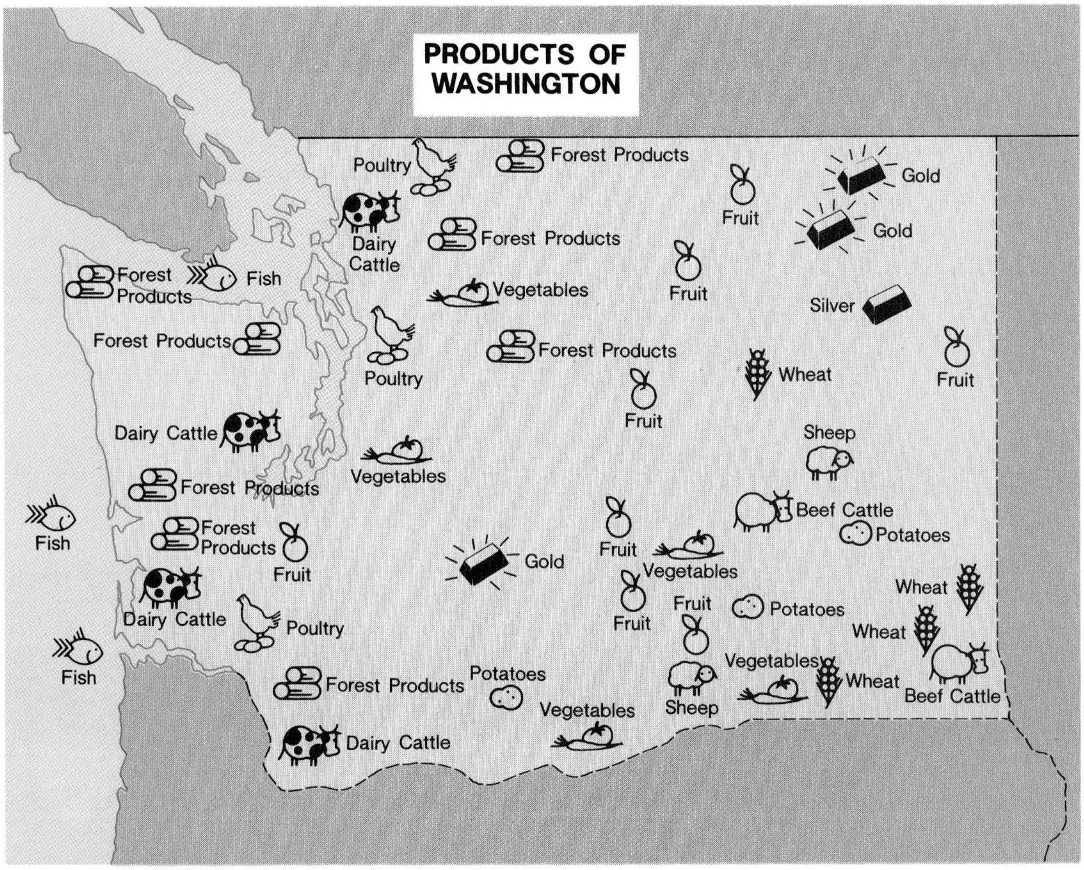

1. What two kinds of cattle are raised in Washington?
2. What other animals are raised in Washington?
3. What symbol shows where fruits are grown?
4. Is there more mining in the northern part or the southern part of the state?
5. Is there more fishing in the eastern part or the western part of the state?
6. What does the symbol  show?

Using a Bar Graph

To follow page 85

This bar graph shows the number of farmers in the United States. Use the graph to answer the questions below. Write your answers on a piece of paper.

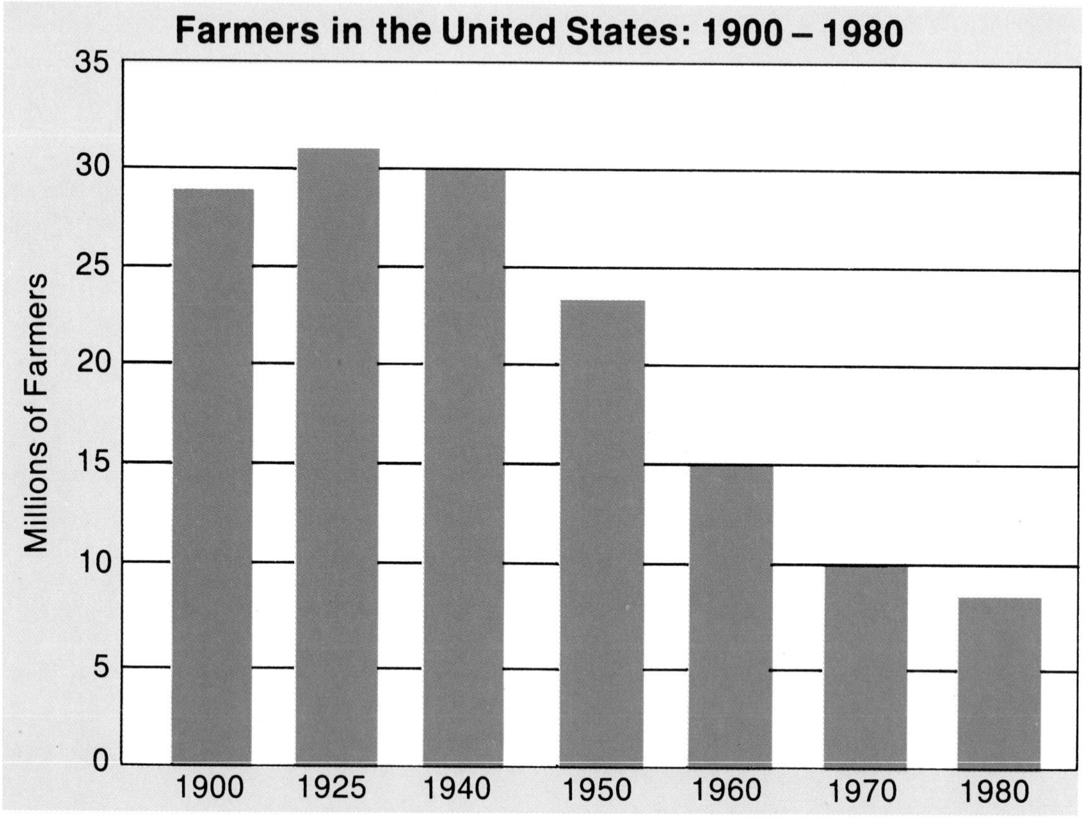

1. What years are shown on this bar graph?

2. In what year did the United States have the most farmers?

3. Between which two years did the number of farmers go up?

4. About how many farmers were there in 1940?

5. Did the number of farmers go up or down between 1940 and 1950?

6. About how many more farmers were there in 1960 than in 1970?

Using a Line Graph

To follow page 87

This line graph shows the average size of farms in the United States. Use the graph to answer the questions below. Write your answers on a piece of paper.

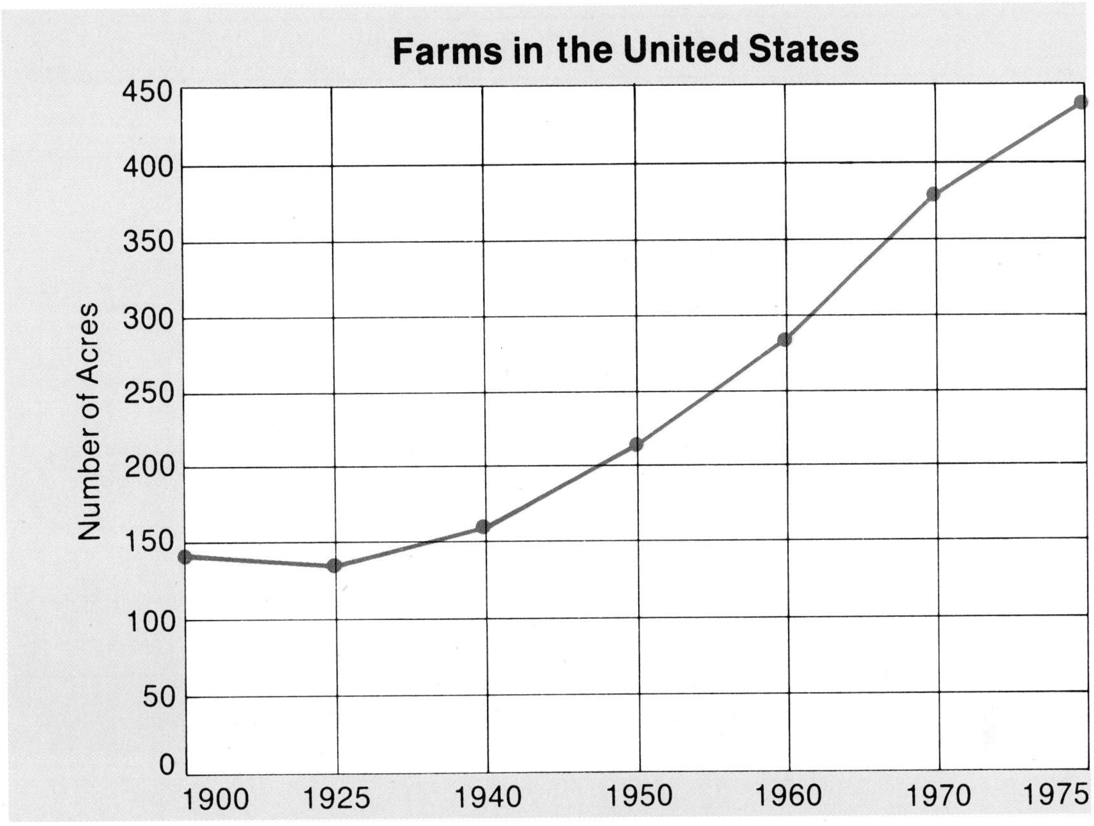

1. What years are shown on this line graph?
2. What is the title of the graph?
3. When was the average size of a farm the smallest?
4. About how big was the average farm in 1900?
5. What happened to the average size of farms after 1925?
6. Compare this line graph with the bar graph on page 260. What happened to the number of farmers after 1925? What happened to the size of farms after 1925?

Using a Chart

To follow page 97

This chart shows some of the parks in our National Park System. Use the chart to answer the questions below. Write your answers on a piece of paper.

National Park System		
National Park	**State**	**Feature**
Grand Canyon	Arizona	Mile-deep canyon; rock forms
Petrified Forest	Arizona	Rock-hard wood
Kings Canyon	California	Giant sequoia trees
Yosemite	California	Waterfalls, deep gorges
Redwood	California	Tallest trees in the world
Mesa Verde	Colorado	Early Indian cliff dwellings
Rocky Mountain	Colorado	High mountains with many peaks
Everglades	Florida	Near tropical wilderness
Mount Rainier	Washington	Huge one-peak glacier system
Grand Teton	Wyoming	Rugged mountains, elk herds
Yellowstone	Wyoming	Geysers, canyons, waterfalls

1. How many national parks are in Arizona?
2. What is the name of the national park in Florida?
3. Where would you go to see giant sequoia trees?
4. If you went to Yosemite National Park, what would you expect to see?
5. Where would you go to see the tallest trees in the world?

Many tourists visit San Francisco every year. Some of the places they visit are shown on this map. Use the landmark map to answer the questions below. Write your answers on a piece of paper.

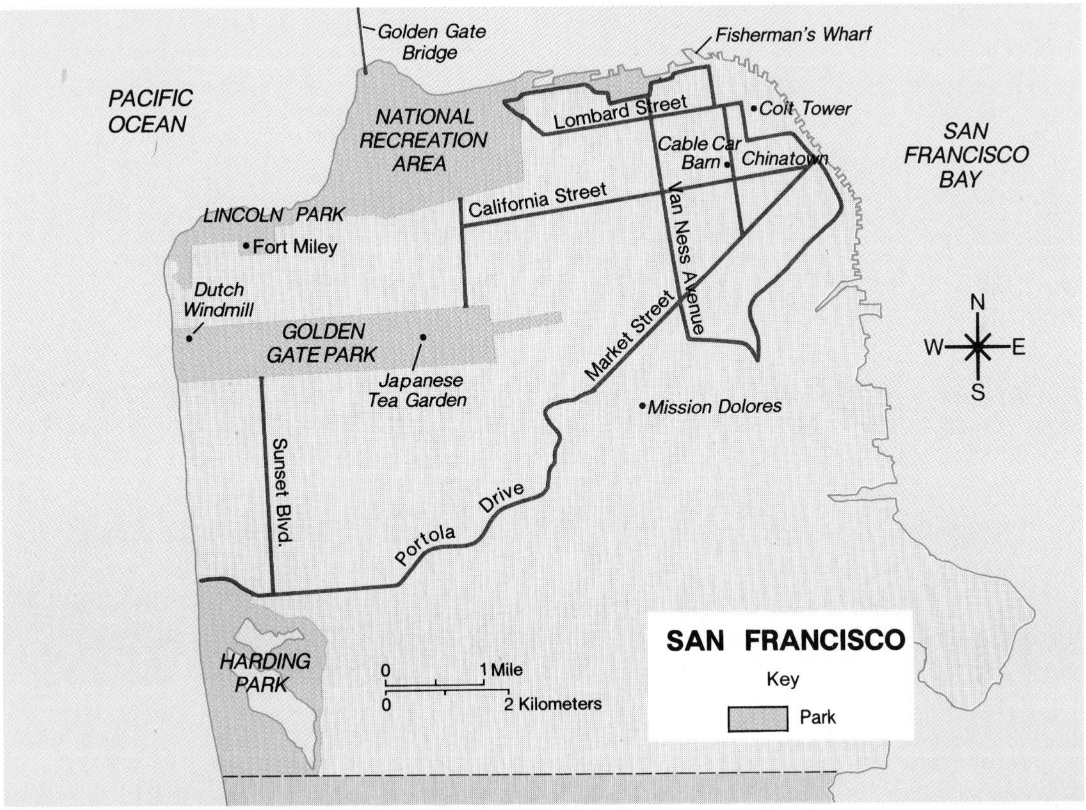

1. In what park could you see a Japanese Tea Garden?
2. Is Chinatown north or south of Coit Tower?
3. Suppose you are visiting Fisherman's Wharf. In which direction would you go to see the Golden Gate Bridge?
4. What fort is located in Lincoln Park?
5. What body of water is west of the Golden Gate Bridge?

Using a Diagram

To follow page 119

This diagram shows some of the different parts of a car. Use the diagram to answer the questions below. Write your answers on a piece of paper.

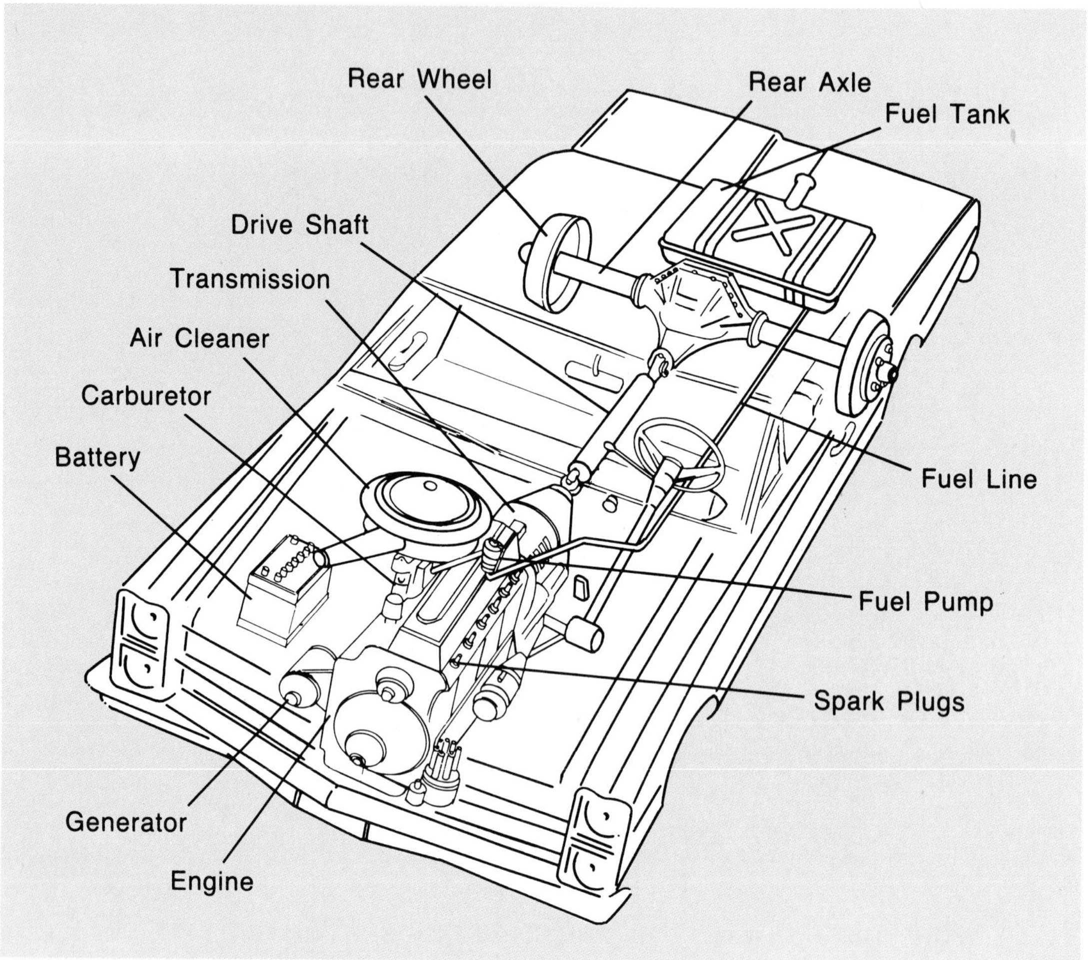

1. Is the fuel tank in the front or the back of the car?
2. What connects the fuel tank to the fuel pump on the engine?
3. Where is the air cleaner located?
4. What connects the transmission to the rear axle?
5. Where are the spark plugs?

Using a Landform Map

To follow page 131

This map shows the different landforms of Kenya. Use the map and the map key to answer the questions below. Write your answers on a piece of paper.

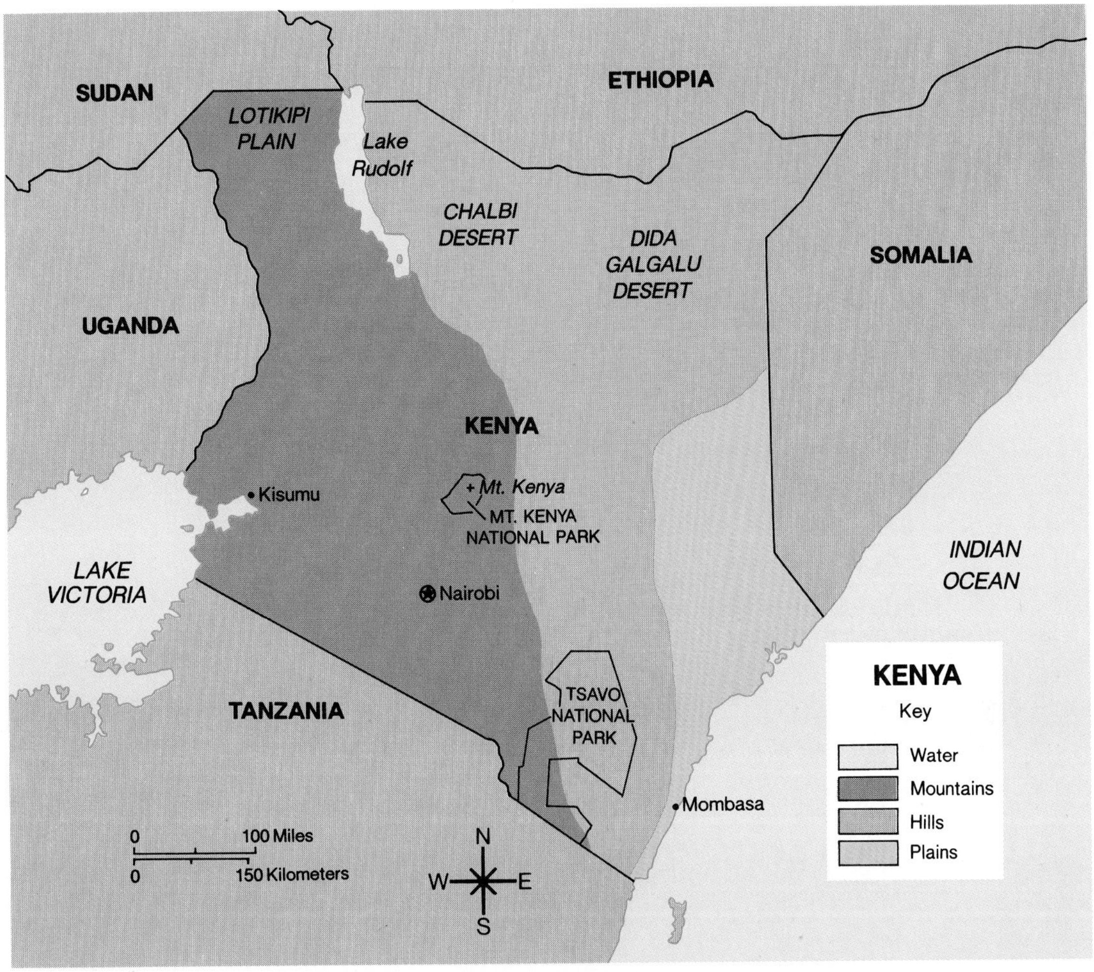

1. What color on the map shows the area along the coast?
2. What body of water borders Kenya to the east?
3. In what kind of landform is Nairobi located?
4. What kind of landform is shown by the color orange?
5. In what part of Kenya are the mountains located?

ENRICHMENT

Using a Route Map

To follow page 143

This map shows the route Lewis and Clark took in exploring the northwestern part of the United States. Use the map to answer the questions below. Write your answers on a piece of paper.

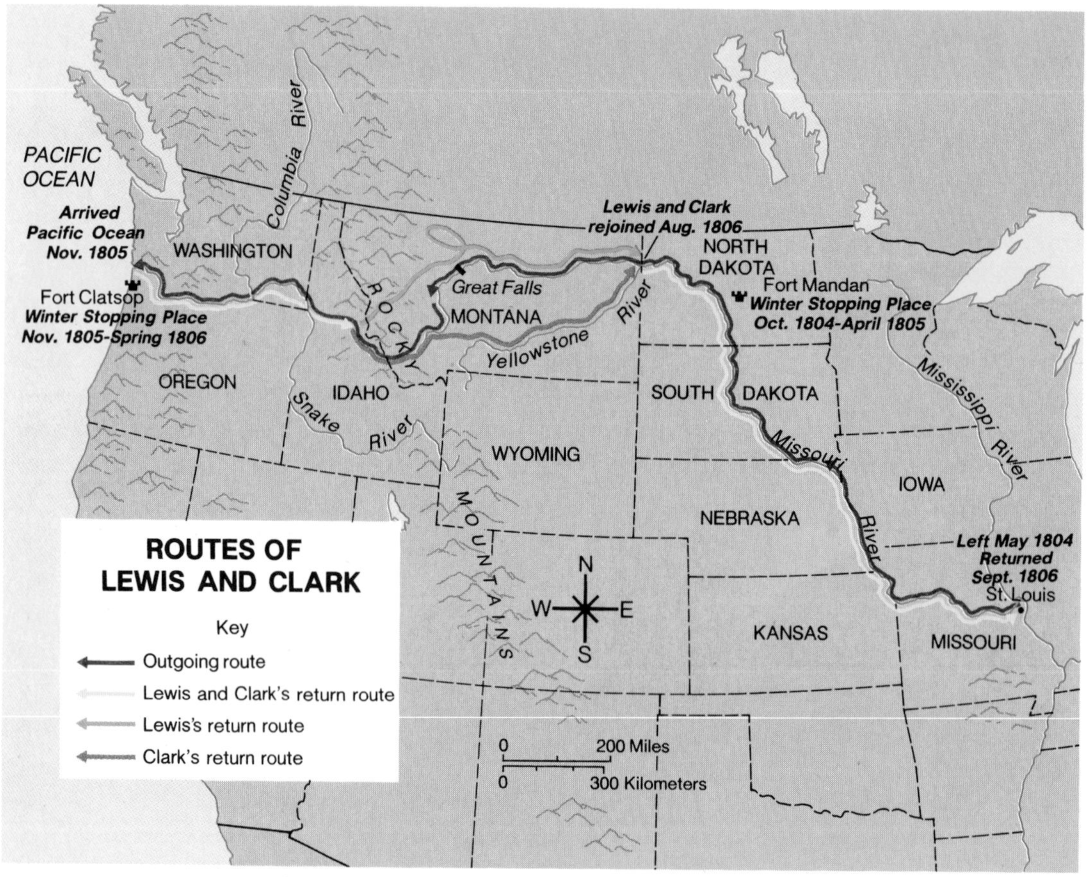

1. When did Lewis and Clark leave St. Louis?
2. Where did they stop for the winter?
3. What mountains did the explorers cross on their trip?
4. What river brought them to the Pacific Ocean?
5. When did they reach the Pacific Ocean?
6. What fort did they build for the winter of 1805?
7. What river did Clark explore on the return trip?

To follow page 143

Read the following paragraphs. Then answer the questions below. Write your answers on a piece of paper.

Jane Addams and Hull House

In 1889 a group of people in Chicago decided to help the immigrants living in their community. They set up a community center in the home of Charles J. Hull. It became known as Hull House.

The two people who worked the hardest to establish Hull House were Jane Addams and Ellen Gates Starr. First Jane Addams studied the needs of the immigrants. Then she set up programs to provide them with food and shelter.

Today Hull House is a group of 24 centers in different parts of Chicago. Most of the early buildings have been torn down. The original Hull mansion has been kept to help us remember the important work done by Jane Addams.

1. Where is Hull House located?
- **a.** New York
- **b.** Detroit
- **c.** Chicago

2. In what year was Hull House founded?
- **a.** 1856
- **b.** 1889
- **c.** 1931

3. Who was the head of Hull House?
- **a.** Charles J. Hull
- **b.** Jane Addams
- **c.** Nicholas Butler

4. What group of people did Hull House help?
- **a.** immigrants
- **b.** rich people
- **c.** college students

Using a Time Line

To follow page 150

This time line shows some important events in the history of Phoenix, Arizona. Use the time line to answer the questions below. Write your answers on a piece of paper.

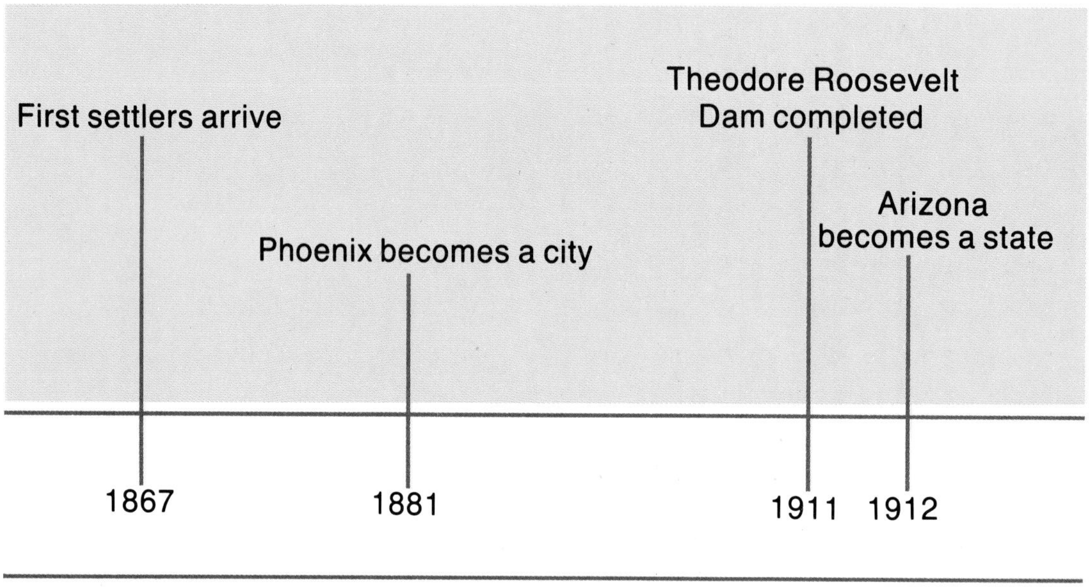

Events in the History of Phoenix, Arizona

1. In what year did settlers first arrive in Phoenix?
2. Did Phoenix become a city before or after Arizona became a state?
3. In what year was the Roosevelt Dam completed?
4. Was the Roosevelt Dam completed before or after Phoenix became a city?
5. How soon after the dam was completed did Arizona become a state?
6. How many years after the first settlers arrived in Phoenix did Arizona become a state?

Reading for Dates

To follow page 151

Read the paragraphs below about the invention of the automobile. Number a paper from **1** through **5**. After each number, write a sentence that tells an important event that happened in the following years:

1770	1885	1890	1894	1908

The History of the Automobile

The very first car was invented by a Frenchman in 1770. It had only three wheels. It was powered by steam and could carry only one person.

Steam-powered cars that could carry several passengers became popular in England in 1830. But they were noisy and dirty. A law was passed in 1865 to limit their use.

Several different steam cars were built in the United States. One popular steam car was the Stanley Steamer, which was built in 1897.

In 1890 a big change in automobiles took place. An American named William Morrison invented the electric car. The electric car was quieter and cleaner than the steam car, but it had to be recharged every 50 miles.

In 1885 two German inventors built an engine that was powered by gasoline. It was very much like the engine used in today's cars. Two Americans used this engine and built the first gas-powered car in 1894. In 1908 Henry Ford began to use the assembly line to manufacture automobiles. Cars made on the assembly line could be made faster and sold for less money.

Using Charts and Graphs

To follow page 163

This chart shows the top winners in the 1980 Winter Olympics. Use the chart to answer the questions below. Write your answers on a piece of paper.

1980 Winter Olympics				
Country	**Gold Medal**	**Silver Medal**	**Bronze Medal**	**Total**
East Germany	9	7	7	23
Norway	1	3	6	10
United States	6	4	2	12
Soviet Union	10	6	6	22

1. How many gold medals did East Germany win?
2. What country won more gold medals than East Germany?
3. How many more gold medals did the United States win than Norway?

After you have answered the questions, copy the unfinished graph shown below. Then make a bar graph that shows the total number of medals won by each country.

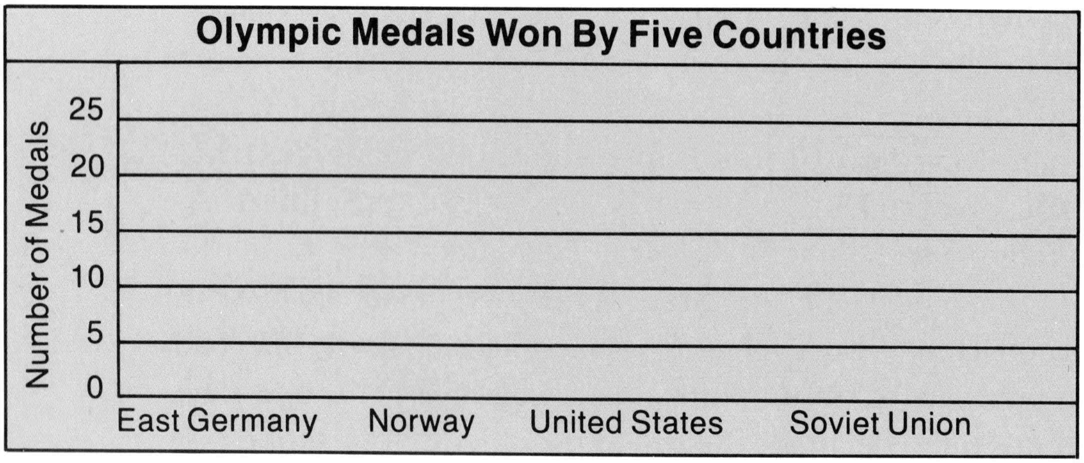

Recognizing Safety Signs

To follow page 171

Traffic signs give drivers important information. They tell about laws that must be obeyed and about the conditions of the road. Some signs have words on them. Others just have pictures, or symbols, to give information.

Read the traffic rules that follow. Number a paper from **1** through **6**. After each number, write the rule that goes with the sign.

- No bicycles allowed
- No left turn
- No trucks allowed
- Slippery when wet
- Steep hill ahead
- Pedestrian crossing

Finding the Facts

To follow page 175

Read about the different kinds of city governments. Then answer the questions that follow. Write your answers on a piece of paper.

Kinds of City Governments

Mayor-Council. In this type of government, the voters elect the mayor and the members of the council. The mayor appoints the heads of each of the different departments, such as Public Safety and Health. The council makes the laws for the city. It is the mayor's job to see that the laws are carried out.

Commission. The commission form of government has a group of commissioners who are elected by the voters. Each commissioner is in charge of a department, such as Health or Public Safety. The commissioners make the laws and carry them out.

Council-Manager. This type of government has a city manager and five to nine council members. The council members are elected by the people. The council hires a city manager. The city manager then hires people to run each city department.

1. In which kind of government does the mayor appoint the heads of the departments?
2. What is the job of a commissioner?
3. In the Council-Manager type of government, who appoints the department heads?

Writing About Jobs

To follow page 179

These pictures show some of the workers needed in a community. Number a paper from **1** through **6**. After each number, write a sentence that tells how each worker helps the community.

1. Firefighter

4. Sanitation Worker

2. Police Officer

5. Librarian

3. Lifeguard

6. Bus Driver

ENRICHMENT

Using a Circle Graph

To follow page 181

This circle graph shows the kinds of work done in Arizona. Use the graph to answer the questions below. Write your answers on a piece of paper.

Kinds of Work Done in Arizona

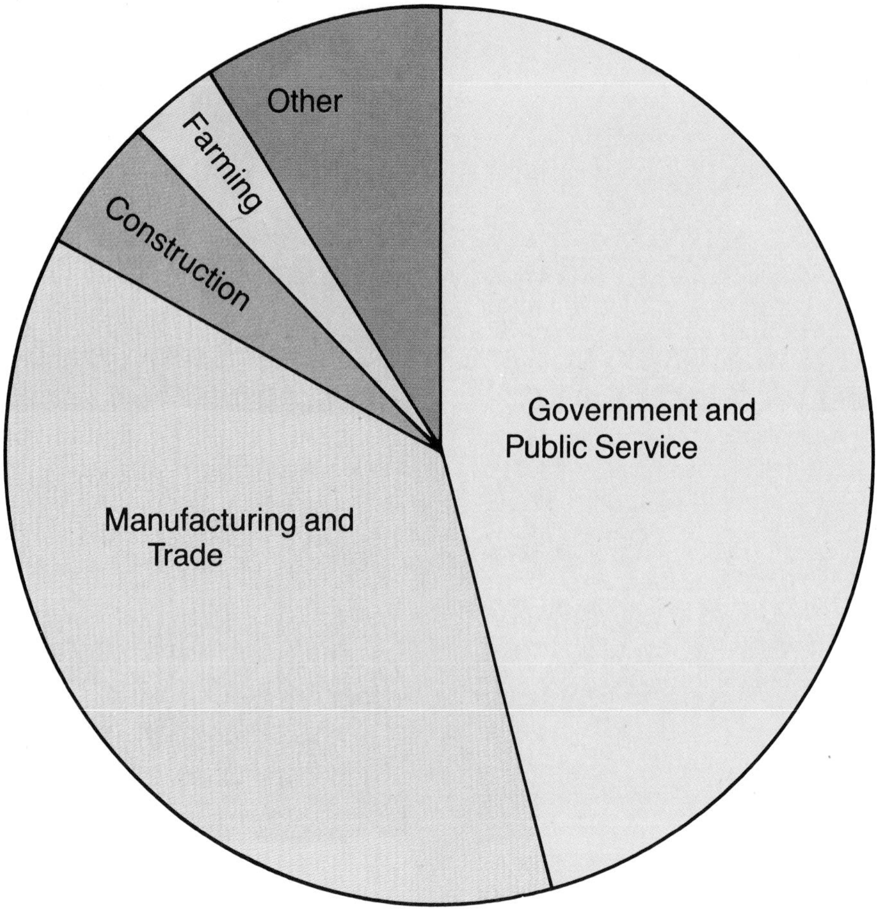

1. In what type of job do most people work?
2. Do more people work in construction or in farming?
3. In what type of job do the fewest number of people work?
4. Name one kind of work that might be included under "Other."

Writing a Letter

To follow page 187

Imagine that you and your friends want to help the public library in your area. Write a letter to the head of the library offering your help. In the first paragraph of the letter, give examples of things you and your friends might do to help. In the second paragraph, ask if there is anything you and your friends could do to get newer books and records for the library. Suggest different ways to raise money for the library. In the last paragraph, ask the librarian if you can meet to talk about your suggestions.

Use this form to help you write your letter:

(Your street address)
(Your city, state, and ZIP code)
(Today's date)

Librarian
Public Library
(Your city, state, and ZIP code)

Dear __________:

(Paragraph 1) ____

____

____

(Paragraph 2) ____

____

____

(Paragraph 3) ____

____

____

Sincerely,

(Your name)

Washington, D.C., has not always been the capital of the United States. Several different cities were used as the capital before Washington, D.C., was built. This time line shows some of the cities that served as capitals of the United States. Use the time line to answer the questions below. Write your answers on a piece of paper.

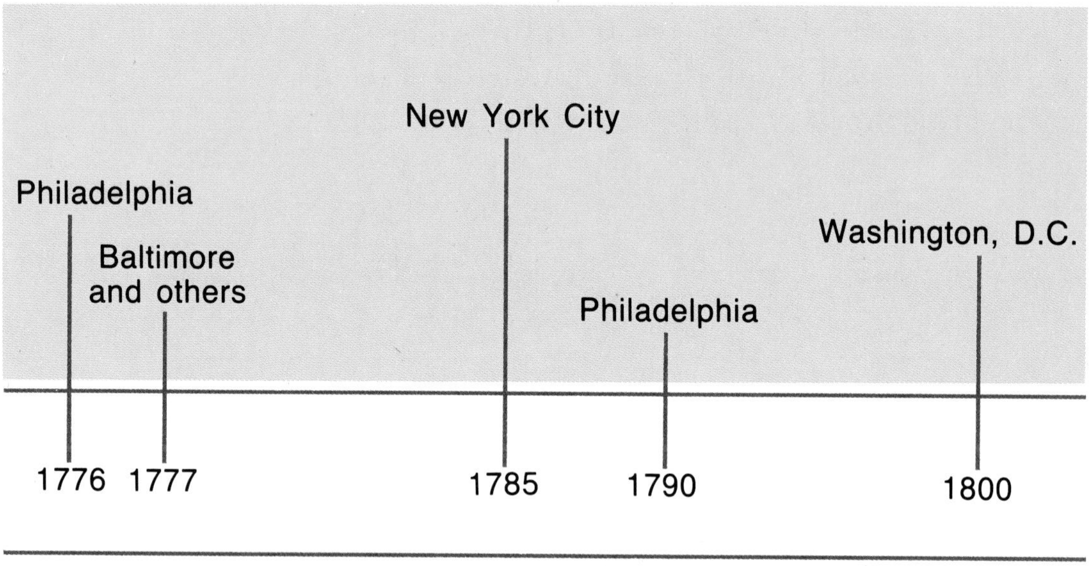

Capitals of the United States

1. What city served as the capital two times?
2. In what year did New York City become the capital of the United States?
3. For how many years was New York City the capital?
4. What city was the capital after New York City?
5. In what year did Washington, D.C., become the capital?

Using a Floor Plan

To follow page 211

A floor plan is a map of the inside of a building. This floor plan shows the five rooms in the White House that tourists may visit. Use the floor plan and the key to answer the questions below. Write your answers on a piece of paper.

Floor Plan of First Floor of the White House

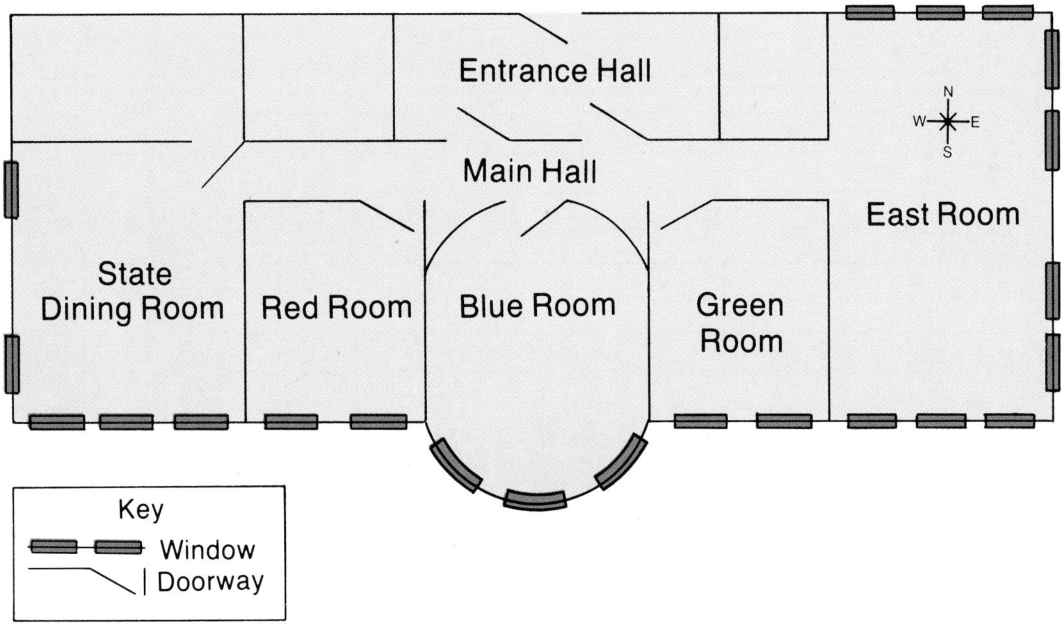

1. In what direction would you walk to go from the State Dining Room to the Red Room?
2. Is the Entrance Hall in the northern part or the southern part of the White House?
3. What area leads to all five rooms?
4. What room is between the Red Room and the Green Room?
5. What room is west of the Red Room?
6. How many windows are in the East Room?

Using a Bar Graph

To follow page 219

This bar graph shows how the population of Washington, D.C., has changed. Use the graph to answer the questions below. Write your answers on a piece of paper.

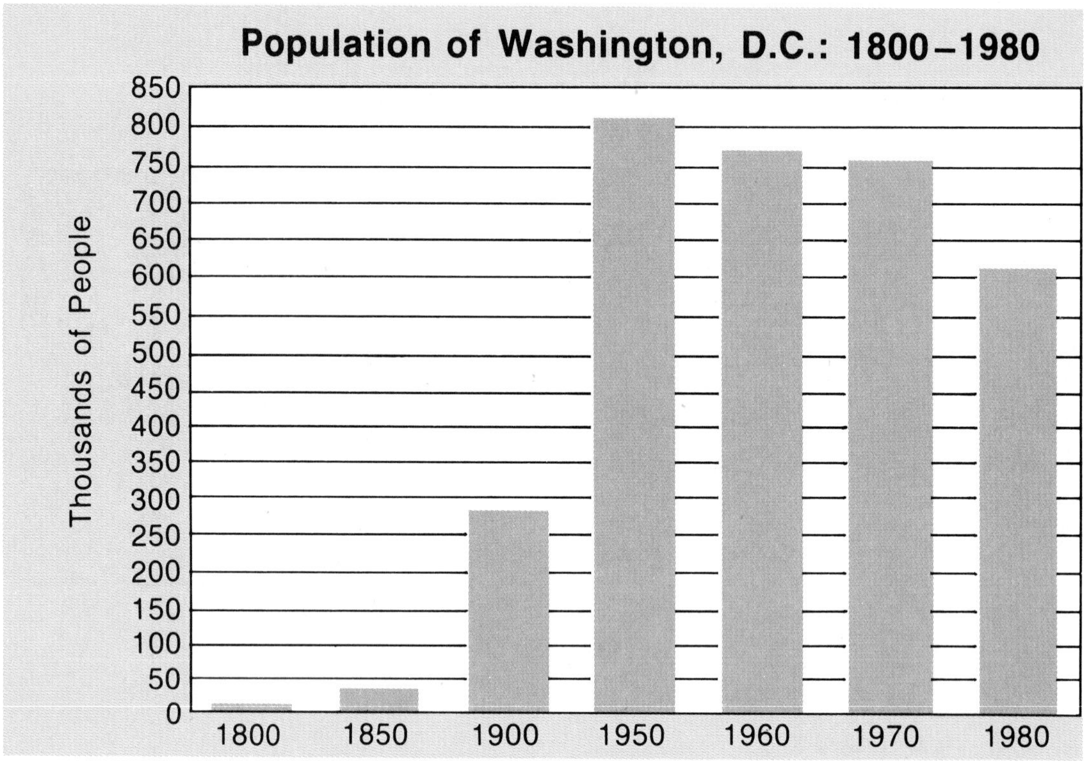

1. In what year did Washington, D.C., have the fewest people?
2. In what year did Washington, D.C., have the most people?
3. What happened to the population between 1850 and 1900?
4. What happened to the population between 1950 and 1960?
5. Between which two years did the population of Washington, D.C., go down the most?

Finding the Facts

To follow page 225

Read the following paragraphs. Then answer the questions below. Write your answers on a piece of paper.

The Statue of Liberty

The Statue of Liberty is located on Liberty Island in New York Harbor. In the past, immigrants came to the United States by boat. The Statue was one of the first things they saw when they arrived in this country. In her right hand the Statue holds a torch welcoming immigrants to the United States. In her left hand is a tablet. On the tablet is the date of the Declaration of Independence—July 4, 1776.

The Statue was given to the United States by France in 1884 as a symbol of friendship. It was made in France and brought here by ship in 214 boxes. In 1924 the Statue of Liberty became an official national monument.

1. Where is the Statue of Liberty located?
2. Who gave the Statue to the United States?
3. How did the Statue get to this country?
4. When did the Statue of Liberty become a national monument?

WORD LIST

This word list will help you to pronounce and understand the meanings of the vocabulary words in this book.

a	b**a**d	k	**k**it	s	**s**it	ə	*stands for*
ā	c**a**ke	l	**l**id	sh	**sh**ip	a	*as in* **a**go
ä	f**a**ther	m	**m**an	t	**t**all	e	*as in* tak**e**n
b	**b**ar	n	**n**or	th	**th**in	i	*as in* penc**i**l
ch	**ch**in	ng	si**ng**	t͟h	**th**at	o	*as in* lem**o**n
d	**d**og	o	h**o**t	u	c**u**p	u	*as in* helpf**u**l
e	p**e**t	ō	**o**pen	ur	t**ur**n		
ē	m**e**	ô	**o**ff	yo͞o	m**u**sic		
f	**f**ive	oo	w**oo**d	v	**v**ery		
g	**g**ame	o͞o	f**oo**d	w	**w**et		
h	**h**it	oi	**oi**l	wh	**wh**ite		
i	**i**t	ou	**ou**t	y	**y**es		
ī	**i**ce	p	**p**ail	z	**z**oo		
j	**j**oke	r	**r**ide	zh	mea**s**ure		

A

assembly line (ə sem′blē līn): workers putting together a product as it passes on a slowly moving track. Many kinds of goods are manufactured on an assembly line.

axis (ak′sis): imaginary line through the center of the earth from the North Pole to the South Pole. The earth turns around on its axis every 24 hours.

C

capital (kap′it əl): a city where the leaders of a state or a country meet and work. Washington, D.C., is our country's capital.

Capitol (kap′it əl): the building where Congress meets and makes our country's laws. The Capitol is in Washington, D.C.

cardinal directions (kärd′ən əl di rek′shənz): the four main directions. North, east, south, and west are the cardinal directions.

central business district (sen′trəl biz′nis dis′trikt): the downtown area of a city. The central business district is the location of most of a city's businesses and stores.

citizen (sit′ə zən): a member of a community and a country. Every citizen of the United States can vote at the age of 18.

city (sit′ē): a very large community. Many people live and work in a city.

climate (klī′mit): the kind of weather a place has over many years. Florida's climate is good for growing oranges.

communication (kə myōō′ni kā′shən): the exchange of information and ideas. Writing a letter is one kind of communication.

community (kə myōō′nə tē): a place and the people who live and work there. Many people live in a community.

commuter (kə myōōt′ər): a person who travels from his or her home to work in a city. Many commuters use mass transit to get to work.

compass rose (kum′pəs rōz): a drawing that shows direction on a map. A compass rose shows cardinal and intermediate directions.

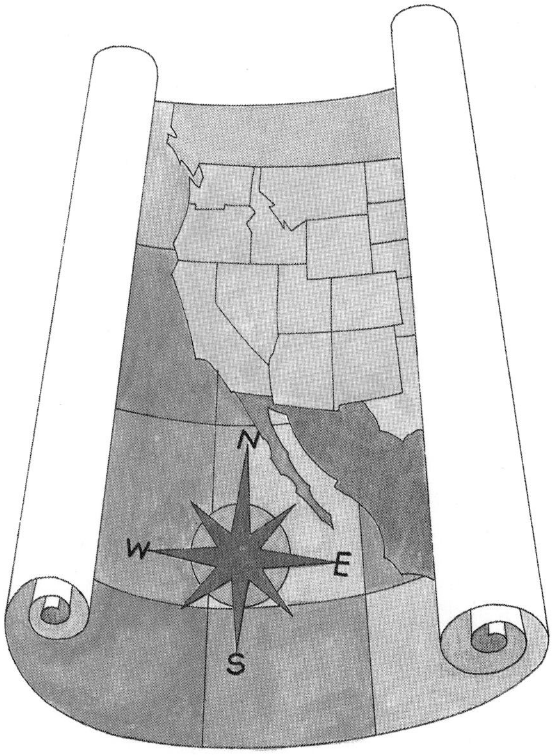

Congress (kong′gris): the group of men and women who make the laws for the United States. Members of Congress are elected by the people.

conservation (kon′sər vā′shən): using natural resources wisely. Everyone must help in the conservation of our natural resources.

council (koun′səl): the group of men and women who make the laws in some communities. The city council voted to build a new park.

culture (kul′chər): the way of life of a group of people. The culture of a group includes its food, clothing, language, and beliefs.

D

dam (dam): a wall built across a river to hold back the water. A dam is used to prevent floods and provide a steady supply of water all through the year.

desert (dez′ərt): a very dry area where few plants can grow. A community in the desert must find a way to meet its need for water.

diplomat (dip′lə mat′): a person who represents his or her country. There are diplomats from many countries in Washington, D.C.

E

election (i lek′shən): the choosing of a leader by voting. There is an election for President every four years in our country.

F

fine (fīn): money that must be paid by a person as punishment for breaking a law. A driver who does not stop at a red light may have to pay a fine.

fuel (fyo͞o′əl): something that is burned to make heat or to provide energy to run machines. Oil is an important fuel.

H

hemisphere (hem′is fēr′): half of the earth. The United States is in the Western Hemisphere.

I

immigrant (im′ə grənt): a person who comes to a new country to live. Immigrants have come to the United States from most countries of the world.

income (in′kum′): money earned from providing goods or services. People use the income from their jobs to buy the things they need and want.

independence (in′di pen′dəns): freedom from the control of others. The United States declared its independence from England on July 4, 1776.

industrial area (in dus′trē əl er′ē ə): the part of a city where there are many factories. Often the industrial area of a city includes a port.

industry (in′dəs trē): the many businesses that make one kind of product. The computer industry is important in many cities in the United States.

intermediate directions (in′tər mē′dē it di rek′shənz): the four directions halfway between the cardinal directions. The intermediate directions are northeast, southeast, southwest, and northwest.

interstate highway (in′tər stat′ hī′wā′): a main road that connects two or more states. Interstate highways link most large cities in our country.

invention (in ven′chən): something that has never been made before. The invention of elevators made possible tall buildings.

irrigation (ir′ə gā′shən): a system for bringing water to dry land. Irrigation makes it possible to grow crops in the desert.

L

location (lō kā′shən): the place where something is. The city grew quickly because of its location near the railroad.

---

a b**a**d, ā c**a**ke, ä f**a**ther; e p**e**t, ē m**e**; i **i**t, ī **i**ce; o h**o**t, ō **o**pen, ô **o**ff; oo w**oo**d; o͞o f**oo**d, oi **oi**l, ou **ou**t; u c**u**p, ur t**ur**n; yo͞o m**u**sic; ə **a**go, tak**e**n, penc**i**l, lem**o**n, helpf**u**l

---

M

manufacturing (man′yə fak′chər ing): the making of large numbers of goods in factories. Many people have jobs manufacturing automobiles.

mass transit (mas tran′sit): transportation for large numbers of people. Buses, trains, and subways are examples of mass transit.

mayor (mā′ər): the head of most community governments. The mayor's job is to see that the laws are carried out.

memorial (mə môr′ē əl): something that is built to honor a person or event. The Lincoln Memorial honors President Abraham Lincoln.

metropolitan area (met′rə pol′ə tən er′ē ə): a large city and the surrounding suburbs and small cities that are linked to it. Phoenix is the center of a growing metropolitan area.

mining (mī′ning): digging minerals from the earth. Coal mining is an important industry in West Virginia.

monument (mon′yə mənt): something that is built to remember a person or event. The Washington Monument was built in memory of George Washington, our country's first President.

museum (myo͞o zē′əm): a building where people go to look at interesting things. You can see old airplanes and new spacecraft in the National Air and Space Museum.

N

national park (nash′ən əl pärk): beautiful lands that are set aside for all the people in a country to enjoy. There are national parks in all parts of the United States.

P

page (pāj): a high school student who helps members of Congress by running errands. Every page is chosen by a member of Congress.

petition (pə tish′ən): a written request made to a leader. Many people in the neighborhood signed a petition asking the city council for a new park.

pipeline (pīp′līn′): a long row of metal tubes. The Alaska pipeline carries oil from the northern part of the state to the port of Valdez in the south.

pollution (pə lo͞o′shən): the many kinds of dirt and garbage that spoil the air, land, and water. Americans are working to prevent pollution.

population (pop′yə lā′shən): the number of people who live in a place. New York City has a very large population.

port (pôrt): a place where ships load and unload goods. St. Louis is a port on the Mississippi River.

R

residential area (rez′ə den′shəl er′ē ə): the part of a city where many people live. There are many residential areas in a large city.

---

a b**a**d, ā c**a**ke, ä f**a**ther; e p**e**t, ē m**e**; i **i**t, ī **i**ce; o h**o**t, ō **o**pen, ô **o**ff; oo w**oo**d; o͞o f**oo**d, oi **oi**l, ou **ou**t; u c**u**p, ur t**ur**n; yo͞o m**u**sic; ə **a**go, tak**e**n, penc**i**l, lem**o**n, helpf**u**l

---

S

scale (skāl): the relation between a distance on a map and that distance on the earth. The map scale shows miles and kilometers.

suburb (sub′urb): a smaller community near a city. Many people who live in a suburb commute to work in a city.

T

tax (taks): money that people pay to the government of a country, community, or state. Tax money provides needed services.

tourist (toor′ist): a person who visits a place on vacation. Each year millions of tourists visit our country's national parks.

town (toun): a small community, usually found in a rural area. Many children who live on farms go to school in a town.

trade (trād): the buying and selling of goods. Cities are important centers of trade.

transportation (trans′pər tā′shən): moving people and goods from place to place. Every community needs transportation.

V

village (vil′ij): a very small community, usually found in a rural area. People in the surrounding area like to shop in the village.

volunteer (vol′ən tēr′): a person who works without being paid. A volunteer uses his or her free time to help others in the community.

W

weather (weth′ ər): what it is like outdoors each day. The weather may be hot or cold, rainy or sunny. What is the weather in your community today?

White House (hwīt hous): the building in Washington, D.C., where the President lives and works. The White House has been the home of every President since John Adams.

Z

ZIP code (zip′kōd): numbers used as part of an address to tell the post office where the mail is going. The ZIP code is used to speed up delivery of the mail.

---

a b**a**d, ā c**a**ke, ä f**a**ther; e p**e**t, ē m**e**; i **i**t, ī **i**ce; o h**o**t, ō **o**pen, ô **o**ff; oo w**oo**d; o͞o f**oo**d, oi **oi**l, ou **ou**t; u c**u**p, ur t**ur**n; yo͞o m**u**sic; ə **a**go, tak**e**n, penc**i**l, lem**o**n, helpf**u**l

---

INDEX

For pronunciations see guide on page 280.

D

E

N

O

P

R

S

T

U

V

W

Z

Acknowledgments

Cover Credit: Illustration by Robert LoGrippo

Grateful acknowledgment is made to the following people for the illustrations, maps and charts:

Illustrators: Robert Jackson, Hima Pamoedjo

Maps: General Cartography, Inc.

Photography Credits: *Abbey Aldrich Rockfeller Folk Art Center,* Williamsburg, Va., 63. *Addison Gallery of American Art,* Phillips Academy, Andover, Md., 168. © *George Ancona,* 34, 37, 38, 39. *Amon Carter Museum,* 140. © *H. Armstrong Roberts:* 14-15, 184-185; © J. Blank, 143; © Michelle Burgess, 208; © R. Krubner, 126; © R. Lloyd, 273 top left. Art Resource: © Jan Lukas, 225; © Naples National Museum, 157; © Andrew Sacks, 82, 116; © Joshua Tree, 154; © Jim Tuten, 54; © Peter Vadnai, 17R. *Bancroft Library,* University of California, Berkeley, 69 right, 88. *Black Star:* © Charles Moore, 89. © *Cameramann Int., Inc.,* 99 left, 123, 127. *Courtesy of Cheyenne Frontier Days,* 68. *Chicago Historical Society,* 141. *Coast & Geodetic Survey,* 197 left. *Colour Library International,* 20, 21, 94 right, 148, 151, 207, 209. *Leo deWys:* 76, 273 top right; © Danilo Boschung, 16; © Ives, 147 right; © Everett C. Johnson, 217, 273 center left; © Messerschmidt, 206 right; © Momatiuk, 77; © Steve Vidler, 33R, 159, 161, 204, 205 left. © Zingel, 130-131. *The Dimock Gallery,* George Washington University, 196. *Dorian Studio:* © Carl Schonbrod, 78, 79. *Design Photographers International:* © Syd Greenberg, 92. *Eastman Kodak,* 95 right. © *The Easton Press, MBI, Inc.,* Norwalk, Ct., 44-45. © *Lloyd Englert,* 238 top right. *Courtesy Ford Motor Company,* 118. © *David R. Frazier,* 93 right. *Courtesy of John Hancock Mutual Life Insurance Company,* Boston, 56. © *Grant Heilman, Photography,* 23, 91. *International Stock Photo:* © Ronn Maratea, 251 bottom left; © Wayne Sproul, 84 bottom. © *Brent Jones,* 187. © *William Loren Katz,* 69 left. © *Ken Lax,* 230 left and right, 232. *Library of Congress,* 175, 195. © *Robert Llewellyn,* 192-193. *Magnum Photos:* © Elliott Erwitt, 84 top; © Erich Hartmann, 97; © Richard Kalvar, 33 left; © Bernard Pierre Wolff, 99 right. *Massachusetts Historical Society,* 198 right. *Metropolitan Museum of Art:* Classical Purchase & Fletcher & Rogers Funds, 158 left; Rogers Fund, 1917, 158 right. © *Lawrence Migdale,* 109, 110, 111, 113, 114. *Monkmeyer Press Photo Service:* © Mimi Forsyth, 17 left; © Michal Heron, 273 center right; © Herbert Lanks, 100; © Hugh Roger, 19; © Rhoda Sidney, 173. *Montana Historical Society,* 61. *Museum of Fine Arts, Boston,* Gift of Mrs. Charles Francis Adams, 198 left. *Museum of the City of New York,* 65, Harry T. Peterson Collection, 62. *Nawrocki Stock Photo,* 46. *New York Public Library:* Stokes Collection, Prints Division, Lenox, Astor & Tilden Foundation, 57, 199; *Philbrook Art Center,* 47. *Photo Researchers, Inc.:* © Richard Hutchings, 18 top, 171; © Fred Maroon, 93 left; © Tom McHugh, 106-107, 136-137; © Joseph Nettis, 115; © Earl Roberge, 22; © Bruce Roberts/Rapho Division, 221; © Katrina Thomas, 101; © USDA, 80. *Courtesy of Ralston Purina,* 142 left and right. © *Leith A. Rohr,* 95 left. *Royal Ontario Museum,* Toronto, Ontario, 50. *The St. Louis Art Museum,* Gift of August A. Busch, Jr., 138 top. *Salt River Project,* 147 left. © *Amla Sanghvi,* 94 left. © *Bob Scott,* 172. © *Robert S. Scurlock,* 201. © Blair Seitz, 18 bottom, 169, 176, 178, 179, 182, 183, 186. *Shostal Associates:* © Bob Glander, 224; © Karl Kummels, 30; © Kurt Scholz, 279; © E. Streichan, 129; © Augusts Upitis, 273 bottom left. *Southern Light:* © Bohdan Hrynewych, 238 bottom left. © *Bob & Ira Spring,* 238 bottom right. *Stock Boston:* © Bill Gillette, 238 top left; © Ellis Herwigh, 217 right, 251 top left; © Stacy Pix, 211. © *Michos Tzovaras,* 160 right. *UNIPHOTO Photo Agency:* © Paul Conklin, 210; © Chris Cross, 214; © Curt W. Kaldor, 112; © Roddey E. Mims, 220; © Les Moore, 273 bottom right; © Stacy Pix, 200; © Tim Ribar, 153; © Jim Scruggs, 160 left; © Roger Watts, 219. *United Press International,* 155. *U.S. Government Printing Office,* Architect of the Capitol under the direction of Joint Committee on the Library, 85. *U.S. House of Representatives,* James T. Molloy, Doorkeeper, 215. *Upstream Productions:* © Yasu Osawa, 52 left, 53. © *Rick Wester,* 150. *West Light:* © Craig Aurness, 74-75, 83, 251 right. *White House Historical Association,* 205 right. *Woodfin Camp & Associates:* © Dick Durrance II, 119; © Timothy Eagan, 206 left; © John Ficara, 216; © Fred Mayer, 124, 125. © Chuck O'Rear, 149. *Yale University Art Gallery,* Mabel Brady Garvan Collection, 64. *Yale University Library,* Beinecke Rarebook & Manuscript Library, 51. © *Jack Zehrt,* 138 bottom. © Philip M. Zito, 166-167.